THE
SPIRIT
OF
CHRIST

THE
SPIRIT
OF
CHRIST
Andrew Murray

BETHANY HOUSE PUBLISHERS
MINNEAPOLIS, MINNESOTA 55438
A Division of Bethany Fellowship, Inc.

Publisher's Note

This edition of Andrew Murray's classic has been newly edited, and the language updated to improve clarity. The reader may be sure that Murray's message remains the same. It is our hope that this new edition will bring blessing to many thousands of people around the world.

The Spirit of Christ
Andrew Murray

New Edition
Copyright © 1979
Bethany House Publishers
All Rights Reserved

Published by Bethany House Publishers
A Division of Bethany Fellowship, Inc.
6820 Auto Club Road, Minneapolis, Minnesota 55438

Printed in the United States of America

Library of Congress Cataloging in Publication Data

Murray, Andrew, 1828–1917.
   The spirit of Christ.

    1. Holy Spirit—Sermons. 2. Sermons, English.
I. Title.
[BT122.M87   1984]   231'.3   83–25768
ISBN 0–87123–589–7

PREFACE

In olden times believers met God, knew Him, walked with Him, had the clear and full consciousness that they had dealings with the God of heaven, and through faith had the assurance that they and their lives were well-pleasing to Him. When the Son of God came to earth, revealing the Father, it was so that fellowship with God and the assurance of His favor might become clearer, and be the abiding portion of every child of God. When He was exalted to the throne of glory, it was that He might send down into our hearts the Holy Spirit, in whom the Father and the Son have their own blessed life in heaven, and to maintain in us through divine power, the blessed life of fellowship with God. It was to be one of the marks of the New Covenant that each member of it should walk in personal communion with God. "They shall teach no more every man his neighbor, Know the Lord: for they shall all know me, from the least to the greatest of them, saith the Lord; for I will forgive their iniquity." The personal fellowship and knowledge of God in the Holy Spirit was to be the fruit of the pardon of sin. The Spirit of God's own Son was sent into our hearts to do a work as divine as the work of the Son in redeeming us. The Spirit displaces our life and replaces it with the life of Christ in power, to make the Son of God divinely and consciously present with us always. This was what the Father had promised as the distinctive blessing of the New Testament. The fellowship of God as the three-in-one was now to be *within us*; the Spirit revealing the Son in us, and through Him the Father.

No one will deny that there are few believers who realize this walk with God, this life in God, such as their Father has prepared for them. And few are willing to discuss what the cause of this failure is. It is also acknowledged on all hands that the Holy Spirit, through whose divine omnipotence this inner revelation comes, is not realized fully in the Church as

He should be. In our preaching and in our practice He does not hold that place of prominence which He has in God's plan and in His promises. While our creed on the Holy Spirit is orthodox and scriptural, His presence and power in the life of believers, in the ministry of the Word, in the witness of the Church to the world, is not what the Word promises or God's plan requires.

There are many who are conscious of this great need, and earnestly ask to know God's mind concerning it, and the way of deliverance out of it. Some feel that their own life is not what it should and might be. Many can look back to some special season of spiritual revival when their whole life was apparently lifted to a higher level. The experience of the joy and strength of the Saviour's presence, as they realized that it was He who would keep them trusting, was for a time very real and blessed. But it did not last: there was a very gradual decline to a lower stage, with much vain effort and sad failure. Many long to know where the evil lies. There can be little doubt that the answer is this: they did not know or honor the indwelling Spirit as the strength of their life, as the power of their faith, to keep them always looking to Jesus and trusting in Him. They did not know what it was, day by day, to wait in lowly reverence for the Holy Spirit to deliver from the power of the flesh, and to maintain the wonderful presence of the Father and the Son within them.

There are many more, tens of thousands of God's dear children, who as yet know little of any temporary experiences of a brighter life than one of never-ending stumbling and rising. They have lived outside of revivals and conferences; the teaching they receive is not particularly helpful in the matter of entire consecration. Their surroundings are not favorable to the growth of the spiritual life. There may be times of earnest longing to live according to the will of God, but the prospect of it actually being possible to walk and please God, worthy of the Lord to all well-pleasing, has hardly dawned upon them. They are strangers to the best part of their birthright as God's children, to the most precious gift of the Father's love in Christ—the gift of the Holy Spirit, to dwell in them, and to lead them.

I would really count it an unspeakable privilege if God would use me to bring to these, His beloved children, the question of His Word: "Know ye not that ye are a temple of God, and that the Spirit of God dwelleth in you?" and then to tell them the blessed news of what that glorious work is, which the Spirit whom they have within them is able to do in each of them. If I could, I would show them what it is that has until now hindered the Spirit from doing His blessed work. I would explain how divinely simple the path is by which each upright soul can enter into the joy of the full revelation of the presence of the indwelling Jesus. I have humbly asked God that He would give, even through my simple words, the quickening of His Holy Spirit, that through them the thoughts, truth, love, and the power of God may enter and shine into the hearts of many of His children. I long that these words may bring in blessed reality and experience the wondrous gift of love which they describe— the life and the joy of the Holy Ghost, as He brings nigh and glorifies within them that Jesus whom until now they have only known at a distance, high above them.

I must confess to still another wish. I have strong fears— and I say it in all humility—that in the theology of our churches the teaching and leading of the Spirit of truth, the anointing which alone teaches all things, is not recognized in a practical sense, which a holy God demands, and which our Saviour meant Him to have. If the religious leaders of our church—teachers, pastors, Bible scholars, writers, and workers—were all fully conscious of the fact that in everything that concerns the Word of God and the church of Christ the Holy Spirit should have the supreme place of honor that He had in the church of the Acts of the Apostles, surely the signs and marks of His holy presence would be clearer and His mighty works more manifest. I trust I have not been presumptuous in hoping that what has been written may help to remind even our masters in Israel of that which is so easily overlooked—the indispensable requirement for what is really to bear fruit for eternity—to be full of the power of the eternal Spirit.

I am well aware of what may be expected by men of intellect and culture, and by scientific theologians, that these writings should bear marks of scholarship, force of thought, and power of expression. To these I cannot dare to lay claim. Yet I venture to ask any of these honored brethren who may read these lines, to regard the book at least as the echo of a cry for light rising from many hearts, and as a display of questions, the solution for which many are longing. There is a deep feeling prevalent that Christ's own promise of what the Church should be, and its actual state, do not correspond.

Of all questions in theology there is none that leads us more deeply into the glory of God, or that is of more intense, vital and practical importance for daily life, than that which deals with the full revelation of God and the work of redemption. Or, in what way and to what extent God's Holy Spirit can dwell in, fill, and make into a holy and beautiful temple of God, the heart of His child, making Christ reign there as an ever-present and almighty Saviour. It is a question of which the solution, if it were sought and found in the presence and teaching of the Spirit himself, would transform all our theology into that knowledge of God which is eternal life.

Of theology, in every possible form, we have no lack. But it is as if, with all our writing, and preaching, and working, there is something lacking. Is it not the power from on high? Could it be that, with all our love for Christ and labor for His cause, we have not made the chief object of our desire that which was the chief object of His heart when He ascended the throne? It was to have His disciples as a company of men waiting for the clothing with the power of the Holy Ghost, that in that power of the felt presence of their Lord they might testify of Him? May God raise up from among our theologians many who will give their lives to see that God's Holy Spirit is fully recognized in the lives of believers, in the ministry of the Word by tongue and pen, and in all the work done in His Church.

I have noticed with deep interest a new thrust for union in prayer—"that Christian life and teaching may be increasingly subject to the Holy Ghost." I believe that one of the first blessings of this united prayer will be to direct attention to the reasons why prayer is not more evidently answered, and to true preparation for receiving abundant answers. In my reading in connection with this subject, in my observation of the lives of believers, and in my personal experience, I have been very deeply impressed with one thought. It is that our prayer for the mighty working of the Holy Spirit through us and around us can only be powerfully answered as *His indwelling in every believer* is more clearly acknowledged and lived out. We have the Holy Spirit within us; only he who is faithful in the lesser will receive the greater. As we first yield ourselves to be led by the Spirit, to confess His presence in us; as believers rise to realize and accept His guidance in their daily lives, God will entrust to us larger measures of His mighty workings. If we give ourselves entirely into His power, as our life, ruling within us, He will give himself to us, take more complete possession of us, and work through us.

If there is one thing I desire, it is that the Lord may use what I have written to make clear and impress this one truth: it is as an indwelling life that the Holy Spirit must be known. In a living, adoring faith, the indwelling must be accepted and treasured until it becomes part of the consciousness of the new man: The Holy Spirit possesses me. In this faith, the whole life, even in the smallest things, must be surrendered to His leading, while all that is of the flesh or self is crucified and put to death. If in this faith we wait on God for His divine leading and working, placing ourselves entirely at His disposal, our prayer cannot remain unheard. There will be operations and manifestations of the Spirit's power in the Church and the world such as we could not dare to hope. The Holy Spirit only demands vessels entirely set apart to Him. He delights to manifest the glory of Christ our Lord.

I commit each beloved fellow believer to the teaching of the Holy Spirit. May we all, as we study His work, be partakers of the anointing which teaches all things.

Andrew Murray

CONTENTS

NOTES

1

A NEW SPIRIT, AND GOD'S SPIRIT

A new heart also will I give you, and a new spirit
will I put *within* you. . . . And I will put my Spirit
within you. . . . —Ezek. 36:26, 27

God has revealed himself in two great dispensations. In
the Old we have the time of promise and preparation, in the
New that of fulfillment and possession. In harmony with the
difference of the two dispensations, there is a twofold working of God's Spirit. In the Old Testament we have the Spirit
of God coming upon men and working on them in special
times and ways: working from above, without, and within.
In the New we have the Holy Spirit entering them and
dwelling within them: working from within, without, and
upward. In the former we have the Spirit of God as the Almighty and Holy One; in the latter we have the Spirit of the
Father of Jesus Christ.

The difference between the twofold operation of the Holy
Spirit is not to be regarded as if with the closing of the Old
Testament the former ceased, and there was in the New no
more of the work of preparation. By no means. Just as there
were in the Old blessed anticipations of the indwelling of
God's Spirit, so now in the New Testament the twofold
working still continues. According to the lack of knowledge,
or of faith, or of faithfulness, a believer may even in these
days get little beyond the Old Testament measure of the
Spirit's working. The indwelling Spirit has indeed been giv-
en to every child of God, and yet he may experience little
beyond the first half of the promise. The new spirit is given
to us in regeneration but we may know almost nothing of
God's own Spirit as a living person put within us. The Spirit's work in convincing of sin and of righteousness, in His
leading to repentance and faith and the new life, is but the
preparatory work. The distinctive glory of the dispensation

of the Spirit is His divine personal indwelling in the heart of the believer, there to reveal the Father and the Son. It is only as Christians understand and remember this that they will be able to claim the full blessing prepared for them in Christ Jesus.

In the words of Ezekiel we find, very strikingly set forth, in the one promise this twofold blessing God bestows through His Spirit. The first is, "I will put within you *a new spirit*"—that is, man's own spirit is to be renewed and quickened by the work of God's Spirit. When this has been done, then there is the second blessing, "I will put *my Spirit* within you," to dwell in that new spirit. Where God is to dwell, He must have a habitation. With Adam He had to create a body before He could breathe the spirit of life into him. In Israel the tabernacle and the temple had to be built and completed before God could come down and take possession. Likewise, a new heart is given and a new spirit put within us as the indispensable condition of God's own Spirit being given to dwell within us. We find the same contrast in David's prayer. First, "Create in me a clean heart, O God! and *renew a right spirit* within me"; then, "Take not *thy Holy Spirit* from me." Look what is indicated in the words, "That which is born of *the Spirit is spirit*": there is the divine Spirit begetting and the new spirit begotten by Him. So the two are also distinguished: "*God's Spirit* beareth witness *with our spirits* that we are the children of God." Our spirit is the renewed, regenerate spirit. God's Spirit dwells in our spirit, yet distinguished from it, witnesses in, with and through it.

The importance of recognizing this distinction can easily be perceived. We shall then be able to understand the true relation between regeneration and the indwelling of the Spirit. The former is the work of the Holy Spirit by which He convinces us of sin, leads to repentance and faith in Christ, and imparts a new nature. Through the Spirit, God thus fulfills the promise: "I will put a new spirit within you." The believer is now a child of God, a temple ready for the Spirit to dwell in. Where faith claims it, the second half of the promise is fulfilled as surely as the first. However, as long as the believer looks only at regeneration, and the renewal wrought in his spirit, he will not come to the life of joy and strength which is meant for him. But when he accepts God's promise that there is something better than even the new nature, than the inner temple, that there is the Spirit of the Father and the Son to dwell within him, there opens up a wonderful prospect of holiness and blessedness. It becomes his one great desire to know this Holy Spirit aright, how He works and what He asks, to know how he may to the full experience His indwelling and that revelation of the Son of God within us, which it is His work to bestow.

The question will be asked, How are these two parts of the divine promise fulfilled—simultaneously or successively? The answer is very simple: From God's side the twofold gift is simultaneous. The Spirit is not divided: in giving the Spirit, God gives himself and all He is. So it was on the day of Pentecost. The three thousand received the new spirit, with repentance and faith, and on the same day, when they had been baptized, they received the indwelling Spirit as God's seal to their faith. Through the word of the disciples, the Spirit, which had come upon them, did a mighty work among the multitudes, changing disposition, heart and spirit. When in the power of this new spirit working in them they had believed and confessed, they received the baptism of the Holy Spirit to abide in them.

Even today, in times when the Spirit of God moves mightily, and the Church is living in the power of the Spirit, the children which are begotten of her receive from the first beginnings of their Christian life the distinct, conscious sealing and indwelling of the Spirit. But we have indications in Scripture that there may be circumstances, dependent either on the enduement of the preacher or the faith of the hearers, in which the two halves of the promise are not so closely linked. So it was with the believers in Samaria converted under Philip's preaching; and so too with the converts Paul met at Ephesus. In their case, the experience of the apostles themselves was repeated. We regard them as regenerate men before our Lord's death; it was only at Pentecost that the promise was fulfilled, "*He* shall be *in you.*" What was seen in them, just as in the Old and New Testaments—the grace of the Spirit divided into two separate manifestations—may still take place in our day.

When the standard of spiritual life in a church is sickly

and low, when neither in the preaching of the Word nor in the testimony of believers is the glorious truth of an indwelling Spirit distinctly proclaimed, we must not wonder that even where God gives His Spirit He will be known and experienced only as the Spirit of regeneration. His indwelling presence will remain a mystery. In the gift of God, the Spirit of Christ in all His fullness is bestowed once for all as an Indwelling Spirit; but He is received and possessed only as far as the faith of the believer reaches.[1]

It is generally admitted in the Church that the Holy Spirit has not the recognition which becomes Him as being the equal of the Father and the Son, the divine person through whom alone the Father and the Son can be truly possessed and known, in whom alone the Church has her beauty and her blessedness. In the Reformation the gospel of Christ had to be vindicated from the terrible misapprehension which makes man's righteousness the ground of his acceptance, and the freedom of divine grace had to be maintained. To the ages that followed was committed the trust of building on that foundation and developing what the riches of grace would do for the believer through the indwelling of the Spirit of Jesus. The Church rested too contentedly in what it had received, and the teaching of all that the Holy Spirit will be to each believer in His guiding, sanctifying, strengthening power has never yet taken the place it ought to have in our evangelical teaching and living.[2] And there is many an earnest Christian who will join in the confession made by a young believer of intelligence: "I think I understand the work of the Father and the Son, and rejoice in them, but I hardly see the place the Spirit has."

Let us unite with all who are pleading that God in His power may grant mighty workings of the Spirit in His church, that each child of God may prove that in him the double promise is fulfilled: "I will put a new spirit within you, and I will put my Spirit within you." Let us pray that we may so apprehend the wonderful blessing of the indwelling Spirit, so that our whole inmost being may be opened up for the full revelation of the Father's love and the grace of Jesus.

"Within you! Within you!" This twice-repeated word of our text is one of the key words of the new covenant. "I will put my law *in their inward parts*,[3] and *in their hearts* will I write it." "I will put my fear *in their hearts*, that they shall not depart from me." God created man's heart for His dwelling. Sin entered and defiled it. Four thousand years God's Spirit strove and worked to regain possession. In the incarnation and atonement of Christ the redemption was accomplished and the kingdom of God established. Jesus could say, "The kingdom of God is come unto you; the kingdom of God is *within you*." It is *within* we must look for the fulfillment of the new covenant, the covenant not of ordinances but of life. In the power of an endless life the law and the fear of God are to be given in our heart; the Spirit of Christ himself is to be within us as the power of our life. Not only on Calvary, or in the resurrection, or on the throne is the glory of Christ the conqueror to be seen—but in our heart. *Within* us is to be the true display of the reality and the glory of His redemption. Within us, in our inmost parts, is the hidden sanctuary where the ark of the covenant is sprinkled with the blood. It contains the law written in an ever-living writing by the indwelling Spirit, and where, through the Spirit, the Father and the Son now come to dwell.

O my God! I do thank Thee for this double blessing. I thank Thee for that wonderful holy temple Thou hast built up in me for thyself—a new spirit given within me. And I thank Thee for that still more wonderful holy presence, Thine own Spirit, to dwell within me and there reveal the Father and the Son.

O my God! I do pray Thee, open my eyes to the mystery of Thy love. Let Thy words *"within you"* bow me low in trembling fear before Thy condescension, and may my one desire be to have my spirit indeed the worthy dwelling of Thy Spirit. Let them lift me up in holy trust and expectation, to look for and claim all that Thy promise means.

O my Father! I thank Thee that Thy Spirit dwells in me. I pray Thee, let His indwelling be in power, in the living fellowship with thyself, in the growing experience of His renewing power, in the ever fresh anointing that witnesses to His presence and the indwelling of my glorified Lord Jesus. May my daily walk be in the deep reverence of His holy presence within me and the glad experience of all He works. Amen.

SUMMARY

1. Have we not here the reason why many fail in the effort to abide in Christ, to walk like Christ, to live as holy in Christ? They do not fully know the wonderful and perfectly sufficient provision God made to enable them to do so. They have not the clear believing assurance that the Holy Spirit will work it in them. Let us seek above everything to get firm hold of the promise, that God who has given us a new spirit also gives His own Spirit within us.

2. The distinction is of the deepest importance. In the new spirit given to me, I have a work of God in me; in God's Spirit given, I have God himself, a living person, to dwell with me. What a difference between having a home built by a rich friend, given me to live in, while I remain poor and weak; or having the rich friend himself come to live with me and fulfill my every want!

3. "The Spirit is given both as a builder and as an inhabitant of this temple. We cannot dwell till He builds and He builds that He may dwell."—Howe

4. There must be harmony between a home and its occupant. The more I know this holy guest, the more will I bow in lowly fear and reverence, giving my inmost being for Him to order and adorn as pleases Him.

5. The Holy Spirit is the inmost self of the Father and the Son. My spirit is my inmost self. The Holy Spirit renews that inmost self, then dwells in it and fills it. He becomes to me what He was to Jesus—the very life of my personality. Let me bow in holy silence and reverence to say: "O my Father! I thank Thee that Thy Holy Spirit dwells in me, in my very self."

Notes

1. "This distinction between the preparatory operation of the Spirit *upon* man, by means of external manifestation, and His actual dwelling *in* man, seems almost effaced from Christian consciousness."—Godet on John 14:17

"The Spirit first works from without *on* and *in* men, in word and deed, before He becomes their inner personal possession, before He dwells in them. We must always distinguish between the inworking and indwelling of the Spirit."—Beck, *Chr. Ethik*

2. "If we review the history of the Church, we notice how many important truths, clearly revealed in Scripture, have been allowed to lie dormant for centuries, unknown and unappreciated except by a few isolated Christians, until it pleased God to enlighten the Church by chosen witnesses, and to bestow on His children the knowledge of hidden and forgotten treasures. For how long a period, even after the Reformation, were the doctrines of the Holy Ghost, His work in conversion, and His indwelling in the believer, almost unknown!"—Saphir, *The Lord's Prayer*

3. The word translated "within" is not a preposition, but the same as is rendered here and elsewhere (Ps. 5:9; 49:11), "inward parts"; "inmost thought."

2

THE BAPTISM OF THE SPIRIT

And John bare record, saying. . . . And I knew him not: but he that sent me to baptize with water, the same said unto me, Upon whom thou shalt see the Spirit descending, and remaining on him, the same is he which baptizeth with the Holy Ghost.—John 1:32, 33

There were two things that John the Baptist preached concerning the person of Christ: The one was that He was the Lamb of God that taketh away the sin of the world; the other, that He would baptize His disciples with the Holy Ghost and with fire. The blood of the Lamb and the baptism of the Spirit were the two central truths of his creed and his preaching. They are, indeed, inseparable: the Church cannot do her work in power, nor can her exalted Lord be glorified in her unless the blood as the foundation-stone and the Spirit as the cornerstone are fully preached.

This has not at all times been done even among those who heartily accept Scripture as their guide. The preaching of the Lamb of God, of His suffering and atonement, of pardon and peace through Him, is more easily apprehended by the understanding of man, and can more speedily influence his feelings, than the more inward spiritual truth of the baptism, indwelling and guidance of the Holy Spirit. The pouring out of the blood took place upon earth; it was something visible and outward, and, in virtue of the types, not altogether unintelligible. The pouring out of the Spirit was in heaven, a divine and hidden mystery. The shedding of the blood was for the ungodly and rebellious; the gift of the Spirit, for the loving and obedient disciple. It is no wonder, when the life of the Church is not very intense in devotion to her Lord, that the preaching and the faith of the baptism of the Spirit should find less entrance than that of redemption and forgiveness.

And yet God would not have it so. The Old Testament promise had spoken of God's Spirit within us. The forerunner at once took up the strain and did not preach the atoning Lamb without telling to what extent it was that we were to be redeemed, and how God's high purpose was to be fulfilled in us. Sin was not only guilt and condemnation; it was defilement and death. It had incurred not only the loss of God's favor; it had made us unfit for the divine fellowship. And without this the wonderful love that had created man could not be content. God really wanted to have us for himself—our hearts and affections, our inmost personality, our very self; a home for His love to rest in, a temple for His worship. The preaching of John included both the beginning and the end of redemption: the blood of the Lamb was to cleanse God's temple and restore His throne within the heart. Nothing less than the baptism and indwelling of the Spirit could satisfy the heart of either God or man.

Of what the baptism of the Spirit meant, Jesus himself was to be the type: He would give only what He himself had received. Because the Spirit abode on Him, He could baptize with the Spirit. And what did the Spirit descending and abiding on Him mean? He had been begotten of the Holy Spirit; in the power of the Spirit He had grown up a holy child and youth; He had entered manhood free from sin and had now come to John to give himself to fulfill all righteousness in submitting to the baptism of repentance. And now, as the reward of His obedience, as the Father's seal of approval on His having thus far yielded to the control of the Spirit, He receives a new communication of the power of the heavenly life. Beyond what He had yet experienced, the Father's conscious indwelling presence and power takes possession of Him and fits Him for His work. The leading and the power of the Spirit become His more consciously (Luke 4:1, 14, 22) than before; He is now anointed with the Holy Ghost and with power.

But though now baptized himself, He cannot yet baptize others. He must first, in the power of His baptism, meet temptation and overcome it. He must learn obedience and suffer, and through the eternal Spirit offer himself a sacrifice unto God and His will—then only would He afresh receive the Holy Spirit as the reward of obedience (Acts 2:32), with the power to baptize all who belong to Him.

What we see in Jesus teaches us what the baptism of the Spirit is. It is not that grace by which we turn to God, become regenerate and seek to live as God's children. When Jesus reminded His disciples (Acts 1:4) of John's prophecy, they were already partakers of this grace. Their baptism with the Spirit meant something more. It was to be to them the conscious presence of their glorified Lord come back from heaven to dwell in their hearts, and their participation in the power of His new life. It was to them a baptism of joy and power in their living fellowship with Jesus on the throne of glory. All that they were further to receive of wisdom, courage and holiness had its root in this: what the Spirit had been to Jesus when He was baptized, as the living bond with the Father's power and presence, He was to be to them. Through Him, the Son was to manifest himself, and Father and Son were to make their abode with them.

"Upon whom thou shalt see the Spirit descending, and abiding upon him, the same is he that baptizeth with the Holy Spirit." This word comes to us as well as to John. To know what the baptism of the Spirit means, how and from whom we are to receive it, we must see *the One* upon whom the Spirit descended and abode. We must see Jesus baptized with the Holy Ghost. We must try to understand how He needed it, how He was prepared for it, how He yielded to it, how in its power He died His death and was raised again.

What Jesus has to give us, He first received and personally appropriated for himself; what He received and won for himself is all for us. He will make it our very own. Upon whom we see the Spirit abiding, He baptizes with the Spirit.

In regard to this baptism of the Spirit there are questions that we may not find it easy to answer and to which all will not give the same answer. Was the outpouring of the Spirit at Pentecost the complete fulfillment of the promise? Is that the only baptism of the Spirit, given once for all to the new-born Church? Or is not the coming of the Holy Spirit on the disciples (Acts 4); on the Samaritans (Acts 8); on the heathen in the house of Cornelius (Acts 10); and on the twelve disciples at Ephesus (Acts 19) also to be regarded as separate fulfillments of the words: "He shall baptize with the Holy Ghost"? Is the sealing of the Spirit, given to each believer in regeneration, to be counted by him as his baptism of the Spirit? Or is it, as some say, a distinct, definite blessing to be received later on? Is it a blessing given only once, or can it be repeated and renewed? In the course of our study we shall find light in God's Word that may help us to a solution of difficulties like these.[1] But it is of great consequence that at the outset we should not allow ourselves to be occupied with points as these, which are, after all, of minor importance. We should fix our whole hearts on the great spiritual lessons that God would have us learn from the preaching of the baptism of the Holy Ghost. There are two lessons in particular.

The first is that this baptism of the Holy Spirit is the crown and glory of Jesus' work; that we need it and must know that we have it if we are to live the true Christian life. We do need it. The holy Jesus needed it. Christ's loving, obedient disciples needed it. It is something more than the working of the Spirit in regeneration. It is the personal Spirit of Christ making himself present within us, always abiding in the heart in the power of His glorified nature, as He is exalted above every enemy. It is the Spirit of the life of Christ Jesus making us free from the law of sin and death and bringing us, as a personal experience, into the liberty from sin to which Christ redeemed us. To so many regenerate it is only a blessing registered on their behalf but not possessed or enjoyed. It is the enduement with power to fill us with boldness in the presence of every danger and give the victory over the world and every enemy. It is the fulfillment of what God meant in His promise: "I will dwell in them, and walk in them."

Let us ask the Father to reveal to us all that His love meant for us until our souls are filled with the glory of the thought: "He baptizeth with the Holy Spirit."

The second lesson is: It is Jesus who thus baptizes. Whether we look upon this baptism as something we already have and of which we only want a fuller apprehension, or something we still must receive, in this all agree: it is only in the fellowship of Jesus, in faithful attachment and obedience to Him, that a baptized life can be received, maintained or renewed. "He that believeth in me," Jesus said, "out of his belly shall flow rivers of living water." The one thing we need is living faith in the indwelling Jesus. The living water will surely and freely flow. Faith is the instinct of the new nature by which it recognizes and receives its divine food and drink. In the power of the Spirit who dwells in every believer, let us trust Jesus, who fills with the Spirit, and cling to Him in love and obedience. It is He who baptizes. In contact with Him, in devotion to Him, in the confidence that He has given and will give himself wholly to us, let us look to Him for nothing less than all that the baptism of the Spirit can imply.

In doing so, let us especially remember one thing: only he that is faithful in the least will be made ruler over much. Be very faithful to what you already have and know of the Spirit's working. Regard yourself with deep reverence as God's holy temple. Wait for and listen to the gentlest whispering of God's Spirit within you. Listen particularly to the conscience, which has been cleansed in the blood. Keep that conscience very clean by simple childlike obedience. In your heart there may be much involuntary sin over which you feel yourself powerless. Humble yourself deeply because of inbred corruption, strengthened as it has been by actual sin. Let every rising of such sin be cleansed in the blood.

But with regard to your voluntary actions say, day by day, to the Lord Jesus, that everything you know to be pleasing to Him you will do. Yield to the reproofs of conscience when you fail; but come again, have hope in God, and renew the vow: What I know God wants me to do, I will do. Ask humbly every morning, and wait, for guidance in your path; the Spirit's voice will become better known, and His strength will be felt. Jesus had His disciples three years in His baptism class, and then the blessing came. Be His loving, obedient disciple and believe in Him on whom the Spirit abode and who is full of the Spirit. Then you too shall be prepared for the fullness of the blessing of the baptism of the Spirit.

Blessed Lord Jesus! with my whole heart I worship Thee, as exalted on the throne to baptize with the Holy Ghost. Oh! reveal thyself to me in this Thy glory that I may rightly know what I may expect from Thee.

I bless Thee that in thyself I have seen what the preparation is for receiving the Holy Spirit in His fullness. During Thy life of preparation for thy work in Nazareth, O my Lord, the Spirit was always in Thee. And yet when Thou hadst surrendered thyself to fulfill all righteousness, and to enter into fellowship with the sinners Thou camest to save, in partaking of their baptism, Thou didst receive from the Father a new inflowing of His Holy Spirit. It was to Thee the seal of His love, the revelation of His indwelling, the power for His service. And now Thou, on whom we see the Spirit descend and abide, doest for us what the Father did for Thee.

My Holy Lord! I bless Thee that the Holy Spirit is in me too. But, oh! I beseech Thee, give me yet the full, the overflowing measure Thou hast promised. Let Him be to me the full unceasing revelation of Thy presence in my heart, as glorious and as mighty as on the throne of heaven. O my Lord Jesus! baptize me, fill me with the Holy Spirit. Amen.

SUMMARY

1. All divine giving and working is in the power of an endless life. And so we can look up to Jesus each day in the blessed light of this world: "He baptizeth with the Holy Spirit." He cleanses with the blood and baptizes with the Spirit, according to each new need.

2. Let us keep inseparably connected in our faith the double truth the Baptist preached: Jesus the Lamb taking away sin, Jesus the Anointed baptizing with the Spirit. It was only in virtue of His shedding His blood that He re-

ceived the Spirit to shed forth. It is as the cross is preached that the Spirit works. It is as I believe in the precious blood, that cleanses from all sin, and walk before my God with a conscience sprinkled with the blood, that I may claim the anointing. The blood and the oil go together. I need both. I have them both in the one Jesus, the Lamb on the throne.

Note

1. See Note 1, p. 211.

3

WORSHIP IN THE SPIRIT

But the hour cometh, and now is, when the true worshippers shall worship the Father in spirit and in truth: for the Father seeketh such to worship him. God is a Spirit, and they that worship him must worship him in spirit and in truth.—John 4:23, 24

For we are the circumcision, which worship God in the spirit and rejoice in Christ Jesus, and have no confidence in the flesh.—Phil. 3:3

To worship is man's highest glory. He was created for fellowship with God: of that fellowship worship is the sublimest expression. All the exercises of the religious life— meditation and prayer, love and faith, surrender and obedience—culminate in worship. Recognizing what God is in His holiness, His glory and His love, realizing what I am as a sinful creature and as the Father's redeemed child, in worship I gather up my whole being and present myself to my God. I offer Him the adoration and the glory which is His due. The truest, fullest and nearest approach to God is worship. Every sentiment and every service of the religious life is included in it: to worship is man's highest destiny, because in it God is all.

Jesus tells us that with His coming a new worship will commence. All that heathen or Samaritans had called worship, all that even the Jews had known of worship, in accordance with the provisional revelation of God's law, would make way for something entirely and distinctively new—the worship in spirit and in truth. This is the worship He was to inaugurate by the giving of the Holy Spirit. This is the worship which now alone is well-pleasing to the Father. It is for this worship in particular that we have received the Holy Spirit. Let us, at the very commencement of our study of the work of the Spirit, take in the blessed thought that the great object for which the Holy Spirit is within us is that we worship in spirit and in truth. "For the Father seeketh such to worship him." For this He sent forth His Son and His Spirit.

In spirit. When God created man a living soul, that soul, as the seat and organ of his personality and consciousness, was linked, on the one side, through the body, with the outer visible world; on the other side, through the spirit, with the unseen and the divine. The soul had to decide whether it would yield itself to the spirit, by it to be linked with God and His will, or to the body and the solicitations of the visible. In the Fall, the soul refused the rule of the spirit and became the slave of the body with its appetites. Man became flesh; the spirit lost its destined place of rule and became little more than a dormant power. It was now no longer the ruling principle but a struggling captive. And the spirit now stands in opposition to the flesh (the name for the life of soul and body together) in its subjection to sin.

When speaking of the unregenerate man in contrast with the spiritual (1 Cor. 2:14), Paul calls him psychical, soulish, or animal, having only the natural life. The life of the soul comprehends all our moral and intellectual faculties, as they may even be directed towards the things of God, apart from the renewal of the divine Spirit. Because the soul is under the power of the flesh, man is spoken of as having *become* flesh, as being flesh. As the body consists of flesh and bone, and the flesh is that part of it which is especially endowed with sensitiveness, and through which we receive our sensations from the outer world, the flesh denotes human nature. It has become subject to the world of sense. And because the whole soul has thus come under the power of the flesh, the Scripture speaks of all the attributes of the soul as belonging to the flesh and being under its power. So it contrasts, in reference to religion and worship, the two principles from which they may proceed. There is a fleshly wisdom and a spiritual wisdom (1 Cor. 2:12; Col. 1:9). There is a service to God, trusting in the flesh and glorying in the flesh, and a service to God by the spirit (Phil. 3:3, 4; Gal. 6:13). There is a fleshly mind and a spiritual mind (Col. 2:18, 1:9). There is a will of the flesh and a will which is of God working by His Spirit (John 1:13; Phil. 2:13). There is a worship which is a satisfying of the flesh, because it is in the power of what flesh can do (Col. 2:18, 23), and a worship of God which is in the spirit. It is this worship Jesus came to make possible, and to realize in us, by giving a new spirit in our inmost part, and then, within that, God's Holy Spirit.

"In spirit and *in truth.*" Such a worship in spirit is worship in truth. Just as the words "in spirit" do not mean internal as contrasted with external observances, but spiritual, worked in us by God's Spirit, as opposed to what man's natural power can effect, so the words *in truth* do not mean hearty, sincere, upright. In all the worship of the Old Testament saints, they knew that God sought truth in the inward parts; they sought Him uprightly with their whole hearts, and yet they attained not to that worship in spirit and truth which Jesus brought us when He rent the veil of the flesh. *Truth* here means the substance, the reality, the actual possession of all that the worship of God implies, both in what it demands and what it promises. John speaks of Jesus as "the only begotten of the Father, full of grace and truth." And he adds, "For the law was given by Moses; grace and truth came by Jesus Christ." If we take truth as opposed to falsehood, the law of Moses was just as true as the gospel of Jesus; they both came from God. But if we understand what it means, that the law gave only a shadow of "good things to come," and that Christ brought us the things themselves, their very substance, we see how He was full of truth, because He was himself *the truth*, the reality, the very life, love and power of God imparting itself to us. We then also see how it is only a worship *in spirit* that can be a worship *in truth*, in the actual enjoyment of that divine power, which is Christ's own life and fellowship with the Father, revealed and maintained within us by the Holy Spirit.

The true worshippers worship the Father in spirit and in truth. All worshippers are not true worshippers. There may be a great deal of earnest, honest worship without its being worship in spirit and in truth. The mind may be intensely occupied, the feelings may be deeply moved, the will may be strongly aroused, while yet there is but little of the spiritual worship which stands in the truth of God. There may be great attachment to Bible truth, and yet through the predominating activity of that which comes not from God's working but from man's effort, it may not be the Christ-given, Spirit-breathed worship which God seeks. There must be accordance, harmony, unity between God, who is a Spirit, and the worshippers drawing near in the spirit. The Father seeks such as these to worship Him. The infinite, perfect, Holy Spirit, which God the Father is, must have some reflection in the spirit which is in the child. And this can only be as the Spirit of God dwells in us.

If we would strive to become such worshippers in spirit and in truth—true worshippers—the first thing we need is a sense of the danger that we are in as a result of worshipping in the flesh. As believers we have in us a double nature—flesh and spirit. The one is the natural part, which is ever ready to intrude itself and to undertake to do what is needed in the worship of God. The other is the spiritual part, which may still be very weak and possibly we do not yet know how to give it full sway. Our mind may delight in the study of God's Word; our feelings may be moved by the wonderful thoughts there revealed. However, see in Romans 7:22 that our wills may delight in the law of God after the inward man, but we may yet be impotent to do that law; to render the obedience and worship that we would like.

We need the Holy Spirit's indwelling for life and worship alike. And to receive this we need, first of all, to have the flesh silenced. "Be silent, all flesh, before the Lord. Let no flesh glory in His presence." To Peter had already been revealed by the Father that Jesus was the Christ, and yet he did not savor the thought of the cross. His mind was not in tune to the things of God but to the things of men. Our own thoughts of divine things, our own efforts to awaken in us or work up the right feelings must be given up; our own power to worship must be brought down and laid low. Every approach to God must take place under a very distinct and very quiet surrender to the Holy Spirit. As we learn how impossible it is, to willfully and at any moment ensure the

Spirit's working, we shall learn that if we would worship in the spirit we must walk in the spirit. "*Ye are* not in the flesh but *in the spirit, if so be* the Spirit of God dwelleth in you." As the Spirit dwells and rules in me, I am in the spirit, and can worship in the spirit.

"The hour cometh, and now is, when the true worshippers shall worship the Father in spirit and in truth: for the Father seeketh such to worship him: Yes, the Father seeks such worshippers, and what He seeks He finds because He himself calls us out. That we might be such worshippers, He sent His own Son to seek and to save the lost; to save us with this salvation, that we should become His true worshippers, who enter in through the rent veil of the flesh and worship Him in the spirit. Then He sent the Spirit of His Son, the Spirit of Christ, to be in us the truth and reality of what Christ had been. His actual presence will communicate within us the very life that Christ had lived. Blessed be God! the hour has come and is now; we are living in it this very moment—the time when true worshippers shall worship the Father in spirit and in truth. Let us believe it; the Spirit has been given and dwells within us for this one reason: because the Father seeks such worshippers. Let us rejoice in the confidence that we can attain to it, we can be true worshippers, because the Holy Spirit has been given.

Let us realize in holy fear and awe that He dwells within us. Let us humbly, in the silence of the flesh, yield ourselves to His leading and teaching. Let us wait in faith before God for His workings. And let us practice this worship. Let every new insight into what the work of the Spirit means, every exercise of faith in His indwelling or experience of His working, terminate in this as its highest glory: the adoring worship of the Father, the giving to Him the praise, thanks, honor, and love which are His alone.

O God! Thou art a Spirit, and they that worship Thee must worship Thee in spirit and in truth. Blessed be Thy name! Thou didst send forth Thine own Son to redeem and prepare us for the worship in the Spirit; and Thou didst send forth Thy Spirit to dwell in us and fit us for it. And now we have access to the Father, as through the Son, so in the Spirit.

Most holy God! we confess with shame how much our

worship has been in the power and the will of the flesh. By this we have dishonored Thee, and grieved Thy Spirit, and brought infinite loss to our own souls. O God! forgive and save us from this sin. Teach us, we pray Thee, never, never to attempt to worship Thee but in spirit and in truth.

Our Father! Thy Holy Spirit dwells in us. We beseech Thee, according to the riches of Thy glory, to strengthen us with might by Him, that our inner man may indeed be a spiritual temple, where spiritual sacrifices are unceasingly offered. Teach us the blessed art, as often as we enter Thy presence, of yielding self and the flesh to the death, and waiting for and trusting the Spirit who is in us, to work in us a worship, a faith and love, acceptable to Thee through Christ Jesus. And, oh! that throughout the universal Church, a worship in spirit and in truth may be sought after, attained, and rendered to Thee day by day. We ask it in the name of Jesus. Amen.

SUMMARY

1. It is in worship that the Holy Spirit most completely attains the object for which He was given; it is in worship He can most fully prove what He is. If I want the consciousness and the power of the Spirit's presence to become strong within me, *let me worship*. The Spirit fits us for worship: worship fits us for the Spirit.

2. It is not only prayer that is worship. Worship is the prostrate adoration of His holy presence. Often without words: "They bowed their heads and worshipped" (Ex. 12:27; Neh. 8:6). "The elders fell down and worshipped" (Rev. 5:14). Or only with an Amen, Hallelujah (Rev. 19:4).

3. There is so much worship, even among believers, that is not in the spirit! In private, family, and public worship, there is so much hasty entering into God's presence in the power of the flesh, with little or no waiting for the Spirit to lift us heavenward! It is only the presence and power of the Holy Spirit that fits us for acceptable worship.

4. The great hindrance to the spirit is the flesh. The secret of spiritual worship is the death of the flesh; giving it up to the accursed death of the cross. In great fear of the flesh's actions, we must humbly and trustfully wait for the Spirit's

life and power to take the place of the life and strength of self.

5. As our life is, so will our worship be. The Spirit must lead and rule in daily life if He is to inspire our worship. A life in obedience to God's will and in His presence fits us for worship. May God cause us to feel deeply the extent, sinfulness and impotence of worship that is not in spirit and in truth.

6. The Spirit is given for worship. In an attitude of worship let us study the thoughts in this book, humbly and reverently waiting upon God. "My soul, be thou silent unto God."

4

THE SPIRIT AND THE WORD

It is the spirit that quickeneth; the flesh profiteth nothing: the words that I speak unto you, they are spirit, and they are life. . . . Lord, to whom shall we go? thou hast the words of eternal life.—John 6:63, 68

Who also hath made us able ministers of the new testament; not of the letter, but of the spirit: for the letter killeth, but the spirit giveth life.—2 Cor. 3:6

Our blessed Lord has been speaking of himself as the bread of life, and of His flesh and blood as the meat and drink of eternal life. To many of His disciples it was a hard saying, which they could not understand. Jesus tells them that it is only when the Holy Spirit is come, and they have Him, that His words will become clear to them. He says, "It is the spirit that quickeneth; the flesh profiteth nothing. The words that I speak unto you, they are spirit, and they are life."

"It is the spirit that quickeneth." In these words and in the corresponding ones of Paul, "The spirit giveth life," we have the nearest approach to what may be called a definition of the spirit. (See 1 Cor. 15:45, "a quickening spirit.") The Spirit always acts, in the first place, whether in nature or grace, as a life-giving principle. It is of the deepest importance to keep firm hold on this. His work in the believer—of sealing, sanctifying, enlightening, and strengthening—is all rooted in this: it is as He is known and honored, and place given to Him; as He is waited on, as the inner life of the soul, that His other gracious workings can be experienced. These are but the outgrowth of the life; it is in the power of the life within that they can be enjoyed. "It is the spirit that quickeneth." In contrast to the spirit, our Lord placed the flesh. He says, "The flesh profiteth nothing." He is not speaking of the flesh as the foundation of sin. In its religious aspect, it is the power in which the natural man, or even the believer who does not fully yield to the Spirit, seeks to serve God, or to know and possess divine things. The futile character of all its efforts our Lord indicates in the words: "profiteth nothing." They are not sufficient; they do not avail us in reaching the spiritual reality—the divine things themselves. Paul means the same when he contrasts with the spirit, the letter that killeth. The whole dispensation of the law was but a dispensation of the letter and the flesh. Though it had a certain glory and Israel's privileges were very great, yet, as Paul says, "Even that which was made glorious had no glory in this respect, by reason of the glory that excelleth." Even Christ himself, as long as He was in the flesh, and until in the rending of the veil of His flesh the dispensation of the Spirit took the place of that of the flesh, could not by His words effect in His disciples what He desired. "It is the spirit that quickeneth; the flesh profiteth nothing."

Our Lord applies this saying especially to the words He had just spoken and the spiritual truth they contained. "The words that I speak unto you, they are spirit, and they are life." He wishes to teach the disciples two things. First of all, that the words are indeed a living seed with a power of germinating and springing up, asserting their own vitality, revealing their meaning, and proving their divine power in those who receive them and keep them abiding in the heart. He did not want them to be discouraged if they could not comprehend them at once. His words are spirit and life; they are not meant for understanding but for life. Coming in the power of the unseen Spirit, higher and deeper than all thought, they enter into the very roots of life. They have themselves a divine life working out effectually with a divine energy the truth they express into the experience of those who receive them. Secondly, as a consequence of this, these words of His need a spiritual nature to receive them. Seed needs a congenial soil: there must be life in the soil as well as in the seed. Not into the mind only, nor into the feelings, nor even into the will alone must the Word be taken, but through them into the life. The center of that life is man's spiritual nature, with conscience as its voice; there the authority of the Word must be acknowledged. But even this is not enough: conscience dwells in man as a captive amid powers it cannot control. It is the Spirit that comes from God, the Spirit that Christ came to bring, becoming our life, receiving the Word and assimilating it into our life, that will make them to become truth and power in us.

In our study of the work of the blessed Spirit, we cannot be too careful to get a clear and firm hold on this blessed truth. It will save us from right-hand and left-hand errors. It will keep us from expecting to enjoy the teaching of the Spirit without the Word, or to master the teaching of the Word without the Spirit.

On the one side we have the right-hand error—seeking the teaching of the Spirit without the Word. In the holy Trinity, the Word and the Spirit are ever in each other—one with the Father. It is not different with the God-inspired words of scripture. The Holy Spirit has for all ages embodied the thoughts of God in the written Word, and lives now for this very purpose in our hearts, there to reveal the power and the meaning of that Word. If you would be full of the Spirit, be full of the Word. If you would have the divine life of the Spirit within you grow strong and acquire power in every part of your nature, let the word of Christ dwell richly in you. If you would have the Spirit fulfill His office of remembrancer, calling to mind at the right moment and applying with divine accuracy what Jesus has spoken to your need, have the words of Christ abiding in you. If you would have the Spirit reveal to you the will of God in each circumstance of life, choosing what you must do from apparently conflicting commands or principles with unerring precision; suggesting His will as you need it, have the Word living in you, ready for His use. If you would have the eternal Word as your light, let the written Word be transcribed on your heart by the Holy Spirit. "The words that I speak unto you, they are spirit, and they are life." Take them and treasure them: it is through them that the Spirit manifests His quickening power.[1]

On the other side we have the left-hand and more common error. Think not for one moment that the Word can unfold its life in you, except as the Spirit within you accepts and appropriates it in the inner life. How much scripture reading, scripture study and scripture preaching has as its first and main object that of reaching the meaning of the Word? Men think that if they know correctly and exactly what it means, there will come as a natural consequence the blessing the Word is meant to bring. This is by no means the case. The Word is a seed. In every seed there is a fleshy part in which the life is hidden. One may have the most precious and perfect seed in its bodily substance; yet unless it be exposed in suitable soil to the influence of sun and moisture, the life may never grow up. We may hold the words and the doctrines of scripture most intelligently and earnestly, and yet know little of their life or power. We need to remind ourselves and the Church unceasingly that the scriptures which were spoken by holy men of old as they were moved by the Holy Spirit can only be understood by holy men as they are taught by the same Spirit. "The words I speak . . . are spirit, and life"; for the apprehending and partaking of them "the flesh profiteth nothing: it is the spirit that quickeneth," the spirit of life within us.

This is one of the serious lessons which the history of the Jews in the time of Christ teaches us. They were exceedingly zealous, as they thought, for God's word and honor and yet it turned out that all their zeal was for their human interpretation of God's Word. Jesus said to them: "Ye search the scriptures, because ye think that in them ye have eternal life; and these are they which testify of me: and ye will not come to me that ye may have life." They did indeed trust to the Scriptures to lead them to eternal life; and yet they never saw that they testified of Christ, and so they would not come to Him. They studied and accepted Scripture in the light and in the power of their human understanding and not in the light and power of God's Spirit as their life.

The weakness in the life of so many believers who read and know much scripture is because they do not know that it is the Spirit that quickeneth; that the flesh, that the human understanding, however intelligent, however earnest, profiteth nothing. They think that in the scriptures they have eternal life. But they know very little of the living Christ in the power of the Spirit, as their life.

What is needed is very simple: the determined refusal to attempt to deal with the written Word without the quickening Spirit. Let us never take scripture into our hand, or mind, or mouth, without realizing the need and the promise of the Spirit. First, in a quiet act of worship, look to God to give and renew the workings of His Spirit within you. Then, in a quiet act of faith, yield yourself to the power that dwells in you, and wait on Him, that not the mind alone but the life in you, may be opened to receive the Word. Let the Holy Spirit be your life. To the spirit and the life coming out from within to meet the Word from without as its food, the words of Christ are indeed spirit and life.

As we further follow the teaching of our blessed Lord as to the Spirit, it will become clear to us that, as the Lord's words are spirit and life, so the Spirit must be in us as the spirit of our life. Our inmost personal life must be the Spirit of God. Deeper down than mind—feeling, or will—the very root of all these and their animating principle—there must be the Spirit of God. If we seek to go lower than these, we see that nothing can equal the spirit of life which there is in the words of the living God. If we wait on the Holy Spirit within us, in the unseen depths of the hidden life, to receive and reveal the words in His quickening power and work them into the very life of our life, we shall know in truth what it means: "It is the Spirit that quickeneth." We shall see how divinely right and becoming it is that the words which are Spirit and Life should be met in us by the Spirit and Life dwelling within, how then alone they will unfold their meaning and impart their substance, and give their divine strength and fullness to the spirit and life already within us.

O my God! again I thank Thee for the wonderful gift of the indwelling Spirit. And I humbly beseech Thee anew that I may indeed know that He is in me, and how glorious the divine work He is carrying on.

Teach me especially, I pray Thee, to believe that He is the life and the strength of the growth of the divine life within me; the pledge and assurance that I can grow up into all my God would have me. As I see this, I shall understand how He, as the Spirit of life within me, will make my spirit hunger for the Word as the bread of life; will receive and assimilate it; will indeed make it life and power.

Forgive me, my God, that I have so much sought to apprehend thy words, which are spirit and life, in the power of human thought and the fleshly mind. I have been so slow to learn that the flesh profiteth nothing. I do desire to learn it now.

O my Father! give me the spirit of wisdom, grant me the mighty workings of the Spirit, that I may know how deeply spiritual each word of thine is, and how spiritual things can only be spiritually discerned. Teach me in all my intercourse with Thy Word to deny the flesh and the fleshly mind, to wait in deep humility and faith for the inward working of the Spirit to quicken the word. Likewise, may all my meditation of Thy Word, all my keeping of it in faith and obedience, be in spirit and in truth, in life and power. Amen.

SUMMARY

1. To understand a book the reader must know the same language as the author. He must in many cases have somewhat of the same spirit in which the author wrote. To understand the scripture, we need the same Holy Spirit dwelling in us which enabled holy men of old to write them.

2. The eternal Word and the eternal Spirit are inseparable. Even so the creative word and the creative Spirit (Gen. 1:2, 3; Ps. 33:6). Also the word and Spirit in redemption (John 1:1-3, 14, 33). Also in the written Word: "The words I speak are spirit." So in the word preached by the apostles (1 Thess. 1:5). So it must be in the word read and meditated on by us; as certainly as the God-breathed word comes from without must the God-breathed spirit meet it from within.

3. The word is the seed. The seed has a hidden life that needs a living soil in which to grow. The word has a divine

life; see that you receive the word not only in the natural mind or will, but in the new spirit, where God's Spirit dwells.

4. I see it more and more: The power of the word and its truth depend upon living fellowship with Jesus. Why is there so often failure instead of victory in the Christian life? It is because the truth is held apart from the power of the Spirit. May God help me to believe these two things: the Word is full of divine Spirit and power and can work mightily; the heart has the same divine Spirit, through whom the living word is accepted in living power. My life must be in the power of the Spirit.

Notes

1. Compare carefully Eph. 5:18, 19 and Col. 3:16, and see how the joyful fellowship of the Christian life, described in identically the same words, is said in the one place to come from being full of the Spirit, in the other from being full of the Word. Let us seek just as much of the Word as of the Spirit, and just as much of the Spirit as of the Word.

5

THE SPIRIT OF THE GLORIFIED JESUS

He that believeth on me, as the scripture hath said, out of his belly shall flow rivers of living water. (But this spake he of the Spirit, which they that believe on him should receive: for the Holy Ghost was not yet given; because that Jesus was not yet glorified).—John 7:38, 39

Our Lord promises here that those who come unto Him and drink, who believe in Him, will not only never thirst, but will themselves become fountains, from which will flow streams of living water of life and blessing. In recording the words, John explains that the promise was a prospective one that would have to wait for its fulfillment—till the Spirit would be poured out. He also gave the double reason for this delay: "The Holy Ghost was not yet given; because that Jesus was not yet glorified." The expression "the Spirit was not yet" appeared strange, so the word *given* has been inserted. But the expression, if accepted as it stands, may guide us into the true understanding of the real significance of the Spirit's not coming until Jesus was glorified.

We have seen that God has given a twofold revelation of himself: first as God in the Old Testament, then as Father in the New. We know how the Son, who had from eternity been with the Father, entered upon a new stage of existence when He became flesh. When He returned to heaven, He was still the same only-begotten Son of God, and yet not altogether the same. For He was now also, as Son of Man, the first-begotten from the dead, clothed with that glorified humanity which He had perfected and sanctified for himself. Likewise, the Spirit of God poured out at Pentecost was indeed something new. Through the Old Testament He was always called the Spirit of God or the Spirit of the Lord; the name of Holy Spirit He did not yet bear as His own proper name.[1] It is only in connection with the work He has to do in preparing the way for Christ, and a body for Him, that the proper name comes into use (Luke 1:15, 35). When poured out at Pentecost, He came as the Spirit of the glorified Jesus, the Spirit of the incarnate, crucified and exalted Christ, the bearer and communicator to us not of the life of God as such, but of that life as it had been interwoven into human nature in the person of Christ Jesus. It is in this capacity especially, that He bears the name of Holy Spirit, for it is as the indwelling one that God is holy.

Of this Spirit, as He dwelt in Jesus in the flesh and can dwell in us in the flesh too, it is distinctly and literally true; the Holy Spirit was not yet. The Spirit of the glorified Jesus; the Son of man become the Son of God—*He* could not be until Jesus was glorified.

This thought opens up to us further the reason why it is not the Spirit of God as such, but the Spirit of Jesus, that could be sent to dwell in us. Sin had not only disturbed our relation to God's law but to God himself; with the divine favor we had lost the divine life. Christ came not only to deliver man from the law and its curse, but to bring human nature itself again into the fellowship of the divine life, to make us partakers of the divine nature. He could do this, not by an exercise of divine power on man, but only in the path of a free, moral, and most real human development. In His own person, having become flesh, He had to sanctify the flesh and make it a fit and willing receptacle for the indwelling of the Spirit of God. Having done this, He had (in accordance with the law that the lower form of life can rise to a higher only through decay and death), in death, both to bear the curse of sin and to give himself as the seedcorn to bring forth fruit in us. From His nature, as it was glorified in the resurrection and ascension, His Spirit came forth as the Spirit of His human life, glorified into the union with the divine, to make us partakers of all that He had personally worked out and acquired, of himself and His glorified life. In virtue of His atonement, man now had a right and title to the fullness of the divine Spirit and to His indwelling as never before.

In virtue of His having perfected in himself a new, holy, human nature on our behalf, He could now communicate what previously had no existence—a life at once human and divine. From henceforth the Spirit, just as He was the personal divine life, could also become the personal life of men. Even as the Spirit is the personal life principle in God himself, so He can be it in the child of God: the Spirit of God's Son can now be the Spirit that cries in our heart, "Abba, Father." Of this Spirit it is most fully true, "The Spirit was not yet, because Jesus was not yet glorified."[2]

But now, blessed be God! Jesus has been glorified; there is now the Spirit of the glorified Jesus; the promise can now be fulfilled: "He that believeth on me, out of him shall flow rivers of living waters." The great transaction which took place when Jesus was glorified is now an eternal reality. When Christ had entered into our human nature, in our flesh, into the holiest of all, there took place that of which Peter speaks, "Being by the right hand of God exalted, *he received of the Father* the promise of the Holy Ghost." In our place and on our behalf, as man and the head of man,

He was admitted into the full glory of the divine, and His human nature constituted the receptacle and the dispenser of the divine Spirit. The Holy Spirit could come down as the Spirit of the God-man—actually the Spirit of God, and yet as truly the spirit of man. He could come down as the Spirit of the glorified Jesus to be in each one who believes in Jesus, the Spirit of His personal life and His personal presence, and at the same time the spirit of the personal life of the believer. Just as in Jesus the perfect union of God and man had been effected and finally completed when He sat down upon the throne and He so entered on a new stage of existence, a glory hitherto unknown; now also, a new era has commenced in the life and the work of the Spirit. He can now come down to witness of the perfect union of the divine and the human. In becoming our life, He makes us partakers of it. *There is now* the Spirit of the glorified Jesus: He has poured Him forth; we have received Him to stream into us, through us and forth from us in rivers of blessing.

The glorifying of Jesus and the streaming forth of His Spirit are intimately connected; in vital organic union the two are inseparably linked. If we would have not only the Spirit of God, but this Spirit of Christ, which "was not yet," but now is, the Spirit of the glorified Jesus, it is particularly with the glorified Jesus we must believingly deal. We must not simply rest content with the faith that trusts in the cross and its pardon; we must seek to know the new life, the life of glory and power divine in human nature, of which the Spirit of the glorified Jesus is meant to be the witness and the bearer. This is the mystery which was hid from ages and generations, but is now made known by the Holy Spirit, *Christ in us:* how He actually can live His divine life in us who are in the flesh. We have the most intense personal interest in knowing and understanding what it means that Jesus is glorified, that human nature shares the life and glory of God, that the Spirit was not yet, as long as Jesus was not glorified. It is important that we understand this not only because we are one day to see Him in His glory and to share in it, but even *now,* day by day, we are to live in it. The Holy Spirit is able to *be* to us just as much as we are willing to *have* of Him and of the life of the glorified Lord.

"This spake Jesus of the Spirit, which they that believed

on him were to receive; for the Spirit was not yet; because Jesus was not yet glorified." God be praised! Jesus has been glorified: there is now the Spirit of the glorified Jesus; we have received Him. In the Old Testament only the unity of God was revealed; when the Spirit was mentioned, it was always as His Spirit, the power by which God was working. He was not yet known on earth as a person. In the New Testament the Trinity is revealed; with Pentecost the Holy Spirit descended as a person to dwell in us. This is the fruit of Jesus' work—that we now have the personal presence of the Holy Spirit on earth. In Christ Jesus, the second person, the Son came to reveal the Father and the Father dwelt and spoke in Him. Likewise, the Spirit, the third person, comes to reveal the Son and in Him the Son dwells and works in us. This is the glory wherewith the Father glorified the Son of man, because the Son had glorified Him. In His name and through Him, the Holy Spirit descends as a person to dwell in believers and to make the glorified Jesus a present reality within them. He it is of whom Jesus said, that whosoever believes in Him shall never thirst but shall have rivers of living waters flowing out of him. This alone satisfies the soul's thirst and makes it a fountain to quicken others—the personal indwelling of the Holy Spirit, revealing the presence of the glorified Jesus.

He that believes on me, rivers of water shall flow out of him. This He said of the Spirit. Here we have once again the blessed key of all God's treasures: *He that believeth on me.* It is the glorified Jesus who baptizes with the Holy Ghost. Let us believe in Him. Let each one who longs for the full blessing here promised only believe. Let us believe in Him, that He is indeed glorified, that all He is and does and wishes to do is in the power of a divine glory. According to the riches of His glory, God can now work in us. Let us believe that He has given His Holy Spirit, that we have the personal presence of the Spirit on earth and within us. By this faith the glory of Jesus in heaven and the power of the Spirit in our hearts become inseparably linked. Let us believe that in the fellowship with Jesus the stream will flow ever stronger and fuller, into us and out of us. Yes, let us believe on Jesus. But let us remember: thinking on these things, understanding them, being very sure of them, rejoicing in a fuller insight into them, all this, though needful, is not in itself *believing*. Believing is that power of the renewed nature which, forsaking self and dying to it, makes room for the divine, for God, for the glorified Christ to come and take possession and do His work. Faith in Jesus bows in lowly stillness and poverty of spirit, to realize that self has nothing and that another, the unseen Spirit, has now come in to be its leader, its strength and its life. Faith in Jesus bows in the stillness of a quiet surrender before Him, fully assured that as it waits on Him, He will cause the river to flow.

Blessed Lord Jesus! I do believe; help Thou mine unbelief. Do Thou, the author and perfecter of our faith, perfect the work of faith in me too. Teach me, I pray Thee, with a faith that enters the unseen, to realize what Thy glory is and what my share in it is even now, according to Thy Word: "The glory which thou gavest me, I have given them." Teach me that the Holy Ghost and His power is the glory which Thou givest us, and that Thou wouldst have us show forth Thy glory in rejoicing in His holy presence on earth and His indwelling in us. Teach me above all, my blessed Lord, not only to take and hold these blessed truths in the mind, but with my spirit that is in my inmost parts, to wait on Thee to be filled with Thy Spirit.

O my glorified Lord! I do even now bow before Thy glory in humble faith. Let all the life of self and the flesh be abased and perish as I worship and wait before Thee. Let the Spirit of Glory become my life. Let His presence break down all trust in self, and make room for Thee. Let my whole life be one of faith in the Son of God, who loved me, and gave himself for me. Amen.

SUMMARY

1. In Christ there was an outward lowly state as Servant, which preceded His state of glory as King. It was His faithfulness in the first that led Him to the second. Let every believer who longs to partake with Christ in His glory, first faithfully follow Him in His denial of self; the Spirit will in due time reveal the glory within Him.

2. Christ's glory was particularly the fruit of His suffer-

ing—the death of the cross. It is as I enter into the death of the cross in its double aspect, Christ's crucifixion for me, my crucifixion with Christ, that the heart is opened for the Spirit's revelation of the glorified Christ.

3. It is not having glorious thoughts and impressions at times of my Lord's glory that can satisfy me; it is *Christ himself glorified in me,* in my personal life, in the way of a divine and heavenly power uniting His life in glory with my life; it is this alone that can satisfy His heart and mine.

4. Again I say: Glory be to God! this Spirit, the Spirit of the glorified One, is within me. He has possession of my inmost life. By His grace I will withdraw that life from the ways of self and sin, wait and worship in the assured confidence that He will take full possession; will prepare my heart; will glorify my Lord in me.

Notes

1. The only three passages (Ps. 51:11; Isa. 63:10, 11) where we have in our translation Holy Spirit, the Hebrew is properly (and Stier, for instance, in his Commentary renders it so) *"the Spirit of His holiness."* It is thus of the Spirit of God that the word is used, and not as the proper name of the third person. Only in the New Testament does the Spirit bear the name of "The Holy Spirit."

2. See Notes 2, p. 221, and 7, p. 246.

6

THE INDWELLING SPIRIT

> And I will pray the Father, and he shall give you another Comforter, that he may abide with you for ever; even the Spirit of truth; whom the world cannot receive, because it seeth him not, neither knoweth him: but ye know him; for he dwelleth with you, and shall be in you.—John 14:16, 17

"He shall be in you." In these simple words our Lord announces that wonderful mystery of the Spirit's indwelling which was to be the fruit and the crown of His redeeming work. It was for this, man had been created. It was for this, God's mastery within the heart, the Spirit had labored in vain with men through the past ages. It was for this, Jesus had lived and was about to die. Without this the Father's purpose and His own work would fail in their accomplishment. For want of this the blessed Master's work with the disciples had effected so little. He had hardly ever ventured to mention it to them because He knew they would not understand it. But then on the last night, when time was running out, He disclosed the divine secret that when He left them, their loss would be compensated by a greater blessing than His bodily presence. Another would come in His place, to abide with them forever and to dwell in them. Dwelling in them He would prepare them to receive himself, their Lord, and their Father too. "He shall be in you."

Our Father has given us a twofold revelation of himself. Through His Son He reveals *His holy image* and setting Him before men invites them to become like Him by receiving Him into their heart and life. Through His Spirit He sends forth His divine power, to enter into us and from within prepare us for receiving the Son and the Father. The dispensation of the Spirit is the dispensation of the inner life. The dispensation of the Word, or the Son, began with the creation of man in God's image and continued through all the preparatory stages down to Christ's appearing in the flesh. This was external and preparatory. There were, at times, special and mighty workings of the Spirit, but the indwelling was unknown; man had not yet become a habitation of God in the Spirit. This still needed to be attained. Eternal life was to become the very life of man, hiding itself within his very being and consciousness and clothing itself in the forms of a human will and life. Just as it is through the Spirit that God is what He is, just as the Spirit is the principle by which the personalities of the Father and the Son have their root and consciousness, likewise this Spirit of the divine life is now to be *in us*. In the deepest sense of the word, He should be the principle of our life, the root of our personality, the very life of our being and consciousness. He is to be one with us in the absoluteness of a divine immanence—dwelling in us, even as the Father in the Son and the Son in the Father. Let us bow in holy reverence to worship and adore Him and to receive the mighty blessing.

If we would enter into the full understanding and experience of what our blessed Lord here promises, we must, above everything, remember that what He speaks of is a *divine* indwelling. Wherever God dwells He hides himself. In nature He hides himself; most men do not see Him there. In meeting His saints of old He usually hid himself under some manifestation in human weakness, so that it was often only after He was gone that they said, "Surely the Lord is in this place, and I knew it not."[1] The blessed Son came to reveal God, and yet He came as a root out of a dry ground, without form or comeliness; even His own disciples were at times offended at Him. Men always expect the kingdom of God to come with observation. They do not know that it is a hidden mystery to be received only as, in His own self-revealing power, God makes himself known in hearts surrendered and prepared for Him. Christians are always ready, when the promise of the Spirit occupies them, to form some conception as to how His leading can be known in their thoughts; how His quickening will affect their feelings; how His sanctifying can be recognized in their will and conduct. They need to be reminded that deeper than mind, feeling and will, deeper than the soul, where these have their seat, in the depths of the spirit that came from God, there comes the Holy Spirit to dwell.

This indwelling is therefore first of all, and all through, to be recognized by faith. Even when I cannot see the least evidence of His working, I am quietly and reverently to believe that He dwells in me. In that faith I am restfully and trustfully to count upon His working, and to wait for it. In that faith I must very distinctly deny my own wisdom and strength, and in childlike self-abnegation depend upon Him to work. His first workings may be so feeble and hidden that I can hardly recognize them as coming from Him; they may appear to be nothing more than the voice of conscience, or the familiar sound of some Bible truth. Here is the time for faith to hold fast to the Master's promise and the Father's gift and to trust that the Spirit is within and will guide. In that faith let me continually yield up my whole being to His rule and mastery; let me be faithful to what appears the nearest to His voice; in such faith and such faithfulness my soul will be prepared for knowing His voice better. Out of the hidden depths His power will move to take possession of mind and will, and the indwelling in the hidden recesses of the heart will grow into a being filled with His fullness.[2]

Faith is the one faculty of our spiritual nature by which we can recognize the divine, in whatever low and unlikely appearances it clothes itself. If this be true of the Father in His glory as God and the Son as the manifestation of the Father, how much more must it be true of the Spirit, the unseen divine life-power come to clothe itself and hide itself away within our weakness? Let us cultivate and exercise our faith in the Father whose one gift through the Son is this— the Spirit in our hearts. Let us look in faith to the Son also whose whole person and work and glory center in the gift of the indwelling Spirit. Likewise, let our faith grow strong in the unseen, sometimes unfelt divine presence of this mighty power. He is a living person, who has descended into our weakness and hidden himself in our smallness, to fit us for becoming the dwelling of the Father and the Son. Let our adoring worship of our glorified Lord ever seek to grasp the wondrous answer He gives to every prayer, as the seal of our acceptance. It is the promise of deeper knowledge of our God, of closer fellowship and richer blessedness: The Holy Spirit dwelleth in you.

The deep importance of a right apprehension of the indwelling of the Spirit is evident from the place it occupies in our Lord's farewell discourse. In this and the two following chapters, He speaks of the Spirit more directly as teacher and witness, as representing and glorifying himself, as convincing the world. At the same time, He connects what He says of His and the Father's indwelling, of the union of the vine and the branches, of the peace and joy and power in prayer which His disciples would have, with "that day," the time of the Spirit's coming. But, before all this, as its one condition and only source, He places the promise: "The Spirit shall be in you." It does not profit us if we know all that the Spirit can do for us, or that we confess our entire dependence on Him, unless we clearly realize and put in proper perspective what the Master has given first place. It is as the indwelling Spirit alone that He can be our teacher or our strength. As the church and the believer accept our Lord's promise: "He shall be in you," and live under the control of this faith, our true relation to the blessed Spirit will be restored. He will take charge and inspire; He will mightily fill and bless the being given up to Him as His abode.

A careful study of the epistles will confirm this. In writing to the Corinthians, Paul had to reprove them for sad and terrible sins and yet he says to all, including the weakest and most unfaithful believer, "Know you not that the Spirit of God dwelleth in you? Know you not that your body is the temple of the Holy Ghost?" He is sure that if this were believed, if truth were given the place God meant it to have, it would not only be the motive but the power of a new and holy life. To the backsliding Galatians, he has no greater plea to address than this: they had *received* the Spirit by the preaching of faith; God had sent forth the Spirit of His Son *into their hearts;* they had their life by the Spirit in them; if they could but understand and believe this, they would also walk in the Spirit.

It is this teaching the church of Christ needs in our days. I am deeply persuaded that very few of us fully realize to what extent believers are ignorant of this aspect of the truth concerning the Holy Spirit, or to what an extent this is the cause of their weakness in holy walk and work. There may be a great deal of praying for the Holy Spirit's working; we may be correct in our confession, both in preaching and prayer, of entire and absolute dependence on Him; but unless His personal, continual, divine indwelling be acknowledged and experienced, we must not be surprised if there is continual failure. The holy dove wants His resting-place free from all intrusion and disturbance. God wants entire possession of His temple. Jesus wants His home all to himself. He cannot do His work there, He cannot rule and reveal himself and His love as He would, unless the whole home, the whole inner being, be possessed and filled by the Holy Spirit.

Let us consent to this. As the meaning of the indwelling dawns upon us in its full extent and claims, as we accept it as a divine reality to be carried out and maintained by nothing less than an almighty power, as we bow low in emptiness and surrender, faith and adoration, to accept the promise and live on it—"He shall be in you—" the Father will for Jesus' sake delight to fulfill it in our experience. We shall know that the beginning, the secret and the power of the life of a true disciple is the indwelling Spirit.

Blessed Lord Jesus! my soul doth bless Thee for Thy precious word: The Spirit shall be in you. In deep humility I

now once again accept it and ask Thee to teach me its full
and blessed meaning.

I ask for myself and all God's children that we may see
how near Thy love would come to us, how entirely and most
intimately Thou wouldst give thyself to us. Nothing can satisfy Thee but to have Thy abode within us, to dwell in us as
the life of our life. To this end Thou hast sent forth, from
Thy glory, Thy Holy Spirit into our hearts, to be the power
that lives and acts in our inmost being and to give in us the
revelation of thyself. O holy Saviour, bring Thy church to
see this truth that has been so much hid and lost, to experience it and to bear witness to it in power. May the joyful
sound be heard throughout her borders, that every true believer has the indwelling and the leading of thy Spirit.

And teach me, my Lord, the life of faith that goes out of
self, to wait on Thee, as in Thy Spirit Thou dost Thy work
within me. May my life from hour to hour be in the holy,
humble consciousness: Christ's Spirit dwelleth in me.

In humility and silence I bow before this holy mystery,
my God, my Lord Jesus, Thine own Spirit dwells in me.
Amen.

SUMMARY

1. The coming of the Son of God in the likeness of sinful
flesh, the Word being made flesh, and His dwelling in our
nature—what a mystery is this! Great is the mystery of
Godliness! But how great then the mystery of the Spirit of
God dwelling in us who are sinful flesh! Blessed are they "to
whom God would make known what is the riches of the glory
of *this mystery*—Christ in you."

2. There is an introspection in which the soul looks at its
own thoughts, feelings and purposes to find the proof of
grace and the ground of peace. This is unhealthy and not of
faith; it turns the eye from Christ to self. But there is another turning inwardly which is one of the highest exercises
of faith. It is when, closing the eye to all it can see in itself,
the soul seeks to realize in faith that there is in its inmost
parts a new spirit, within which the Spirit of Christ now
dwells. In this faith in unreservedly gives itself up to be renewed by the Spirit and yields every faculty of the soul to be
sanctified and guided by this Spirit within. Without such

consciousness of a temple within and its occupant daily renewed in holy silence, there cannot be the clear believing prayer to the Father to work mightily by His Spirit, or the confidence in Jesus to give the living streams from within.

3. *Within you! Within you!* in your inmost parts!—this was God's promise. Thank God, His Holy Spirit dwells within me!

4. The first thought connected with the entrance into a temple is reverence—the head uncovered. The first and abiding thought connected with the Spirit's dwelling in me as His temple is this also—deep reverence and awe before the holy presence.

5. "He *abideth* with you, and shall be *in you.*" Hold fast the two thoughts: the *permanence* of His presence with the Church, the *intimacy* of His presence in every believer.

Notes

1. In the tabernacle and the temple God dwelt in the darkness; He was there, but behind a veil, to be believed in and feared, but not to be seen.

2. See Note 3, p. 227.

7

THE SPIRIT GIVEN TO THE OBEDIENT

If ye love me, keep my commandments. And I will pray the Father, and he shall give you another Comforter . . . even the Spirit of truth. . . .—John 14:15, 16, 17

. . . the Holy Ghost, whom God hath given to them that obey him.—Acts 5:32

The truth which these words express has often suggested the question: How can this be? We need the Spirit to make us obedient. We long for the Spirit's power because we regret so much the disobedience we will find in ourselves, and we desire to be otherwise. And how is this? The Saviour claims obedience as the condition of the Father's giving and our receiving the Spirit.

The difficulty will be resolved if we remember what we have more than once seen: that there is a twofold manifestation of the Spirit of God corresponding to the Old and New Testament. In the former, He works as the Spirit of God preparing the way for the higher revelation of God, as the Father of Jesus Christ. In this way He had worked in Christ's disciples, as the Spirit of conversion and faith. What they were now about to receive was something higher—the Spirit of the glorified Jesus communicating the power from on high, the experience of His full salvation. Although now to all believers under the New Testament economy, the Spirit in them is the Spirit of Christ, there is still something that corresponds to the twofold dispensation. Where there is not much knowledge of the Spirit's work or where His workings in a Church or an individual are weak even there believers will not get beyond the experience of His preparatory workings in them. Though He be in them, they know Him not in His power as the Spirit of the glorified Lord. He is in them to make them obedient. It is only as they yield obedience to this His more elementary work, the keeping of Christ's commandments, that they will be promoted to the higher experience of His conscious indwelling, as the representative and revealer of Jesus in His glory. "If ye love me, keep my commandments: and I will pray the Father, and he will send you another Comforter."

The lesson is one we cannot study too attentively. In paradise, in the angels of heaven, in God's own Son, by obedience and obedience alone, could the relationship with the divine being be maintained and admission secured to closer experience of His love and His life. God's will revealed is the expression of His hidden perfection and being. Only in accepting and doing His will, to the entire giving up of our will to be possessed and used as He pleases, are we fitted for entering the divine presence. Was it not so with the Son of God? It was when, after a life of holy humility and obedience for thirty years, He had spoken that word of entire consecration, "It becometh us to fulfill all righteousness," and given himself to a baptism for the sins of His people, that He was baptized with the Spirit. The Spirit came because of His obedience. And again, it was after He had learned obedience in suffering and became obedient to the death of the cross that He again received the Spirit from the Father (Acts 2:33) to pour out on His disciples. The fullness of the Spirit for His body, the Church, was the reward of obedience. This law of the Spirit's coming, as revealed in the head, holds for every member of the body. Obedience is the indispensable condition of the Spirit's indwelling. "If ye love me, keep my commandments: and the Father will send you the Spirit."

Christ Jesus had come to prepare the way for the Spirit's coming. Or rather, His outward coming in the flesh was the preparation for His inward coming in the Spirit to fulfill the promise of a divine indwelling. The outward coming appealed to the soul with its mind and feeling and it affected the same. It was only as Christ in His outward coming was accepted, as He was loved and obeyed, that the inward and more intimate revelation would be given. Personal attachment to Jesus, the personal acceptance of Him as Lord and Master to love and obey, was the disciples' preparation for the baptism of the Spirit. Even now, it is in the tender listening to the voice of conscience and a faithful effort to keep the commands of Jesus that we prove our love to Him and our hearts are prepared for the fullness of the Spirit. Our attainments may fall short of our aims; we may have to admit that what we would we do not. But, if the Master sees the wholehearted surrender to His will and the faithful obedience to what we already have of the leadings of His Spirit, we may be sure that the full gift will not be withheld.

Don't these words suggest to us the two great reasons why the presence and the power of the Spirit in the Church are so little realized? We do not understand that although the obedience of love must precede the fullness of the Spirit, we must wait for the fullness of the Spirit to follow. They err who want the fullness of the Spirit before they obey, no less than those who think that obedience is already a sign that the fullness of the Spirit is there.

Obedience must precede the baptism of the Spirit. John had preached Jesus as the true baptist—baptizing with the Holy Spirit and with fire. Jesus took His disciples as candidates for this baptism into a three-year training course. First of all, He attached them to himself personally. He taught them to forsake all for Him. He called himself their Master and Lord and taught them to do what He said. Then in His farewell discourse He, time after time, spoke of obedience to His commands as the one condition for all further spiritual blessing. I am afraid that the Church has not given this word obedience the prominence that Christ gave it. The causes have been: wrong views of the danger of self-righteousness and the way in which free grace is to be exalted; the power of sin and the natural reluctance of the flesh to accept a high standard of holiness. While the freedom of grace and the simplicity of faith have been preached, the absolute necessity of obedience and holiness has not been equally insisted upon. The general thought has been that only those who had the fullness of the Spirit could be obedient. We must realize that obedience is the first step—that the baptism of the Spirit, the full revelation of the glorified Lord as the indwelling one working in us and through us His mighty works, is God's part—His presence is given to the obedient. It was not understood that simple and full allegiance to every dictate of conscience and every precept of the word, that to "walk worthy of the Lord to all well-pleasing," is to be the passport to that full life in the Spirit in which He can witness to the abiding presence of the Lord in the heart.

As the natural consequence of the neglect of this truth, the companion truth was also forgotten: *The obedient must and may look for the fullness of the Spirit.* The promise to the obedient, of the actual conscious, active indwelling of the Spirit is a fact unknown to many Christians. The greater part of life is spent in regret over disobedience, regret over the lack of the Spirit's power and prayer for the Spirit to *help* us obey, instead of rising in the strength of the Spirit already in us to obedience—as indeed possible and necessary. The fact of the Holy Spirit being particularly sent to the obedient to give them the presence of Jesus as a continuous reality that He might do in them the greater works, even as the Father had worked in Him, was hardly thought of. The meaning of the life of Jesus as our example is not understood. How distinctly Jesus lived the outward lowly life of trial and obedience in preparation for the hidden spiritual life of power and glory! It is of this inner life that we are made partakers in the gift of the Spirit of the glorified Jesus. But, in our inner personal participation of that gift, we must walk in the way He prepared for us. Through the crucifixion of the flesh we yield ourselves to God's will for Him to do in us what He wills and for us also to do what He wills. We shall then experience that God is to be found nowhere but in His will. His will in Christ, accepted and done by us with the same heart with which He did it, is the home of the Holy Spirit. The revelation of the Son in His perfect obedience was the condition of the giving of the Spirit; the acceptance of the Son in love and obedience is the path to the indwelling of the Spirit.

It is this truth which has in recent years come home with power to the hearts of many, described by the terms full surrender and entire consecration. As they understood that the Lord Jesus did indeed claim implicit obedience, that the giving up of all to Him and His will is absolutely necessary; that in the power of His grace it is truly possible; and as in the faith of His power they did it; they found the entrance to a life of peace and strength previously unknown. Many are learning, or have to learn, that they do not yet fully know the lesson. They will find that there are applications of this principle beyond what we have conceived. As we see how in the all-pervading power of the Spirit, as we already possess Him, every movement of our life must be brought into allegiance to Jesus; and as we give ourselves to it in faith, we shall also see that the Spirit of the glorified Lord can make Him present and work His mighty works in us and through us in a way far beyond what we can ask or think. The indwelling of the Holy Spirit was intended by God and Christ to be to the Church more, oh! so much more, than we have yet known. Oh! shall we not yield ourselves in a love and obedience that will sacrifice anything for Jesus that our hearts may be enlarged for the fullness of His blessing prepared for us.

Let us cry to God very earnestly that He may awaken His Church and people to take in this double lesson: A living obedience is indispensable to the full experience of the indwelling; the full experience of the indwelling is what a loving obedience may certainly claim. Let each of us even now say to our Lord that we do love Him and desire to keep His commandments. However weak and faltering it may sound, let us still speak it out to Him as the one purpose of our souls—this He will accept. Let us believe in the indwelling of the Spirit as already given to us, when in the obedience of faith we gave ourselves to Him. Let us believe that the full indwelling, with the revelation of Christ within, can be ours. Let us be content with nothing less than the loving, reverent, trembling, but blessed consciousness that we are the temples of the living God because the Spirit of God dwells in us.

Blessed Lord Jesus! with my whole heart do I accept the teaching of these words of Thine. And most earnestly do I beseech Thee to write the truth ever deeper in my heart, as one of the laws of Thy kingdom, that loving obedience may look for a loving acceptance, sealed by an ever-increasing experience of the power of the Spirit.

I thank Thee for what Thy Word teaches of the love and obedience of Thy disciples. Though still imperfect—for did they not all forsake Thee?—yet Thou didst cover their shortcomings with the cloak of Thy love: "The Spirit is willing, but the flesh is weak"; and accept them, weak as they were. Savior! with my whole heart I say I do love Thee and would keep each one of Thy commandments.

Afresh I surrender myself to Thee for this. In the depths of my soul Thou seest there is but one desire: that Thy will should be done in me as in heaven.

To every reproof of conscience I would bow very low; to every moving of Thy Spirit I would yield implicit obedience. I give my will and life unto Thy death, that being raised with Thee, the life of another, even of Thy Holy Spirit, which dwells in me, and reveals Thee, may be my life. Amen.

SUMMARY

1. When God commanded Israel to build Him a holy place that He might dwell among them, He said to Moses: "According to all I show thee, the pattern of the dwelling, even so shall ye make it." And so we find in the last two chapters of Exodus, eighteen times the expression that all had been made "as the Lord commanded." It was in a house thus built after God's pattern, to His mind, the perfect expression of His will, that God came to dwell. In the will of God, carried out by man, God finds a home. God comes down to dwell in the obedience of His people.

2. In this house, the throne of God, He placed His

mercy-seat and the ark in which were kept the tables of the law. In the new spirit, where God writes His law and where it is kept, there the Lord will reveal His immediate presence.

3. Before God came down to dwell, it cost Israel time and sacrifice to prepare a house for Him. Believer, if you pray for the revelation of Jesus, look inside and see if your heart is prepared as His temple. Does conscience testify that you seek with your whole heart to know and do the will of the Lord?

4. It is only when God's will has been accepted as our only law, and the commands of Jesus are by the Holy Spirit written in the heart, that the glory of God can fill His temple.

5. If you would know the indwelling of the Spirit as a blessed reality, let conscience be kept very pure, let your rejoicing every day be in the testimony that your behavior has been " . . . in simplicity and godly sincerity . . . by the grace of God" (2 Cor. 1:12).

8

KNOWING THE SPIRIT

Even the Spirit of truth; whom the world cannot receive, because it seeth him not, neither knoweth him: but ye know him; for he dwelleth with you, and shall be in you.—John 14:17

Know ye not that ye are a temple of God, and that the Spirit of God dwelleth in you?—1 Cor. 3:16

The value of knowledge, that is, true spiritual knowledge, in the life of faith can hardly be exaggerated. Just as a man on earth is none the richer for an inheritance that comes to him, or a treasure in his field, as long as he does not know of it, or does not know how to get possession of it, and to use it—so the gifts of God's grace cannot bring their full blessing until we know and, in knowing, truly apprehend and possess them. In Christ are *hid* all the treasures of wisdom and knowledge; it is the excellency of the *knowledge* of Christ Jesus, his Lord, for which the believer is willing to count all things but loss. It is because of the lack of a true knowledge of what God in Christ has prepared for us that the lives of believers are so low and weak. The prayer Paul offered for the Ephesians—that the Father would give them *the Spirit of wisdom* and revelation in the *knowledge* of Him, the eyes of their heart being enlightened, that they might *know* the hope of their calling the riches of the inheritance and the exceeding goodness of the power working in them—is a prayer we never can offer enough, whether for ourselves or for others. But it is of special importance that we should know the teacher through whom all the other knowledge is to come! The Father has given each one of His children not only Christ, who is the truth, the reality of all life and grace, but the Holy Spirit, who is the very Spirit of Christ and the truth. "We received the Spirit, which is of God, that we might know the things which are freely given us by God."

But now comes the important question: How do we know when it is the Spirit that is teaching us? If our knowledge of divine things is to be to us a certainty and a comfort, we must know the teacher himself. It is only by knowing Him that we will have the full evidence that the value we place on our spiritual knowledge is no deception. Our blessed Lord meets this question, with all the solemn issues depending upon it, by assuring us that we shall *know* the Spirit. When a messenger comes to tell of a king, when a witness gives a testimony for his friend, neither speaks of himself. And yet, without doing so, both the messenger and the witness, in the very fact of giving their evidence, draw our attention to themselves, and claim our recognition of their presence and trustworthiness. So likewise, the Holy Spirit, when He testifies of Christ and glorifies Him, must be known and acknowledged in His divine commission and presence. It is only then that we can have the assurance that the knowledge we receive is indeed of God and not what our human reason has gathered from the Word of God. To know the King's seal is the only safeguard against a counterfeit image. To know the Spirit is the divine foundation of certainty.

How can we presently know the Spirit in this way? Jesus says: "Ye know him, for he abideth with you, and shall be in you." The abiding indwelling of the Spirit is the condition of knowing Him. His presence will be self-evident. As we allow Him to dwell in us, as we give Him full liberty in faith and obedience and allow Him to testify of Jesus as Lord, He will bring His credentials: He will prove himself to be the Spirit of God. "It is the Spirit beareth witness, because the Spirit is truth." It is because the presence of the Spirit as the indwelling teacher of every believer is so little known and recognized in the Church and because, as the result of this, the workings of the Spirit are sparse and weak that there is so much difficulty and doubt, so much fear and hesitation about the recognition of the witness of the Spirit. As the truth and experience of the indwelling of the Spirit are restored among God's people, and the Spirit is free again to work in power among us, His blessed presence will be its own sufficient proof: we shall indeed know Him. "Ye know him, for he shall be in you."[1]

But meanwhile, as long as His presence is so little recognized and His working limited, how can we now know Him? The answer to this question is very simple. To every one who honestly desires to know that he has the Spirit and to know Him in His person as a personal possession and teacher, we say: Study the teaching of the Word in regard to the Spirit. Be not content with the teaching of the Church or of men about the Spirit, but go to the Word. Do not be content with your ordinary reading of the Word, or what you already know of its doctrines. If you are in earnest to know the Spirit, go and search the Word with this in view as one thirsting to drink deeply of the water of life. Gather together all that the Word says of the Spirit, His indwelling and His work and hide it in your heart. Be determined to accept nothing but what the Word teaches, but also to accept heartily all that it teaches.

Study the Word with dependence upon the Spirit's teaching. If you study it with your human wisdom, your study of it may only confirm to you your mistaken views. If you are a child of God, you have the Holy Spirit to teach you, even though you do not yet know how He works in you. Ask the Father to work through Him in you and to make the

Word life and light to you. If, in the spirit of humility and trusting in God's guidance, you submit heartily to the Word, you will find the promise surely fulfilled: you will be taught of God. We have more than once spoken of the progress from the outward to the inward: be wholehearted in giving up all your thoughts and men's thoughts as you accept the Word; ask God to reveal in you by His Spirit His thoughts concerning His Spirit. He will surely do so.

What will be the chief marks to be found in the Word by which the Spirit can be known in us. They will be mainly two. The first will be more external—referring to the work He does. The second, more in the inner life—in the disposition that He seeks in those in whom He dwells.

We have just heard how Jesus spoke of a loving obedience as the condition of the Spirit's coming. Obedience is also the abiding mark of His presence. Jesus gave Him as a teacher and guide. All Scripture speaks of His work as demanding the surrender of the whole life. "If by the Spirit ye *mortify the deeds of the body,* ye shall live; for as many as *are led* by the Spirit of God, these are the sons of God. . . . Your body is a temple of the Holy Ghost: glorify God therefore in your body. . . . If we live in the Spirit, let us also walk in the Spirit. . . . We are changed into the same image, even as by the Spirit of the Lord." Words like these define very distinctly the operations of the Spirit. As God is first known in His works, so it is with the Spirit. He reveals God's will, Christ doing that will and calling us to follow Him in it. As the believer surrenders himself to a life in the Spirit and willingly consents to the leading of the Spirit, the mortifying of the flesh, the obedience to the rule of Christ, without limit or exception, he shall become what he gives himself up to. As he waits on the Spirit, he will find and know the Spirit working in him. It is as we simply make the aim of the Holy Spirit our aim and give ourselves up entirely to what He has come to work in us that we are prepared to know His indwelling. It will be the Spirit himself bearing witness with our spirit, as we are led by Him to obey God even as Christ did, that He dwells in us.

We shall also know Him more certainly and intimately as we not only yield ourselves to that life He works in us, but also as we study the personal relationship that a believer has with Him and the way in which His working may most fully be experienced. The habit of soul that the Spirit desires in us is contained in the one word—faith. Faith always has to do with the invisible, with what appears to man most unlikely. When the divine appeared in Jesus, it was hidden in a lowly form! Thirty years He lived in Nazareth and they had seen nothing in Him but the son of a carpenter. It was only with His baptism that His divine sonship came into complete and perfect consciousness. Even to His disciples His divine glory was often hidden. How much more when the life of God enters the depths of our sinful being will it be a matter of faith to recognize it! Let us meet the Spirit in holy, humble faith. Let us not be content just to know that the Spirit is in us: that will profit us little. Let us cultivate the habit, in each religious exercise, of bowing reverently in silence before God, to give the Spirit the recognition that is His due and keep down the will of the flesh that is so ready with its service to God. Let us wait on the Spirit in deep dependence. Let us have a season of quiet meditation in which we enter the inner temple of our heart to see that all that is there is indeed surrendered to the Spirit. Let us there bow before the Father to ask and expect from Him the mighty working of the Holy Spirit. However little we see or feel, let us believe. The divine is always first known by believing. As we continue believing, we shall be prepared to know and to see.

There is no way of knowing a fruit unless we taste it. There is no way of knowing the light unless we are in it and use it. There is no way of knowing a person except by close fellowship with him. There is no way of knowing the Holy Spirit unless we possess Him and are possessed of Him. To live in the Spirit is the only way to know the Spirit. To have Him in us, doing His work and giving us His fellowship, is the pathway the Master opens to us when He says: "Ye know him, for he shall be in you."

Believer! for the excellency of the knowledge of Christ Jesus, Paul counted all things but loss. Shouldn't we do so too? Shouldn't we give up everything to know the glorified Christ through the Spirit? Oh, let us think of it! the Father has sent the Spirit that we might fully share in the glory of the glorified Christ! Shouldn't we give ourselves up to have

Him in us, to let Him have all in us, that we may fully know Him, through whom alone we can know the Son and the Father? Let us even now yield ourselves fully to the indwelling and teaching of the blessed Spirit whom the Son hath given us from the Father.

Blessed Father, who hast, in the name of Christ, sent us Thy Holy Spirit, graciously hear my prayer and grant that I may know Him indeed by having Him within me. May His witness to Jesus be divinely clear and mighty, may His leading and sanctifying be in such holy power, may His indwelling in my spirit be in such truth and life that the consciousness of Him as my life may be as simple and sure as of my natural life. As the light is the sufficient witness to the sun, may His light be its own witness to the presence of Jesus.

Lead me, O my Father, in knowing Him to know fully the mystery of Thy love in giving Him within. May I understand how it was not enough for Thee to work in me by Thy secret, unknown, almighty power, nor even to work through Him who came to the earth to reveal Thee. Thy Son had something more and better for us—the Spirit, the blessed third in the godhead was sent, that Thy personal presence, the most intimate union and unbroken fellowship with Thee, might be my portion. The Holy Spirit, Thy very life and self, has come to be now the life of my very self, and so take me wholly for Thine own.

O my God, do teach me and all Thy people to know Thy Spirit. Not only to know that He is in us, not only to know somewhat of His working, but to know Him as in His very person He reveals and glorifies the Son and in Him Thee, the Father. Amen.

SUMMARY

1. A church or a believer may have a correct apprehension of all that Scripture says of the Holy Spirit, may know all about Him, and yet know little of himself as the divine revelation of a present Christ as Saviour and King.

2. The Word alone cannot teach us to know the Spirit. The Word is indeed the test. But to apply the test of the Word with certainty, we need with certainty to know the Spirit and that He is teaching us.

3. "The world cannot receive him, for it seeth him not, neither knoweth him. . . . We received not the spirit of the world, but the Spirit which is of God, that we might *know.*" The spirit of the world and its wisdom cannot possibly know the Spirit of God. There must be a very unworldly spirit to know the Spirit that comes from heaven.

4. Brother! would you know the Spirit? Remember He will reveal himself if you will submit to the laws of His indwelling. These are very simple. Believe that He dwells in you and exercise this faith continually. Yield yourself wholeheartedly to His leading, as to one who has the sole and whole guidance of your life. Wait then, in very lowly humility and dependence, on His further teaching and the fuller experience of His indwelling and work. You may be sure of it, this word will be fulfilled: "Ye know him, for he shall be in you."

5. "If we believe He is a person in the Trinity, let us treat Him as a person, apply ourselves to Him as a person, glorify Him in our hearts as a person, give Him full expression of our love, and converse with Him as a person. Let us fear to grieve Him, let us believe on Him as a person." —Goodwin

Note

1. See Note 4, p. 232.

9

THE SPIRIT OF TRUTH

But when the Comforter is come, whom I will send unto you from the Father, even the Spirit of truth, which proceedeth from the Father, he shall testify of me.—John 15:26

Howbeit when he, the Spirit of truth, is come, he will guide you into all truth: for he shall not speak of himself; but whatsoever he shall hear, that shall he speak. . . .—John 16:13

God created man in His image, to become like himself, capable of holding fellowship with Him in His glory. In Paradise two ways were set before man for attaining to this likeness to God. These were typified by the two trees—that of life and that of knowledge. God's way was the former—through life would come the knowledge and likeness of God; in abiding in God's will and partaking of God's life, man would be perfected. In recommending the other, Satan assured man that knowledge was the one thing to be desired to make us like God. When man chose the light of knowledge above the life in obedience, he entered upon the terrible path that leads to death.[1] The desire to know became his greatest temptation; his whole nature was corrupted, and knowledge was to him more than obedience and more than life.

Under the power of this deceit, that promises happiness in knowledge, the human race is still led astray. Nowhere does it show its power more terribly than in connection with true religion and God's own revelation of himself. Even when the Word of God is accepted, the wisdom of the world and of the flesh still enters in; even spiritual truth is robbed of its power when held, not in the life of the Spirit, but in the wisdom of man.

Where truth enters into the inward parts, as God desires, there it becomes the life of the spirit. But it may only reach the outer parts of the soul, the intellect and reason. While it may occupy a place there and satisfy us with the imagination that it will exercise its influence and its power, it is nothing more than human argument and wisdom that never reaches to the true life of the spirit. There is a truth of the understanding and feelings, which is only natural, the human image or form, the shadow of divine truth. There is a truth which is substance and reality, communicating to him who holds it, the actual possession of the *life* of the things which others only think and speak of. The truth in shadow, in form, in thought, was all the law could give; and in that the religion of the Jews consisted. The truth of substance, the truth as a divine life, was what Jesus brought as the only-begotten, full of grace and truth. He is himself "the truth."[2]

In promising the Holy Spirit to His disciples, our Lord

speaks of Him as the Spirit of truth. That truth, which He himself is, that truth and grace and life which He brought from heaven as a substantial spiritual reality to communicate to us, has its existence in the Spirit of God: He is the Spirit, the inner life of that divine truth. When we receive Him, and just as far as we receive Him and give ourselves up to Him, He makes Christ and the life of God to be truth in us divinely realized. In His teaching and guiding into the truth, He does not give us only words, thoughts, images and impressions, coming to us from without, from a book or a teacher outside of us. He enters the secret roots of our life and plants the truth of God there as a seed and dwells in it as a divine life. When, in faith, expectation and surrender, this hidden life is cherished and nourished there, He quickens and strengthens it, so that it grows stronger and spreads its branches through the whole being. Therefore, not from without but from within, not in word but in power, in life and truth, the Spirit reveals Christ and all He has for us. He makes the Christ, who has been to us so often only an image, a thought, a Saviour outside and above us, to be truth within us. The Spirit brings with His incoming the truth into us; and then, having possessed us from within, guides us, as we can bear it, into all the truth.

In His promise to send the Spirit of truth from the Father, our Lord very definitely tells us what His principal work would be. "He shall bear witness of ME." He had just before said, "I am the truth"; the Spirit of truth can have no work but to reveal and impart the fullness of grace and truth that there are in Christ Jesus. He came down from the glorified Lord in heaven to bear witness within us, and so through us, of the reality and the power of the redemption which Christ has accomplished there. There are Christians who are afraid that thinking too much of the Spirit's presence within us will lead us away from the Saviour above us. A looking within ourselves may do this, but we may be sure that the silent, believing, adoring recognition of the Spirit within us will only lead to a fuller, a more true and spiritual apprehension that Christ alone is indeed all in all. "He shall bear witness of me. . . . He shall glorify me." It is He that will make our knowledge of Christ life and truth—an experience of the power with which He works and saves.[3]

To know what the disposition or state of mind is in which we can fully receive this guiding into all truth, note the remarkable words our Lord uses concerning the Spirit: "He shall guide you into all the truth, *for* he shall not speak from himself; but whatsoever things he shall hear, these shall he speak." The mark of this Spirit of truth is a wondrous divine teachableness. In the mystery of the holy Trinity there is nothing more beautiful than this: that with a divine equality on the part of the Son and the Spirit, there is also a perfect subordination. The Son could claim that men should honor Him even as they honored the Father and yet counted it no derogation from that honor to say, "The Son can do nothing of himself; as I hear, so I speak." Likewise, the Spirit of truth never speaks from himself. We may think He surely could speak from himself; but no, only what He hears, He speaks. The Spirit that fears to speak out of its own, that listens for God to speak, and only speaks when God speaks, this is the Spirit of truth.

This is the disposition He works, the life He breathes, in those who truly receive Him—that gentle teachableness which marks the poor in spirit, the broken in heart, who have become conscious that as worthless as their righteousness is so is their wisdom or power of apprehending spiritual truth. They acknowledge that they need Christ as much for the one as the other and that the Spirit within them alone can be the Spirit of truth. He shows us how, even with the Word of God in our hands and on our tongues, we may be utterly wanting in that waiting, docile, submissive spirit to which alone its spiritual meaning can be revealed. He opens our eyes to the reason why so much Bible reading, Bible knowledge, and Bible preaching has so little fruit unto true holiness; because it is studied and held with a wisdom that is not from above, that was not asked for and waited for from God. The mark of the Spirit of truth was wanting. He speaks not, He thinks not from himself; what He hears, that He speaks. The Spirit of truth receives everything day by day, step by step, from God in heaven. He is silent and does not speak, except and until He hears.

These thoughts suggest to us the great danger of the Christian life—seeking to know the truth of God in His Word without the distinct waiting on the Spirit of truth in the heart. The tempter of paradise still moves about among men. Knowledge is still his great temptation. How many Christians there are who could confess that their knowledge of divine truth does but little for them: it leaves them powerless against the world and sin; they know little of the light and the liberty, the strength and the joy the truth was meant to bring. It is because they take to themselves God's truth in the power of human wisdom and human thought, and wait not for the Spirit of truth to lead them into it. Most earnest efforts to abide in Christ, to walk like Christ, have failed because their faith stood more in the wisdom of man than in the power of God. Most blessed experiences have been short-lived, because they knew not that the Spirit of truth was within them to make Christ and His holy presence an abiding reality.

These thoughts suggest the great need of the Christian life. Jesus said, "If any man will come after me, let him deny himself . . . and follow me." Many follow Jesus without denying themselves. There is nothing that needs more denying than our own wisdom, the energy of the fleshly mind, as it exerts itself in the things of God.

Let us learn that in all our fellowship with God, in His word or prayer, in every act of worship, the first step ought to be a solemn act of abnegation, in which we deny our power to understand God's Word, or to speak our words to Him, without the special divine leading of the Holy Spirit. Christians need to deny even more than their own righteousness, their own wisdom; this is often the most difficult part of the denial of self. In all our worship we need to realize the all-sufficiency and the absolute indispensability, not only of the blood, but also the Spirit of Jesus. This is the meaning of the call to be silent unto God and in quiet to wait on Him; to hush the rush of thoughts and words in God's presence; in deep humility and stillness to wait, listen, and hear what God will say. The Spirit of truth never speaks from himself; what He hears, that He speaks. A lowly, listening, teachable spirit is the mark of the presence of the Spirit of truth.

Then, when we do wait, let us remember that even then the Spirit of truth may not first, or all at once, speak in thoughts that we can apprehend and express. These are but on the surface. To be true they must be deeply rooted. They must have hidden depth in themselves. The Holy Spirit is the Spirit of truth because He is the Spirit of life: His life is the light. First, He does not speak to thought or feelings, but to the hidden man of the heart, in the spirit of a man which is within him, in his inmost parts. It is only to faith that it is revealed what His teaching means and of His guidance into the truth. Let our first step, therefore, be to believe; that is, to recognize the living God in the work He undertakes to do. Let us believe in the Holy Spirit as the divine quickening and sanctifying power that is already within us, and yield our all to Him. He will prove himself the divine enlightener: His life is the light. Let the confession that we have no life or goodness of our own be accompanied by the confession that we have no wisdom either; the deeper our sense of this, the more precious will the promise of the Spirit's guidance become. The deep assurance of having the Spirit of truth within us will work in us the holy teacher's likeness and our quiet listening will reveal the secrets of the Lord.

O Lord of truth! who seeks truth in the inward parts in them that worship Thee, I do bless Thee again that Thou hast given me too the Spirit of truth and that He now dwells in me. I bow before Thee in lowly fear to ask that I may know Him fully and walk before Thee in the living consciousness that the Spirit of truth, the Spirit of Christ, who is the truth, is indeed within me, the innermost self of my new life. May every thought and word, every disposition and habit, be the proof that the Spirit of Christ, who is the truth, dwells and rules within me.

Especially do I ask Thee that He may witness to me of Christ Jesus. May the truth of His atonement and blood, as it works with living efficacy in the upper sanctuary, dwell in me and I in it. May His life and glory no less be truth in me, a living experience of His presence and power. O my Father! may the Spirit of Thy Son, the Spirit of truth, indeed be my life. May each word of Thy Son through Him be made true in me.

I do thank Thee once again, O my Father, that He dwells within me. I bow my knees that Thou wouldst grant, that according to the riches of Thy glory, He may work mightily in me and all Thy saints. Oh, that all Thy people may know this their privilege and rejoice in it: the Holy Spirit within them to reveal Christ, full of grace and truth, as truth in them. Amen.

SUMMARY

1. As bodily sight is a function of healthy animal life, so spiritual light comes only out of a healthy spiritual life. Life truths can only be known by living them; the Spirit of life only by living in the Spirit. Where faith exercises itself in accepting and yielding to the life of the Spirit in the hidden part, the new spirit, there its ear will be opened and the voice of the Spirit will be heard. The Spirit of life is the Spirit of truth. *Within you*, in your innermost being, this is what God says.

2. Sin has a twofold effect: it is not only guilt, but death; it not only works legal condemnation from above, but moral corruption within. Redemption is not only righteousness but life: not only objective but subjective restoration to God's favor and fellowship. The first is the work of the Son for us, the second of the Spirit of the Son within us. There are many who cling most firmly to the work of the Son for us and yet fail to receive the peace and the power He gives, because they do not fully yield to the work of the Spirit in us. As full and clear as our acceptance of the divine atoning Saviour must be our assurance of the divine indwelling Spirit, to make that Saviour's work truth in us. The Spirit of truth within us, this is the Spirit of Christ.

3. "Behold, thou desirest truth in the inward parts, and in the hidden part thou shalt make me to know wisdom." The truth and wisdom were not to be in the mere understanding, but in the inward hidden life of the Spirit. The Spirit of truth, now dwelling in us, is the fulfillment of this prophecy.

Notes

1. After I had found the illustration of the two trees elsewhere, and written the comment, I noticed the following in Godet on John 1:4: "Is it not natural in such a context to see in the two words *life* and *light*, and in the relations which John establishes between them, an allusion to the tree of life and to that of knowledge? After

having eaten of the former, man would have been called to feed on the second. John initiates us into the real essence of these primordial and mysterious facts and gives us in this verse, as it were, the philosophy of paradise."

2. "The word *true* in John, as in classical writers, signifies not the *true* in opposition to the *false*, but the *veritable*, the perfect realization of the idea in opposition to all its imperfect manifestations."— Godet, John 1:9. See Note 5, p. 236.

3. See Note 6, p. 238.

10

THE EXPEDIENCY OF THE SPIRIT'S COMING

> Nevertheless I tell you the truth; It is expedient for you that I go away: for if I go not away, the Comforter will not come unto you; but if I depart, I will send him unto you.—John 16:7

As our Lord is leaving this world, He promises the disciples here that His departure will be their gain; the Comforter will take His place and be to them far better than He ever had been or could be in His bodily presence. This would be true particularly in two aspects. His fellowship with them had never been unbroken, but liable to interruption; now it would even be broken off by death and they would see Him no more. But, the Spirit would abide with them forever. His own communion with them had been very much external and in consequence of this, had not resulted in what might have been expected. The Spirit would be in them; His coming would be as an indwelling presence, in the power of which they should have Jesus too in them as their life and their strength.

During the life of our Lord on earth, each of His disciples was dealt with by Him in accordance with his individual character and the special circumstances in which he might be placed. The fellowship with each was intensely personal. In everything He proved that He knew His sheep by name.

For each there was a thoughtfulness and a wisdom that met just what was required. Would the Spirit supply this need too and give back that tenderness of personal interest and that special individual dealing which had made the guidance of Jesus so precious? We cannot doubt it. All that Christ had been to them the Spirit was to restore in greater power and in a blessedness that would not cease. They were to be far happier, safer, and stronger with Jesus in heaven than they ever could have been with Him on earth. The chief beauty and blessedness of their discipleship of such a Master who was so wise and patient to give to each one just what he needed and to make each one feel that he had in Him his best friend could never be left out. The indwelling of the Spirit was meant to restore Christ's most personal communion and guidance, His direct personal friendship.

It is to many a matter of great difficulty to conceive of this or to believe it; much less do they experience it. The thought of Christ walking with men on earth, living in them and guiding them, is so clear. The thought of a Spirit hiding himself within us and speaking not in distinct thoughts but in the secret depths of the life makes His guidance more difficult to understand.

And yet just what constitutes the greater difficulty of the new spiritual communion and guidance is what gives it its greater worth and blessedness. It is the same principle we see in daily life: difficulty calls out the powers, strengthens the will, develops character, and makes the man. In a child's first lessons he has to be helped and encouraged; as he goes on to what is more difficult, the teacher leaves him to his own resources. A youth leaves his parents' home to have the principles that have been instilled in him tested and strengthened. In each case it is expedient that the outward presence and help be withdrawn and the soul be thrown upon itself to apply and assimilate the lessons it has been taught.

God indeed wants to educate us to a perfect manhood—not ruled by an outward law but by the inner life. As long as Jesus was with the disciples on earth, He had to work from without inward and yet could never effectually reach or master the innermost being. When He went away He sent the Spirit to be in them, that now their growth might be from within outward. Taking possession first of the inner-most, secret recesses of their being by His Spirit, He would have them, in the voluntary consent and surrender to His inspiration and guidance, personally become what He himself is, through His Spirit in them. So they would have the framing of their life—the forming of their character—in their own hands, in the power of the divine Spirit, who really had become their spirit. They would grow up to true self-confidence, true independence from outward influences, in which they should become like Christ who is a true, separate person, having life in himself and yet living in full dependence on the Father.

As long as the Christian asks only for what is easy and pleasant, he will never understand that it is expedient, really better for us, that Christ should not be on earth. But as soon as the thoughts of difficulty and sacrifice are set aside, in the honest desire to become a truly Godlike man, bearing the full image of the Son, and living well-pleasing to the Father, the thought of Jesus' departure that His Spirit may now become our very own will be welcomed with gladness and gratitude. If to follow the leading of the Spirit, and particularly the personal friendship and guidance of Jesus in it, be a more difficult and dangerous path than it would have been to follow Him on earth, we must remember the privilege we enjoy, the nobility we attain, the intimacy of fellowship with God we enter into—all these are infinitely greater. To have the Holy Spirit of God coming through the human nature of our Lord, entering into our spirits, identifying himself with us, and becoming our very own just as He was the Spirit of Christ Jesus on earth—surely this is a blessedness worth any sacrifice, for it is the beginning of the indwelling of God himself.

To see that it is such a privilege and to desire it very earnestly does not remove the difficulty. So the question comes up again: the fellowship of Jesus with His disciples on earth—so condescending in its tenderness, so particular and minute in its interest, so consciously personal in its love—how can this be ours in the same degree now that He is absent and the Spirit is to be our guide? The answer is this—by faith. With Jesus on earth, the disciples, when once they had believed, walked by sight. We walk by faith. In faith we must accept and rejoice in the word of Jesus: "It is expedient for you that I go away." We must take time distinctly to believe it, to approve of it, to rejoice that He is gone to the Father. We must learn to thank and praise Him that He has called us to this life in the Spirit. We must believe that in this gift of the Spirit the presence and fellowship of our Lord are fully provided for us most certainly and effectually. It may indeed be in a way we do not yet understand, because we have so little believed and rejoiced in the gift of the Holy Spirit. But faith must believe and praise for what it does not yet understand. Let us believe confidently and joyfully that the Holy Spirit and Jesus himself through Him, will teach us how the fellowship and guidance are to be enjoyed.

"Will teach us." Beware of misunderstanding these words. We always connect teaching with thoughts. We want the Spirit to suggest to us certain conceptions of how Jesus will be with us and in us. This is not what He does. The Spirit does not dwell in the mind, but in the life, not in what we know, but in what we are does the Spirit begin His work. Do not let us seek or expect at once a clear apprehension, a new insight, into this or any divine truth. Knowledge, thought, feeling, action—all this is a part of that external religion which the external presence of Jesus had also wrought in the disciples. The Spirit was now to come, and deeper down than all these, He was to be the hidden presence of Jesus within the depths of their personality. The divine life was in a newness of power to become their life. The teaching of the Spirit would begin, not in word or thought, but in power. In the power of a life working in them secretly, but with divine energy; in the power of a faith that rejoiced that Jesus was really near, was really taking charge of the whole life and every circumstance of it, the Spirit would inspire them with the faith of the indwelling Jesus. This would be the beginning and the blessedness of His teaching. They would have the life of Jesus within them and they would by faith know that it was Jesus. Their faith would be at once the cause and effect of the presence of the Lord in the Spirit.

It is by such a faith—a faith which the Spirit breathes, which comes from His being and living in us—that the presence of Jesus is to be as real and all sufficient as when He was on earth. Why then is it that believers who have the

Spirit do not experience it more consciously and fully? The answer is very simple: they know and honor the Spirit who is in them so little. They have much faith in Jesus who died, or who reigns in heaven, but little faith in Jesus who dwells in them by His Spirit. It is this we need: faith in Jesus as the fulfiller of the promise, "He that believeth in me, rivers of living water shall flow out of him." We must believe that the Holy Spirit is within us as the presence of our Lord Jesus. And we must not only believe this with the faith of our understanding—as it seeks to persuade itself of the truth of what Christ says. We must believe with the heart—a heart in which the Holy Spirit dwells. The whole gift of the Spirit, the whole teaching of Jesus concerning the Spirit is to enforce the word: "The kingdom of God is within you." If we would have the true faith of the heart, let us look within and very gently and humbly yield to the Holy Spirit to do His work in us.

To receive this teaching and this faith, which stands in the life and power of the Spirit, let us above all fear that which hinders Him most—the will and the wisdom of man. We are still surrounded by a life of self—of the flesh; in the service of God, even in the effort to exercise faith, the flesh is ever putting itself forward and putting forth its strength. Every thought—not only every evil thought—but every thought, however good, in which our mind runs before the Spirit, must be brought into captivity. Let us lay our own will and our own wisdom captive at the feet of Jesus and wait there in faith and holy stillness of soul. The deep consciousness will grow strong that the Spirit is within us and that His divine life is living and growing within us. As we thus honor Him and give ourselves up to Him; as we bring our fleshly activity into subjection and wait on Him, He will not put us to shame, but do His work within us. He will strengthen our inner life; He will quicken our faith; He will reveal Jesus; and we shall, step by step, learn that the presence and personal communion and guidance of Jesus are ours as clearly and sweetly—yes, even more truly and mightily—than if He were with us on earth.[1]

Blessed Lord Jesus! I do rejoice that Thou art no longer here on earth. I do bless Thee that in a fellowship more real, more near, more tender, more effectual than if Thou wert still here on earth, Thou dost manifest thyself to Thy disciples. I do bless Thee that Thy Holy Spirit dwells within me and gives me to know what that fellowship is, and the reality of Thy holy indwelling.

Most holy Lord! forgive that I have not known Thy Spirit sooner and better, that I have not praised and loved Thee fully for this most wonderful gift of thine and the Father's love. Do teach me in the fullness of faith to believe in Thee from whom, day by day, the fresh anointing flows and fills the life.

Hear me, Lord, when I cry to Thee on behalf of so many of Thy redeemed ones, who do not yet even see what it is to give up and lose the life after the flesh; to receive in its place the life that is in the power of the Spirit. With many of Thy saints, I do beseech Thee, oh, grant that the Church may be wakened to know the one mark of her election. The secret of her enjoyment of Thy presence, the power for fulfilling her calling, is that each believer be led to know that the Spirit dwells within him. The abiding presence of his Lord with him as keeper, guide and friend is indeed his sure portion. Grant it, Lord, for Thy name's sake. Amen.

SUMMARY

1. This, "the Comforter will not come if I go not," is a convincing proof that the gift of the Spirit at and since the day of Pentecost is something totally distinct from anything before that time: a new and loftier dispensation."—Alford

2. The knowledge which the disciples had of Jesus on earth was something so blessed and divine that they could not conceive of there being anything better. They could only think with sorrow of the prospect of losing what they knew to be of God. There are many evangelical Christians who must also give up the knowledge they have previously had of Christ, if He is indeed to be revealed in them in the power of the Holy Spirit. "Because I go away, sorrow has filled your heart: I tell you the truth, it is expedient for you that I go away."These words can only be fully understood when they have become a personal experience. The more external knowledge of Christ, with its life of effort and failure, must

make way for the spiritual indwelling.

3. The law of the Kingdom is—through death to life—losing all to gain all. The great hindrance with Christians is their trust in the orthodoxy and sufficiency of their religious knowledge. If they, so they say, could only be more earnest and faithful. Do let us notice, the disciples had not to be more earnest and faithful in the use of their privilege in having such a Master; new and more strenuous efforts would only have led to new and more bitter failure. They, though true disciples, had to let go, to lose, to die to their old way of knowing Christ, and to receive as a gift an entirely new life of fellowship with Him. Oh, if Christians could only see the more excellent way of living a holy life! The indwelling Spirit of Christ himself dwelling within them, revealing and maintaining the presence of their Lord in power.

Note

1. See Note 7, p. 246.

11

THE SPIRIT GLORIFYING CHRIST

> It is expedient for you that I go away: for if I go not away, the Comforter will not come unto you; but if I depart, I will send him unto you. . . . He shall glorify me: for he shall receive of mine, and shall shew it unto you.—John 16:7, 14

There is a twofold glorifying of the Son of which Scripture speaks. The one is by the Father, the other by the Spirit: the one takes place in heaven, the other here on earth. By the one He is glorified "in God himself"; by the other, "in us" (John 13:32; 17:10). Of the former Jesus spake: "If God be glorified in him [the Son of Man], God shall also glorify him in himself, and shall straightway glorify him." And again, in the high-priestly prayer, "Father, the hour is come; glorify thy Son. . . . And now, O Father, glorify me with thyself." Of the latter He said: "The Spirit shall glorify me. I am glorified in him."

To glorify is to manifest the hidden excellence and worth of an object. Jesus, the Son of Man, was to be glorified when His human nature was admitted to the full participation of the power and glory in which God dwells. He entered into the perfect spirit-life of the heavenly world, of the divine being. All the angels worshipped Him as the Lamb on the throne. Of this heavenly, spiritual glory of Christ, the human mind cannot conceive or apprehend in truth. It can only be truly known by experience, by being communicated to and appropriated in the inner life. This is the work of the Holy Spirit, as the Spirit of the glorified Christ. He comes down as the Spirit of glory and reveals the glory of Christ in us by dwelling and working in us, in the life and the power of that glory in which Christ dwells. He makes Christ glorious to us and in us. Likewise, He glorifies Him in us and through us in them who have eyes to see. The Son seeks not His own glory: the Father glorifies Him in heaven, the Spirit glorifies Him in our hearts.

But before this glorifying of Christ by the Spirit could take place, He first needed to go away from His disciples. They could not have Him in the flesh and in the Spirit too; His bodily presence would hinder the spiritual indwelling. They had to part with the Christ they had before they could receive the indwelling Christ glorified by the Holy Spirit. Christ himself had to give up the life He had before He could be glorified in heaven or in us. Even so, in union with Him, we must give up the Christ we have known, the measure of the life we have had in Him, if we are indeed to have Him glorified to us and in us by the Holy Spirit.

I am persuaded that at this point many of God's dear children need the teaching: "It is expedient that I go away." Like His disciples, they have believed in Jesus; they love and obey Him; they have experienced much of the inexpressible blessedness of knowing and following Him. And yet they feel that the deep rest and joy, the holy light and the divine power of His abiding indwelling, as they see it in Holy Scripture, is not yet theirs. Now in secret and then under the blessed influence of the fellowship of the saints, or the teaching of God's servants in church or conferences, they have been helped and wonderfully blessed. Christ has become very precious. And yet they see something still before them—promises not perfectly fulfilled; wants not fully satisfied. The only reason can be this: they have not yet fully inherited the promise "The Comforter shall *abide* with you, and he shall be *in you.* He shall *glorify* me." They do not fully understand the expediency of Christ's going away to come again glorified in the Spirit. They have not yet been able to say: "Even though we have known Christ after the flesh, yet now we do not know Him as such."

"Knowing Christ after the flesh" must come to an end—we must make way for knowing Him in the power of the Spirit. After the flesh means in the power of the external, of words and thoughts, of efforts and feelings, of influences and aids coming from within, from men and means. The believer who has received the Holy Spirit but does not know fully what this implies, and so does not give up entirely to His indwelling and leading, still, to a great extent, has confidence in the flesh. Admitting that he can do nothing without the Spirit, he still labors and struggles vainly to believe and live as he knows he should. Confessing most heartily, and at times experiencing most blessedly, that Christ alone is his life and strength, it grieves and almost wearies him to think how often he fails in the maintenance of that attitude of trustful dependence in which Christ can live out His life in him. He tries to believe all there is to be believed of Christ's nearness and keeping and indwelling, and yet, somehow, there are still breaks and interruptions; it is as if faith is not what it should be—the substance of the things we had hoped for. The reason must be that the faith itself was still too much the work of the mind, in the power of the flesh, in the wisdom of man. There has indeed been a revelation of Christ the faithful keeper, the abiding friend, but that revelation has been, in part, taken hold of by the flesh and the fleshly mind. This has made it powerless. Christ, the Christ of glory, the doctrine of the indwelling Christ, has been received into the mixed life—partly flesh and partly spirit. It is only the Spirit that can glorify Christ. We must give up and cast away the old way of knowing and believing and having Christ. We must know Christ no more after the flesh. "The Spirit shall glorify me."

But what does it mean that the Spirit glorifies Christ? What is this glory of Christ that He reveals, and how does He do it? We learn from Scripture what the glory of Christ is. We read in Hebrews, "We see not yet all things made subject to him. But we see Jesus crowned with glory and honour." To Him all things have been made subject. So our Lord connects His being glorified, in both the passages we have taken as our text, with all things being given to Him. "He shall glorify me, for he shall take of mine. All things, whatsoever the Father hath, are mine; therefore, said I, that he taketh of mine, and shall declare it unto you." "All things that are mine are thine, and thine are mine; and I am glorified in them." In exalting Him above all rule and power and dominion, the Father has put all things in subjection under His feet: He gave unto Him the name which is above every name, that in the name of Jesus every knee should bow. The kingdom and the power and the glory are ever one: Unto Him that sits on the throne, and to the Lamb in the midst of the throne, be the glory and the dominion for ever. It is as sitting on the throne of the divine glory, with all things put in subjection under His feet (Eph. 1:20-22), that Jesus has been glorified in heaven.[1]

When the Holy Spirit glorifies Jesus in us, He reveals Him to us in His glory. He takes of the things of Christ and declares them to us. It is not that He gives us a thought, or image, or vision of that glory as it is above us in heaven; but He shows it to us as a personal experience and possession. He makes us partake of it in our innermost being. He shows Christ as present in us. All the true, living knowledge we have of Christ is through the Spirit of God. When Christ comes into us as a weak infant; when He grows and increases and is formed within us; when we learn to trust and follow and serve Him—this is all of the Holy Spirit. All this, however, may consist, even as in the disciples, with much darkness and failure. But when the Holy Spirit does His perfect work and reveals the glorified Lord, the throne of His glory is set up in the heart and He rules over every enemy. Every power is brought into subjection, every thought into captivity to the obedience of Christ. Through the whole of the renewed nature there rises the song, "Glory to Him that sitteth on the throne." Though the confession holds true to the end. "In me, that is, in my flesh, dwelleth no good thing," the holy presence of Christ as ruler and governor so fills the heart and life that His dominion rules over all. Sin has no dominion. The law of the Spirit of the life in Christ Jesus has made me free from the law of sin and death.

If this be the glorifying of Christ which the Spirit brings, it is easy to see the way that leads to it. The enthronement of Jesus in His glory can take place only in the heart that has promised implicit and unreserved obedience. It is in the heart that has had the courage to believe that He will take His power and reign, and in faith that expects that every enemy will be kept under His feet. It feels that it needs and it is willing to have; it claims and accepts Christ as Lord of all, with everything in life, great or small, taken possession of and guided by Him, through His Holy Spirit. It is in the loving, obedient disciple the Spirit is promised to dwell; in him the Spirit glorifies Christ.

This can take place only when the fullness of time has come to the believing soul. The history of the Church, as a whole, repeats itself in each individual. Until the time appointed of the Father, who has the times and seasons in His own hands, the heir is under guardians and stewards, and does not differ from a bondservant. When the fullness of time is come and faith is perfected, the Spirit of the glorified one enters in power and Christ dwells in the heart. Yes, the history of Christ himself repeats itself in the soul. In the temple there were two holy places—the one before the veil, the other within the veil, the Most Holy. In His earthly life Christ dwelled and ministered in the Holy Place without the veil: the veil of the flesh kept Him out of the Most Holy. It was only when the veil of the flesh was rent, and He died to sin completely and forever, that He could enter the inner sanctuary of the full glory of the Spirit-life in heaven.

Likewise, the believer who longs to have Jesus glorified within by the Spirit, must, however blessed his life has been in the knowledge and service of his Lord, learn that there is something better. In him too, the veil of the flesh must be rent; he must enter into this special part of Christ's work through the new and living way into the Holiest of All. "He that hath suffered in the flesh hath ceased from sin." The soul must see how completely Jesus has triumphed over the flesh, and entered with His flesh into the Spirit-life. It must realize how perfect, in virtue of that triumph, is His power over all in our flesh that could hinder and it must know also how perfect in the power of the Spirit the entrance and the indwelling of Jesus as keeper and king can be. The veil is taken away and the life before lived in the Holy Place is now one in the Most Holy, in the full presence of His glory.

This rending of the veil, this enthronement of Jesus as the glorified one in the heart, is not always with the sound of trumpet and shouting. It may be so at times, and with some, but in other cases it takes place amid the deep awe and trembling of a stillness where not a sound is heard. Zion's king still comes meek and lowly with the kingdom to the poor in spirit. Without form or comeliness He enters in, and when thought and feeling fail, the Holy Spirit glorifies Him to the faith that sees not but believes. The eye of flesh did not see Him on the throne; to the world it was a mystery; so, just when all within appears hopeless and empty, the Spirit secretly works the divine assurance, and then the blessed experience that Christ, the glorified, has taken up His abode within. The soul knows, in silent worship and adoration, that Jesus is master; that His throne in the heart is established in righteousness; that the promise is now fulfilled: "The Spirit shall glorify me."

Blessed Lord Jesus, I worship Thee in the glory which the Father has given Thee. I bless Thee for the promise that that glory shall be revealed in the hearts of Thy disciples to dwell in them and fill them. This is Thy glory, that all that the Father has is now Thine: of this Thy glory in its infinite fullness and power Thou hast said the Holy Spirit shall take to show it unto us. Heaven and earth are full of Thy glory. The hearts and lives of Thy beloved may be filled with it too. Lord, let it be so!

Blessed be Thy holy name for all in whom the rich beginnings of the fulfillment have already come! Lord, let it go on from glory to glory.

To this end teach us, we pray Thee, to maintain our separation to Thee unbroken: heart and life shall be Thine alone. To this end teach us to hold fast our confidence without wavering, that the Spirit who is within us will perfect

His work. Above all, teach us to yield ourselves in ever-increasing dependence and emptiness to wait for the Spirit's teaching and leading. We do desire to have no confidence in the flesh, its wisdom, or its righteousness. We would bow ever lower and deeper before Thee in the holy fear and reverence of the truth that Thy Spirit, the Holy Spirit, the Spirit of Thy glory, is within us to do His divine work. Blessed Lord! let Him rise in great power, and have dominion within us, that our heart may by Him be fully made the temple and the kingdom in which Thou alone art glorified, in which Thy glory fills all. Amen.

SUMMARY

1. It was the true Christ these disciples knew; and it was a true knowledge of Christ they had, as far as it went (Matt. 16). It was a knowledge that influenced them mightily, drawing them to follow and love Him. But it was not the full knowledge—the knowledge in Spirit and truth; nor yet the spiritual knowledge of Christ glorified and abiding in them through the Holy Spirit. This is the true second blessing: "If that which passeth away was with glory, much more that which remaineth is in glory, by reason of the glory that surpasseth."

2. Oh, that God may teach us this lesson: the one great work of the Spirit, as the Spirit of Christ, is to make the glorified Christ always present in us—not in thoughts or memory only but within us, in our innermost being, in our life and experience.

3. Can it be? Jesus, the glorified one, always present with us, dwelling in us? It can be. The Holy Spirit has been given by the Father for this one work. And He dwells in us. Let us believe; let us live in that wonderful indwelling.

4. Let us bow very low in submission to His leading, waiting for His teaching, reverently honoring His holy presence within us, even when we cannot see or feel. "Said I not unto thee, that, if thou believest, thou shouldest see the glory of God?"

Note

1. See Note 8, p. 248.

12

THE SPIRIT CONVINCING OF SIN

But if I depart, I will send him unto you. And when he is come, he will reprove the world of sin [speaking of the Comforter].—John 16:7, 8

The close connection between the two statements in these words of our Lord is not always noticed. Before the Holy Spirit was to convince the world of sin, He was first to come into the disciples. He was to make His home, to take His stand in them, and then from out of them and through them to do His conviction work on the world. "He shall bear witness of me, and ye shall also bear witness." The disciples were to realize that the great work of the Holy Spirit—striving with man and convincing the world of sin—could be done only as He had a firm footing on earth *in them*. They were to be baptized with the Holy Ghost and with fire; to receive the power from on high with the one purpose of being the instruments through whom the Holy Spirit could reach the world. The mighty, sin-convicting power of the Spirit to dwell in them and work through them: it was for this our blessed Lord sought to prepare them and us by these words. The lessons they teach are very thought-provoking.

1. The Holy Spirit comes to us, that through us He may reach others. The Spirit is the Spirit of the holy one, of the redeeming God. When He enters us, He does not change His nature or lose His divine character. He is still the Spirit of God striving with man and seeking his deliverance. Wherever He is not hindered by ignorance or selfishness, He radiates from our hearts, as His temple, for the work He has to do on the world. He makes us willing and bold to do that work; to testify against sin and *for* Jesus, the Saviour from sin. He does this particularly as the Spirit of the crucified and exalted Christ. For what purpose was it that He received the Spirit without measure? "The Spirit of the Lord is upon me, because he anointed me to preach good tidings to the poor. He hath sent me to proclaim release to the cap-

tives." It was this same Spirit—through whom Christ had offered himself unto God, and through whom as the Spirit of holiness, He had been raised from the dead—that He sent down on the Church. Thus the Spirit might have a home in them as He had had in Christ. And in no lesser way than in Christ would the divine Spirit in them pursue His divine work. As a light shining in the darkness, revealing, condemning, and conquering—and as "the Spirit of burning and the Spirit of judgment," He is to the world the power of a divine conviction and conversion. Not so much directly from heaven as the Spirit of God, but as the Holy Spirit dwelling in the Church, would He convince the world. "I will send him *to you*, and when he is come, he will convince the world." It is in and through us that the Spirit can reach the world.

2. The Spirit can reach others only through us by first bringing us into perfect harmony with himself. He enters into us to become so *one* with us that He becomes as a disposition or life within us. Then His work in us and through us to others becomes identical with our work.

The application of this truth to the conviction of sin in the world is one of great importance. The words of our Lord are frequently applied to believers, in reference to the continued conviction of sin which He must work within them. In this sense they are most applicable. This first work of the Spirit remains throughout, the undertone of all His comforting and sanctifying work. It is only as He keeps alive a sensitiveness to the danger and shame of sinning that the soul will be kept in a humble place before God—hiding in Jesus as its only safety and strength. As the Holy Ghost reveals and communicates the holy life of Christ within, the sure result will be a deeper sense of the sinfulness of sin. But the words mean more. If the Spirit through us, through our testimony, whether by word or walk, is to convince the world, He must first convince us of its sin. He must first give us personally a sight and sense of the guilt of the world's unbelief and rejection of our Saviour. We must see and sense of each of its sins as being the cause, the proof, and the fruit of that rejection, so that we shall in some measure think and feel in regard to the sin as He does. There will then be that inner-readiness in us for the Spirit to work through us; that inner-unity between our witness and His witness *against* sin and *for* God, which will reach the conscience and carry conviction with a power that is from above.

We know how easy it is, in the power of the flesh, to judge others in the spirit which sees not the beam in our own eye. And if we are indeed free from what we condemn, we say by our actions, "Stand by. I am holier than thou." We either testify and work in a wrong spirit and in our own strength, or we don't have courage to work at all. It is because we see the sin and the sinfulness of others without a conviction that comes from the Holy Spirit. When He convinces us of the sin of the world, His work bears two marks. The first is a sacrifice of self, in the jealousy for God and His honor, combined with a deep and real grief for the guilty. The second is a firm, strong faith in the possibility and power of deliverance. We see each sin in its terrible relation to the whole; we see the whole in the double light of the cross. We see sin unspeakably hateful in its awful affront against God and its fearful power over the weak soul; we see sin condemned, atoned for, put away, and conquered in Jesus. We learn to look on the world as God looks upon it in His holiness. We hate sin with an infinite hatred, but love the sinner with the love that sent His Son. The Son gives life, destroys sin and sets its captive free.

May God give His people a true and deep conviction of the sin of the world in its rejection of Christ, as the fitting preparation for the Spirit's using them in convicting the world of sin.

3. To obtain this conviction of sin, the believer must not only pray for it but also have his whole life under the leading of the Holy Spirit. We cannot too earnestly declare that the various gifts of the Spirit depend upon His personal indwelling and supremacy in the inner life, and the revelation in us of the Christ that gave His life to have sin destroyed. When our Lord spoke that word of inexhaustible meaning, "He shall be in you," He opened up the secret of all the Spirit's teaching, sanctifying, and strengthening. The Spirit is the life of God. He enters in and becomes our life. It is as He can influence and inspire the life that He will be able to work in us all He wills. It is desirable and necessary to direct the attention of the believer to the various operations of the Spirit,

that he not neglect or lose anything through ignorance. But it is even more necessary, with each new insight into what the Spirit can work, to get a firmer grasp of the truth. Let your life be in the Spirit and the special blessing will not be withheld. If you would like to have this deep spiritual conviction of the sin of the world—such an affecting sense of its terrible reality and power and its exceeding sinfulness—such as will fit you for being the man through whom the Spirit can convince sinners, just yield your whole life and being to the Holy Spirit. Let the thought of the wondrous mystery of the indwelling God quiet your mind and heart into humble fear and worship. Surrender the great enemy that opposes Him—the flesh, the self-life—day by day to Him to mortify and keep dead. Be content to aim at nothing less than being filled with the Spirit of the Man who gave himself to death to take away sin; having our whole being and action under His control and inspiration. As your life in the Spirit becomes healthy and strong, and your spiritual constitution gets invigorated, your eye will see more clearly and your heart feel more keenly just what sin is. Your thoughts and feelings will be those of the Holy Spirit breathing in you—your deep horror of sin, your deep faith in the redemption from it, and your deep love of the souls who are in it. You will become willing, like your Lord, to give your life to free men from sin. And He will make you a fit instrument for the Spirit to convince the world of its sin.

4. There is one more lesson. We are seeking, in this book, to show the way by which all can be filled with the Spirit. Here is one condition: He must dwell in us as the world's convincer of sin. "I will send him *unto you*, and he will convince *the world*." Offer yourself to Him to comprehend, feel, and bear the sins of those around you. Let the sins of the world be as much your concern as your own sin. Do not their sins dishonor God as much as yours? Are they not equally provided for in the great redemption? And does not the Spirit dwelling in you long to convince them too? Just as the Holy Spirit dwelt in the body and nature of Jesus and was the source of what He felt, said, and did; just as God through Him worked out the will of His holy love; so the Spirit now dwells in believers: they are His abode. The one purpose for which there has been a Christ in the world, and

for which there is now a Holy Spirit, is that sin may be conquered and brought to naught. This is the great object for which the baptism of the Spirit and of fire was given—that in and through believers He might convince of sin and deliver from it. Put yourself into contact with the world's sin. Meet it in the love and faith of Jesus Christ, as a servant and helper of the needy and despondent. Give yourself to prove the reality of your faith in Christ by your likeness to Him: so will the Spirit convince the world of its unbelief. Seek the full experience of the indwelling Spirit, not for your own selfish enjoyment, but for this purpose that He can do the Father's work through you as He did through Christ. Live in unity of love with other believers, to work and pray, that men may be saved out of sin. "Then will the world believe that God hath sent Him." It is the life of believers in self-sacrificing love that will prove to the world that Christ is a reality and so convince it of its sin of unbelief.

The comfort and success with which a man lives and carries on his business depends much upon his having a suitable building for it. When the Holy Spirit in a believer finds the whole heart free and given up to Him to fill it with God's thoughts of sin and God's power of redemption, He can through such a life do His work. Be assured that there is no more certain way to receive a full measure of the Spirit than to be wholly yielded to Him; to let the very mind of Christ in regard to sin work in us. "He took away sin by the sacrifice of himself" through the eternal Spirit. What the Spirit was in Him, He seeks to be in us. What was true of Him must in the same measure be true of us.

Christians, would you be filled with the Holy Spirit and seek to have a clear understanding of the Holy Spirit in you, convincing the world of sin? If you identify thoroughly with Him in this; if He sees that He can use you for this; if you make His work in this matter your work too, you may be sure He will dwell in you richly and work in you mightily. The one object for which Christ came was to put away sin; the one work for which the Holy Ghost comes to men is to persuade them to give up sin. The one object for which the believer lives is to join in the battle against sin; to seek the will and the honor of his God. Do let us be at one with Christ and His Spirit in their testimony against sin. An exhibition of the life and Spirit of Christ will have its effect: the holiness and the joy, the love and the obedience to Christ will convince the world of its sin of unbelief. Just as Christ's death, as His sacrifice for sin, was the entrance to His glory in the power of the Spirit, so our experience of the Spirit's indwelling will become fuller as our whole life is given up to Him for His holy work of convincing the world of sin. The presence of Christ in us through the Spirit will carry its own conviction.

Blessed Lord Jesus, it is by the presence and power of the Holy Spirit in Thy people that the world is to be convinced of its sin in rejecting Thee, and that sinners are to be brought out of the world to accept of Thee. It is in men and women full of the Holy Ghost, testifying in the power of a holy joy to what Thou hast done for them, that the proof is to be given that Thou art indeed at the right hand of God. It is in a body of living witnesses to what Thou hast done for them that the world is to find the irresistible conviction of its sin and guilt.

Lord, how little the world has seen of this. We do call upon Thee, in deep humiliation, Lord Jesus, make haste and awaken Thy Church to the knowledge of its calling. Oh, that every believer in his personal life, and all Thy believing people in their fellowship, might prove to the world what reality, what blessedness, what power there is in thy faith! May the world believe that the Father has sent Thee and has loved them as He loved Thee.

Lord Jesus, lay the burden of the sin of the world so heavily upon the hearts of Thy people that it may become impossible for them to live for anything but this: to be the members of Thy body in whom Thy Spirit dwells and prove Thy presence to the world. Take away everything that hinders Thee from manifesting Thy presence and saving power in us. Lord Jesus, Thy Spirit is come to us to convince the world. Let Him come and work in ever-increasing power. Amen.

SUMMARY

1. The great sin of the world is unbelief—the rejection of

Christ. This is the very spirit of the world. It is from this standpoint I must decide my whole view of the world, my relation to it: it is a world that by its very nature rejects Christ.

2. This rejected Christ has left this world and gone to the Father. But He has left His people in it and dwells in them by His Spirit that the power of their holy life and their confession of Him to whom they owe that life may convince the world of its guilt and sin. What fullness of surrender to the Holy Spirit is needed if in me, by my life, He is to convince the world of the sin of unbelief!

3. "What is here promised is such an outpouring of the Spirit of God as shall not only reveal itself in the consciousness of the disciples, but also substantiate itself as an undeniable and wonderful fact to the onlooking world. Is not the great thing needed that the Spirit of God should be so poured out on Christ's people that men should be made aware of His presence with them, and of His presence at the right hand of God?"—Bowen

4. To convince the world of the truth of Christianity, it must first be convinced of sin. It is only sin that renders Christ intelligible. And for this there is not so much needed evidences and arguments, but, in the first place, the manifest presence of the Holy Ghost, as coming from Christ, on the throne of God, to believers. And for this there is needed intense, continued, united, believing prayer that the Father would, according to the riches of His glory, strengthen us all with might by His Spirit.

13

WAITING FOR THE SPIRIT

. . . commanded them that they should not depart from Jerusalem, but wait for the promise of the Father, which, saith he, ye have heard of me.—Acts 1:4

In the life of the Old Testament saints, *waiting* was one

of the common words by which they expressed the attitude of their souls toward God. They waited *for* God and *upon* God. Sometimes we find this in Holy Scripture as the language of an experience: "Truly my soul waited upon God." "I wait for the Lord, my soul doth wait." At other times it is a plea in prayer: "Lead me; on thee do I wait all the day. Be gracious unto us; we have waited for thee." Frequently it is an injunction, encouraging perseverance in a work that is not without difficulty: "Wait on the Lord; wait, I say, on the Lord. Rest in the Lord, and wait patiently for him." And then again there is the testimony to the blessedness of the exercise itself: "Blessed are they that wait upon him. They that wait upon the Lord shall renew their strength."

All this blessed teaching and experience of the saints who have gone before, our Lord gathers and relates particularly, in His use of the word, with the promise of the Father the Holy Spirit.[1] What had been so deeply woven into the very substance of the religious life and language of God's people was now to receive a new and a higher application. As they had waited for the manifestation of God, either in the light of His countenance on their own souls, or in special intervention for their deliverance, or in His coming to fulfill His promises to His people; so we too have to wait. But now that the Father has been revealed in the Son, and the Son has perfected the great redemption, waiting is particularly to be occupied with the fulfillment of the great promise by which the love of the Father and the grace of the Son are revealed and made one—the gift, the indwelling, the fullness of the Holy Spirit. We wait on the Father and the Son for ever-increasing inflowing and working of the blessed Spirit. We wait for the blessed Spirit himself—His moving, leading, and mighty strengthening, to reveal the Father and the Son within, and to work in us all the holiness and service to which the Father and the Son are calling us.

"He charged them *to wait* for the promise of the Father, which ye have heard of me." It may be asked whether these words have not exclusive reference to the outpouring of the Spirit on the day of Pentecost, and whether, now that the Spirit has been given to the Church, the charge still holds good. It may be argued that, for the believer who has the Holy Spirit within him, waiting for the promise of the Father is hardly consistent with the faith and joy of the consciousness that the Spirit has been received and is dwelling within.

The question and the argument open the way to a lesson of deepest importance. The Holy Spirit is not given to us as a possession of which we have control and which we can use at our discretion. The Holy Spirit is given to us to be *our* Master and to have control of *us*. It is not we who are to use Him; He must use us. He is indeed ours, but ours as God; and our position towards Him is that of deep and full dependence on Him who gives to every one "even as he will." The Father has indeed given us the Spirit; but He still is, and only works as the Spirit of the Father. Our asking for His working, that the Father would grant unto us to be strengthened with might by His Spirit, and our waiting for this, must be as real and definite as if we were asking for Him for the first time. When God gives His Spirit, He gives His inmost self. He gives with a divine giving—that is, in the power of the eternal life, continuous, uninterrupted, and never-ceasing. When Jesus gave to those who believe in Him the promise of an ever-springing fountain of ever-flowing streams, He spake not of a single act of faith that was once for all to make them the independent possessors of the blessing. But He spoke of a life of faith that, in never-ceasing receptivity, would always and only possess His gifts in living union with himself. And so this precious word *wait*—"He charged them to wait"—with all its blessed meaning from the experience of the past, is woven into the very web of the new Spirit dispensation. All that the disciples did and felt during those ten days of waiting, and all that they got as its blessed fruit and reward, becomes to us the path and pledge of the life of the Spirit in which we can live. The fullness of the Spirit, for such is the Father's promise, and our waiting are inseparably and forever linked together.

Have we not now an answer to the question why so many believers know so little of the joy and power of the Holy Spirit? They never knew to wait for it; they never listened carefully to the Master's parting words: He charged them to wait for the promise of the Father, "which ye have heard of me." The promise they have heard. For its fulfillment they have longed. In earnest prayer they have pleaded for it.

They have gone burdened and grieving under the felt need. They have tried to believe, tried to lay hold, and tried to be filled with the Spirit. But they have never known what it was to wait. They have never here said, or even truly heard, "Blessed are all they that wait for him. They that wait on the Lord shall renew their strength."

But what is this waiting? And how are we to wait? I look to God by His Holy Spirit to teach me to start in the simplest way possible what may help some child of His to obey this command. Let me first say that, as a believer, what you are to wait for is the fuller manifestation of the power of the Spirit within you. On the resurrection morn Jesus had breathed on His disciples and said, Receive the Holy Ghost. They were to wait for the full baptism of fire and of power. As God's child you have the Holy Ghost. Study the passages in the Epistles addressed to believers full of failings and sins (1 Cor. 3:1-3, 16; 6:19, 20; Gal. 3:2, 3; 4:6). Begin in simple faith in God's Word to cultivate this quiet assurance: the Holy Spirit is dwelling within me. If you are not faithful in the little, you cannot expect the greater. Acknowledge in faith and thanks that the Holy Spirit is in you. Each time you enter your closet to speak to God, first sit still to remember and believe that the Spirit is within you, as the Spirit of prayer who cries, "Father!" Appear before God and confess to Him distinctly until you become fully conscious that you are a temple of the Holy Ghost.

Now you are in the right position for taking the second step—that is, asking God very simply and quietly, there and then, to grant you the workings of His Holy Spirit. The Spirit is in God and is in you. Ask your Father that His almighty Spirit may come forth from Him in greater life and power, that the indwelling Spirit may work more mightily in you. As you ask this on the ground of the promises, or on some special promise you lay before Him, you believe that He hears and that He does it. You must not look to see whether you feel anything in your heart; all may be dark and cold there. You are to believe, that is, to rest, in what God is going to do, even is doing, though you may not feel it.

And then comes the waiting. Wait on the Lord; wait for the Spirit. In great quietness be still before God and give the Holy Spirit time to quicken and deepen in you the assurance that God will grant the Spirit to work mightily in you. We are a "holy priesthood to offer up spiritual sacrifice." The slaying of the sacrifice was an essential part of the service. In each sacrifice you bring there must be the slaying, the surrender and sacrifice of self and its power to death. As you wait before God in holy silence, He interprets the confession that you have nothing—no wisdom to pray aright, no strength to work aright. Waiting is the expression of need, of emptiness. All through the Christian life these go together, the sense of poverty and weakness, and the joy of all-sufficient riches and strength. It is in waiting before God that the soul sinks down into its own nothingness, and is lifted up into the divine assurance that God has accepted its sacrifice and will fulfill its desires.

After the soul has waited upon God, it has to go forward to the daily walk or the special task that waits it, in the faith that God will watch over the fulfillment of His promise and His child's expectation. If you give yourself to prayer after waiting for the Spirit, or to the reading of the Word, do it in the trust that the Holy Spirit within guides your prayer and your thoughts. If your experience appears to prove that nothing has happened, be assured that this is simply to lead you onward to a simpler faith and a more entire surrender. You have become so accustomed to worship in the power of human understanding and the carnal mind that truly spiritual worship does not come at once. But wait on: "He charged them to wait." Keep up the waiting disposition in daily life and work. "On thee do I wait all the day."

It is to the three-in-one God we speak; the Holy Spirit brings Him near and unites us to Him. Renew your faith each day and, as you are able to do it, extend your exercise of waiting upon God. The multitude of words and the fervency of feelings in prayer have often been more hindrance than help. God's work in you must become deeper, more spiritual, more directly wrought of God himself. Wait for the promise in all its fullness. Don't count the time lost that you give to the blessed expression of humility and emptiness, of faith and expectation, of full and real surrender to the dominion of the Spirit. Pentecost is meant to be for all times the proof of what the exalted Jesus does for His Church from His throne. The ten days' waiting is meant to be for all time the position before the throne, which secures in continuity the Pentecostal blessing. The promise of the Father is sure. It is Jesus from whom you have it. The Spirit himself is already working in you. His full indwelling and guidance is your portion as His child. Oh, keep the charge of your Lord! Wait on God: wait for the Spirit. "Wait, I say, on the Lord. Blessed are all they that wait for him."

Blessed Father, from Thy beloved Son we have heard Thy promise. In a streaming forth that is divine and never-ceasing, the river of the water of life flows from under the throne of God and the Lamb. Thy Spirit flows down to quicken our thirsty souls. "For we have not heard, neither hath the eye seen, O God, beside Thee, what He hath prepared for him that waiteth for Him."

We have heard His command to wait for the promise. We thank Thee for what has already been fulfilled to us of it. But our souls long for the full possession, the fullness of the blessing of Christ. Blessed Father, teach us to wait on Thee, daily watching at the posts of thy doors.

Teach us each day, as we draw near to Thee, to wait for Him. In the sacrifice of our own wisdom and our will, in the holy fear of the workings of our own nature, may we learn to lie humbly before Thee that Thy Spirit may work with power. Oh, teach us that as the life of self is laid before Thee day by day, the holy life that flows from under the throne will rise in power, and our worship will be in spirit and in truth. Amen.

SUMMARY

1. The disciples were not to proceed to do their work in the faith of the promise that the Spirit would be given: they were to wait until they could joyfully testify and prove that Christ in heaven had given His Spirit within them. *"Tarry, until."*

2. "We are not to look back for our Pentecost. The Pentecost of the Acts is simply given to make the church of Christ acquainted with the privileges belonging to this dispensation. The Spirit of God comes as the rain, that must still come and come again: as the wind, that must still blow and blow again."—Bowen

3. *Waiting!* the all-comprehensive word to indicate the attitude of the disciples toward the promise of the Father. *Waiting!* It includes the denial of self, its wisdom or strength; separation from all else; surrender and preparedness for all the Spirit would claim; joyful faith in what Christ is, and confident expectation of what He is going to do. *Wait! Tarry!* the one final condition imposed by the ascending Lord for the fulfillment of the promise.

4. *Wait!* Let this be the deep undergirding of his daily life in relation to the Spirit, for each one who knows that the Spirit is in him, and longs to be mightily strengthened with Him from above. *Wait!* Let this be the attitude of the Church as she expects her Lord, in answer to her prayer, mightily to manifest His power in the world. "He charged them to wait. Tarry, until ye be clothed with power from on high."

5. "As Christ was the fulfiller of the law, and the end of the law, so the Spirit is the complement, the fulfiller and maker good of all the Gospel. Otherwise all that Christ did would have profited us nothing, if the Holy Ghost did not come into our hearts, and bring it all home to us."— Goodwin.

Note

1. The Greek word is the same that the Septuagint uses in giving the prayer of Jacob, "I have waited for thy salvation, O Lord."

14

THE SPIRIT OF POWER

But ye shall be baptized with the Holy Ghost not many days hence. But ye shall receive power, after that the Holy Ghost is come upon you; and ye shall be my witnesses. . . .—Acts 1:5, 8

Tarry ye in the city of Jerusalem, until ye be endued with power from on high.—Luke 24:49

The disciples had heard from John of the baptism of the Spirit. Jesus had spoken to them of the Father's giving of the Spirit to them that ask Him and of the Spirit of their Father speaking in them. And on the last night he had spoken of the Spirit dwelling in them, witnessing with them, having come to them to convince the world of sin. All these thoughts of what this coming of the Holy Spirit would be was connected in their mind with the work they would have to do and the power for it. When our Lord summed up all His teaching in the promise, "Ye shall receive the power of the Holy Ghost coming upon you, and shall be my witnesses," it must have been to them the simple summing up of what they looked for: a new divine power for the new divine work of being the witnesses of a crucified and risen Jesus.

This was in perfect harmony with all they had seen in Holy Scripture of the Spirit's work. In the days before the flood He had been striving with men. In the ministry of Moses He equipped him, and the seventy who received of His Spirit, for the work of ruling and guiding Israel and giving wisdom to those who built God's house. In the days of the judges He gave the power to fight and conquer the enemies. In the times of kings and prophets He gave boldness to testify against sin, and power to proclaim a coming redemption. Every mention of the Spirit in the Old Testament is connected with the honor and kingdom of God and the equipping for service in it. In the great prophecy of the Messiah, with which the Son of God opened His ministry at Nazareth, His being anointed with the Spirit had the sole purpose of bringing deliverance to the captives and gladness to the sorrowing. To the mind of the disciples, as students of the Old Testament and followers of Christ Jesus, the promise of the Spirit could have but one meaning—power for the great work they had to do for their Lord when He ascended the throne. All that the Spirit would be to them personally in His work of comforting, teaching, sanctifying the soul, and glorifying Jesus were but a means to an end—their enduement with power for the service of their departed Lord.

I would to God that the church of Christ understood this in our day! All prayers for the guiding and encouraging influence of the Holy Spirit in the children of God ought to have this as their aim: power to witness for Christ and do effective service in conquering the world for Him. Waste of power is always a cause of regret to those who witness it. The economy of power is one of the great moving springs in all organization and industry. The Spirit is the great power of God; the Holy Spirit the great power of God's redemption, as it comes down from the throne of Him to whom all power has been given. Can we imagine that God would waste this power on those who seek it only for their own sake, with the desire to be beautifully holy, wise, or good? No, the Holy Spirit is the power from on high for carrying on the work for which Jesus sacrificed His throne and His life. The essential condition for receiving that power is that we be found ready and willing to do the work the Spirit has come to accomplish.

"My witnesses": these two words surely contain a divine and inexhaustible wealth of meaning. They are the perfect description of the Spirit's work and our work; the work for which nothing less than His divine power is needed; the work by which our weakness is made strong. There is nothing so effective as an honest witness. Even the learned eloquence of a lawyer must be convinced by it. There is nothing so simple: just telling what we have seen and heard, or, perhaps in silence, witnessing to what has been done in us. It was the great work of Jesus himself: "To this end have I been born, and to this end am I come into the world, that I should bear witness unto the truth." And yet, simple and easy as it appears, to make us witnesses of Jesus is what the almighty power of the Spirit is needed for, and what He was sent to do. If we are, in the power of the eternal life, the power of the world to come, and in heavenly power, to witness of Jesus as He reigns in heaven, we need nothing less than the divine power of the heavenly life to strengthen the testimony of our lips and life.

The Holy Spirit makes us witnesses because He himself is a witness. "He shall witness of me," Jesus said. On the day of Pentecost when Peter preached that Christ, when He had ascended into heaven, had received from the Father the Holy Ghost, and had poured Him forth, he spake of what he knew: the Holy Ghost witnessed to him and in him of the glory of his exalted Lord. It was this witness of the Spirit to the reality of Christ's power and presence that made him so bold and strong to speak before the council: "God did exalt him to be a prince and a saviour; and we are witnesses of these things; and so is the Holy Ghost." When the Holy Spirit, in a divine life and power, witnesses to us what Jesus is at the present moment in His glory, our witness will be in His power. We may know all that the Gospels record and all that Scripture further teaches of the person and work of Jesus; we may even speak from past experience of what we once knew of the power of Jesus. This is not the witness of power that is promised here and that will have effect in the world. It is the presence of the Spirit at the present moment, witnessing to the presence of the personal Jesus, that gives our witness that breath of life from heaven that makes it mighty through God to the casting down of strongholds. You can witness to as much of Jesus as the Holy Spirit is witnessing to you in life and truth.

The baptism of power, the enduement of power, is sometimes spoken of and sought after as a special gift. If Paul asked very distinctly for the Ephesians, who had been sealed with the Holy Spirit, that the Father would still give them "the Spirit of wisdom" (Eph. 1:17), we cannot be wrong in praying as definitely for "the Spirit of power." He who searches the hearts knows what is the mind of the Spirit, and He will not give according to the perfection of our words but the Spirit-breathed desire of our hearts. Or let us use the other prayer of Paul (Eph. 3:16), and plead that "He would grant us to be mightily strengthened by his Spirit." However we formulate our prayer, one thing is certain: It is in unceasing prayer, it is in bowing our knees, it is in waiting on God that from himself will come what we ask, whether it be the Spirit of power or the power of the Spirit. The Spirit is never separate from God; in all His going about and working He is still the innermost being of God. It is God himself who, according to the riches of His glory, is mighty to do above what we ask or think, who will in Christ clothe us with the power of the Spirit.

In seeking for this power of the Spirit, let us note the mode of His working. There is one mistake we must particularly beware of. It is that of always expecting to feel the power when it works. Scripture links power and weakness in a wonderful way, not as succeeding each other, but as existing together. "I was with you in weakness; my preaching was in power. When I am weak, then am I strong." (See I Cor. 2:3-5; 2 Cor. 4:7, 16, 6:10, 12:10, 13:3, 4.) The power is the power of God, given to faith; and faith grows strong in the dark. The Holy Spirit hides himself in the weak things that God hath chosen, that flesh may not glory in His presence. Spiritual power can be known only by the Spirit of faith. The more distinctly we feel and confess our weakness and believe in the power dwelling within us, ready to work as the need arises, the more confidently we may expect its divine operation even when nothing is felt. Christians lose much not only by not waiting for the power, but by waiting in the wrong way. Seek to combine the faithful and ready obedience to every call of duty, however little your power appears to be, with a deep, dependent waiting and expectation of power from on high. Let your intervals of rest and communion be the exercise of prayer and faith in the power of God dwelling in you and waiting to work through you. Your time of exertion and effort will bring the proof that, by faith, through weakness we are made strong.

Let us also see and make no mistake about *the condition* of the working of this divine power. He that would command nature must first, and most absolutely, obey her. It does not need much grace to long and ask for power, even the power of the Spirit. Who would not be glad to have power? Many pray earnestly for power in or with their work and do not receive it because they do not accept the only position through which the power can work. We want to get possession of the power and use it. God wants the power to get possession of us and use us. If we give up ourselves to the power to rule in us, the power will give itself to us to rule through us. Unconditional submission and obedience to the power in our inner life is the one condition of our being clothed with it. God gives the Spirit to the obedient. "Power belongeth unto God," and remains His for ever. If you would have His power work in you, bow in humble reverence before the holy presence that dwells in you, that asks your surrender to His guidance even in the smallest things. Walk very humbly in holy fear, lest in anything you should fail to know or do His holy will. Live as one given up to a power that has entire control over you, that has complete possession of your inmost being. Let the Spirit and His power have possession of you and you shall know that His power works in you.

Let us be clear, too, as to *the object* of this power, the work it is to do. Men are very careful to economize power and to channel it where it can do its work most effectively. God does not give this power for our own enjoyment, or to save us from trouble and effort. He gives it for one purpose, to glorify His Son. Those who in their weakness are faithful to this one object, who in obedience and testimony prove to God that they are ready at any cost to glorify God—they will receive the power from on high. God seeks for men and women whom He can thus clothe with power. The Church is looking around for them on every side, wondering at the futility of so much of its ministry and worship. The world waits for it, to be convinced that God in indeed in the midst of His people. The perishing millions are crying for deliverance, and the power of God is waiting to deliver. Let us not be content to pray to God to visit and to bless them, or to try to do the best we can for them. Let us give up ourselves, each individual believer, wholly and undividedly, to live as witnesses for Jesus. Let us plead with God to show His people what it means to be Christ's representatives just as He was the Father's. Let us live in the faith that the Spirit of power is within us, and that the Father will, as we wait on Him, fill us with the power of the Spirit.[1]

Most blessed Father, we thank Thee for the wonderful provision Thou hast made for Thy children—that out of weakness they should be made strong, and that in their faltering Thy mighty Spirit should be glorified. We thank Thee for the Holy Spirit, as the Spirit of power, coming down to make Jesus, to whom all power is given, present with His Church, and to make His disciples the witnesses of that presence.

I ask Thee, O my Father, to teach me that I have the power, as I have the living Jesus. May I not look for it to come so that I can see or feel it. May I consent that it shall ever be a divine strength in human weakness, so that the glory may be Thine alone. May I learn to receive it in a faith that allows the mighty Lord Jesus to hold the power and do the work in the midst of weakness. And may, by the Holy Spirit, He be so present with me that my witness may be of Him alone.

O my Father I desire to submit my whole being to this holy power. I would bow before its rule every day and all day. I would be its servant and humble myself to obey its hardest command. Father, let the power rule in me that I may be made meet for it to use. And my one object in life be that Thy blessed Son may receive the honor and the glory. Amen.

SUMMARY

1. There is a presence in the church of Christ as omnipotent and divine as Christ himself when He was on earth; rather, as He is now on the throne of power. As the Church wakes up to believe this, and rises out of the dust to put on her beautiful garments, as she waits on her Lord to be "clothed with power from on high," her witness for Christ will be in living power. She will prove that her almighty Lord is in her.

2. This "clothing with power from on high," this "receiving the power of the Holy Ghost," takes place in a way quite contrary to all our natural expectations. It is a divine power working in weakness. The sense of weakness is not taken away: the power is not given as something we possess. We only have the power as we have the Lord himself. He exerts the power in and through our weakness.

3. Our great danger is waiting for the sight or sense of power. Our one need is faith that spiritually recognizes the mighty Lord as present and knows that He will work in weakness. Being clothed with power, or receiving the power, is appropriating the Lord Jesus, receiving Him in faith, so that our souls rejoice in His hidden presence, and know that His power is working in our weakness.

4. As the character of a body depends upon the different particles of which it is composed, so the power of the church of Christ will be decided by the state of its individual members. The Holy Spirit cannot work mightily through the church of God in the world until the mass of individual believers give themselves wholly to their Lord to be filled with His Spirit. Let us labor and pray for this.

5. A personal power, with a will and a purpose, has control within me, ready to work His will into mine in all things. Another will than my own, now ruling in the depths of my

being, is to be waited on. As I submit and obey, His power will work through me. I live under the power of another.

6. "I also am a man under authority, having under me soldiers; and I say to this one, Go, and he goeth." The man who is himself under a higher power, has that power to rule those under him. To be over others, to conquer, I must first be under the highest power.

Note

1. See Note 9, p. 251.

15

THE OUTPOURING OF THE SPIRIT

> And when the day of Pentecost was fully come . . . they were all filled with the Holy Ghost, and began to speak. . . as the Spirit gave them utterance.— Acts 2:1, 4

In the outpouring of the Holy Spirit, the work of Christ culminates. The adorable mystery of the incarnation in Bethlehem, the great redemption accomplished on Calvary, the revelation of Christ as the Son of God in the power of the eternal life by the resurrection, His entrance into glory in the ascension—these are all preliminary stages; their goal and their crown was the coming down of the Holy Spirit. Pentecost is the last and the greatest of the Christian feasts; in it the others find their realization and their fulfillment. It is because the Church has hardly acknowledged this, and has not seen that the glory of Pentecost is the highest glory of the Father and the Son, that the Holy Spirit has not yet been able to reveal and glorify the Son in her as He would. Let us see if we can realize what Pentecost means.

God made man in His own image and for His likeness, with the distinct object that he should become like himself. Man was to be a temple for God to dwell in; he was to become the home in which God could rest. The closest and most intimate union, the indwelling of love: this was what the Holy One longed for and looked forward to. What was very inadequately set forth in type in the temple in Israel became a divine reality in Jesus of Nazareth: God had found a man in whom He could rest, whose whole being was opened to the rule of His will and the fellowship of His love. In Him there was a human nature, possessed by the divine Spirit; and such God would have had all men to be. And such all would be, who accepted this Jesus and His Spirit as their life. His death was to remove the curse and power of sin and make it possible for them to receive His Spirit. His resurrection was the entrance of human nature, free from all the weakness of the flesh, into the life of Deity, the divine Spirit-life. His ascension was admittance as man into the very glory of God; the participation by human nature of perfect fellowship with God in glory in the unity of the Spirit. And yet, with all this, the work was not yet complete. The chief thing was still lacking. How could the Father dwell in men the same as He had dwelt in Christ? This was the great question to which Pentecost gives the answer.

Out of the depths of the Godhead, the Holy Spirit is sent forth in a new character and a new power, such as He never had before. In creation and nature He came forth from God as the Spirit of life. In the creation of man particularly He acted as the power in which his God-likeness was grounded, and after man's fall still testified for God. In Israel He appeared as the Spirit of the theocracy, distinctly inspiring and equipping certain men for their work. In Jesus Christ He came as the Spirit of the Father, given to Him without measure, and abiding in Him. All these are manifestations, in different degrees, of one and the same Spirit. But now there comes the last, long-promised, entirely new manifestation of the divine Spirit. The Spirit that dwelt in Jesus Christ, and in His life of obedience, has taken up His human spirit into perfect fellowship and unity with himself, is now the Spirit of the exalted God-man. As the man Christ Jesus enters the glory of God and the full fellowship of that Spirit-life in which God dwells, He receives from the Father the right to send forth His Spirit into His disciples, that is, in the Spirit to descend himself and dwell in them. The Spirit comes in a new power, which before had not been possible, because Jesus had not been crucified or glorified. He comes as the very Spirit of the glorified Jesus. The work of the Son, the longing of the Father, receives its fulfillment. Man's heart is now indeed the home of his God.

Didn't I say that Pentecost is the greatest of the Church's feasts? The mystery of Bethlehem is indeed incomprehensible and glorious, but when once I believe it, there is nothing that does not appear possible and forthcoming. That a pure, holy body should be formed for the Son of God by the power of the Holy Spirit, and that in that body the Spirit should dwell, is indeed a miracle of divine power. But that the same Spirit should now come and dwell in the bodies of sinful men, that in them also the Father should take up His abode, this is a mystery of grace that passes all understanding. But this, glory be to God, is the blessing Pentecost brings and receives. The entrance of the Son of God into the likeness of our flesh in Bethlehem, into the curse and death of sin in our place, in human nature as first-begotten from the dead into the power of eternal Life, and His entrance into the very glory of the Father—these were but the preparatory steps: here is the consummation for which all the rest was accomplished. The word now begins to be fulfilled: "Behold! the tabernacle of God is with men, and He shall dwell with them." [1]

It is only in the light of all that preceded Pentecost—of the great sacrifice, which God did not consider too great if He might dwell with sinful men—that the narrative of the outpouring of the Spirit can be understood. It is the earthly reflection of Christ's exaltation in heaven, the participation He gives to His friends of the glory He now has with the Father. To be understood fully we need a spiritual enlightening. In the story that is so simply told, the deepest mysteries of the Kingdom are unfolded, and the title-deeds given to the Church of her holy heritage until her Lord's return. What the Spirit is to be to *believers* and the Church, to the *ministers* of the Word and their work, and to the unbelieving *world*, are the three main emphases.

1. Christ had promised to His disciples that in the Comforter He himself would again come to them. During His life on earth, His personal manifested presence, as revealing the

unseen Father, was the Father's great gift to men—the one thing the disciples longed for and needed. This was to be their portion now in greater power than before. Christ had entered glory with this very purpose, that now, in a divine way, "He might fill all things," He might particularly fill the members of His body with himself and His glorified life. When the Holy Spirit came down, He gave, as a personal life within them, what had previously only been a life near them, but yet outside their own natural life. The very Spirit of God's own Son, as He had lived and loved, obeyed and died, was raised and glorified by almighty power, was now to become their personal life. The wondrous transaction that had taken place in heaven, in the placing of their friend and Lord on the throne of heaven, this the Holy Spirit came to be the witness of, even to communicate it and maintain it within them as a heavenly reality. It is indeed no wonder that, as the Holy Ghost came down from the Father through the glorified Son, their whole nature was filled to overflowing with the joy and power of heaven, with the presence of Jesus, and their lips overflowed with the praise of the wonderful works of God.

Such was the birth of the church of Christ; such must be its growth and strength. The first and essential element of the true succession of the Pentecostal church is a membership baptized with the Holy Ghost and with fire; every heart filled with the experience of the presence of the glorified Lord; every tongue and life witnessing to the wonderful work God has done in raising Jesus to the glory of His throne and then filling His disciples with that glory too. It is not so much the baptism of power for our preachers that we must seek; it is that every individual member of Christ's body may know, possess, and witness to the presence of an indwelling Christ through the Holy Spirit. This is what will draw the attention of the world and compel a confession to the power of Jesus.

2. It was amid the interest and the questionings which the sight of this joyous praising company of believers awakened in the multitude that Peter stood up to preach. The story of Pentecost teaches us the true position of the ministry and the secret of its power. A church full of the Holy Ghost is the power of God to awaken the careless and

attract all honest, earnest hearts. It is to such an audience, awakened by the testimony of believers, that the preaching will come with power. It is out of such a church of men and women full of the Holy Ghost that Spirit-led preachers will rise up, bold and free, to point to every believer as a living witness to the truth of their preaching and the power of their Lord.

Peter's preaching is a most remarkable lesson of what all Holy Ghost preaching will be. He preaches Christ from the Scriptures. In contrast with the thoughts of man, who had rejected Christ, He sets forth the thoughts of God, who had sent Christ, who delighted in Him, and had now exalted Him at His right hand. All preaching in the power of the Holy Spirit will do the same. The Spirit is the Spirit of Christ, the Spirit of His personal life, taking possession of our personality and witnessing with our spirit to what Christ has won for us. The Spirit has come for the very purpose of continuing the work Christ had begun on earth, of making men partakers of His redemption and His life. It could not be otherwise; the Spirit always witnesses to Christ. He did so in the Scriptures; He does so in the believer; the believer's testimony will ever be according to Scripture. The Spirit in Christ, the Spirit in Scripture, the Spirit in the Church; as long as this threefold cord is kept intertwined, it cannot be broken.

3. The effect of this preaching was marvelous, but not more marvelous than might be expected. The presence and power of Jesus were a reality in the company of disciples. The power from on high, from the throne filled Peter. The sight and experience he had of Christ, as exalted at the right hand of God, was such a spiritual reality that power went out from him. As his preaching reached its application: "Know assuredly that God hath made him both Lord and Christ, this Jesus whom ye crucified," thousands bowed in brokenness of spirit, ready to acknowledge the crucified one as their Lord. The Spirit had come to the disciples and through them convinced the hearers of unbelief. The penitent inquirers listened to the command to repent and believe, and they received the gift of the Holy Ghost. The greater works that Christ had promised to do through the disciples, He had done. In one moment, lifelong prejudice

and even bitter hatred gave way to surrender, love, and adoration. From the glorified Lord, power filled his body and from it power went forth to conquer and to save.

Pentecost is the glorious sunrise of "that day," the first of "those days" of which the prophets and our Lord had so often spoken, the promise and the pledge of what the history of the Church was meant to be. It is universally admitted that the Church has ill-fulfilled her destiny, that even now, after eighteen centuries, she has not risen to the height of her glorious privileges. Even when she strives to accept her calling, to witness for her Lord unto the ends of the earth, she does not do it fully in the faith of the pentecostal Spirit and the possession of His mighty power. Instead of regarding Pentecost as sunrise, she too often speaks and acts as if it had been noonday, from which the light must soon begin to fade. Let the Church return to Pentecost, and Pentecost will return to her. The Spirit of God cannot take possession of believers beyond their capacity of receiving Him. The promise is waiting; the Spirit is now available in all His fullness. Our capacity of reception needs to be enlarged. While believers continue with one accord in praise, love, and prayer (delay only intensifies the spirit of waiting and expectation), holding fast the promise in faith and gazes upon the exalted Lord in the confidence that He will make himself known in power, in the midst of His people, it is at the footstool of the throne that Pentecost comes. Jesus Christ is still Lord of all, crowned with power and glory. His longing to reveal His presence in His disciples—to make them share the glory-life in which He dwells—is as fresh and full as when He first ascended the throne. Let us take our place at the footstool. Let us yield ourselves in strong, expectant faith to be filled with the Holy Ghost and to testify for Jesus. Let the indwelling Christ be our life, our strength, and our testimony. Out of such a Church, Spirit-filled preachers will rise with the power that will make Christ's enemies bow at His feet.

O Lord God, we worship before the throne on which the Son is seated with Thee, crowned with glory and honor. We thank and bless Thee that it is for us, the children of men, that Thou hast done this; that He in whom Thou delightest belongs as much to earth as to heaven as much to us as to Thee. O God, we adore Thy love; we praise Thy holy name.

We beseech Thee, O our Father, to reveal to Thy Church how that our blessed head considers us as His own body, sharing with Him in His life, His power, and His glory, and how the Holy Spirit, as the bearer of that life and power and glory, is waiting to reveal it within us. Oh, that Thy people might be awakened to know what the Holy Spirit means—as the real presence of the glorified Lord within them and as the clothing with power from on high for their work on earth. Oh that all Thy people might learn to gaze on their exalted King until their whole being is opened up for His reception and His Spirit fills them to their utmost capacity!

Our Father, we plead with Thee, in the name of Jesus, revive Thy Church. Make every believer be a temple full of the Holy Ghost. Make every church, in its believing members, a consecrated company ever testifying of a present Christ; ever waiting for the fullness of the power from on high. Make every preacher of the word a minister of the Spirit. Let Pentecost, throughout the earth, be the sign that Jesus reigns; that the redeemed are His body; that His Spirit works; that one day every knee shall bow to Him. Amen.

SUMMARY

1. Let us try to grasp the concept that when Jesus went to heaven, He could not bear the thought that His returning to glory should cause the slightest separation between himself and His faithful followers. The mission of the Spirit was to secure and give to them His promised presence. This is the blessedness of the Spirit's work; this makes Him the power of God in us for our work.

2. The perfect health of a body means the health of every member. The healthy action of the Spirit in the Church requires the health of every individual believer. Let us pray to this end that the presence of Christ, by the indwelling Spirit in every believer, shall make our seasons of worship a repeated Pentecost: the waiting, receptive, worshipping company on earth met by the Spirit of Christ from heaven.

Note

1. See Note 10, p. 252.

16

THE HOLY SPIRIT AND MISSIONS

> Now there were in the church that was at Antioch cer-
> tain prophets and teachers. . . . As they ministered to
> the Lord, and fasted, the Holy Ghost said, Separate
> me Barnabas and Saul for the work whereunto I have
> called them. And when they had fasted and prayed,
> and laid their hands on them, they sent them away.
> So they, being sent forth by the Holy Ghost, departed
> unto Seleucia.—Acts 13:1-4

It has been rightly said that the Acts of the Apostles
might well have borne the name, "the Acts of the exalted
Lord," or "the Acts of the Holy Spirit." Christ's parting
promise, "Ye shall receive power when the Holy Ghost is
come upon you; and ye shall be my witnesses, both in Jerusalem and in all Judea and Samaria, and unto the uttermost
parts of the earth," was indeed one of those divine seed-
words in which is contained the kingdom of heaven in the
power of an infinite growth, with the law of its manifestation
and the prophecy of its final perfection. In the book of the
Acts we have the way traced in which the promise received
its incipient fulfillment on its way from Jerusalem to Rome.
It gives us the divine record of the coming, dwelling, and
working of the Holy Spirit, as the power given to Christ's
disciples to witness for Him before Jews and heathen; and of
the triumph of the name of Christ in Antioch and Rome as
the centers for the conquest of the uttermost parts of the
earth. The book reveals, as with a light from heaven, that
the one aim and purpose of the descent of the Spirit from
our glorified Lord in heaven to His disciples—to reveal in
them His presence, His guidance, and His power—is to
equip them to be His witnesses even to the uttermost parts
of the earth. Missions to the heathen is the one object of the
mission of the Spirit.

In the passage we have as our text, we have the first record of the part the Church is definitely called to take in the
work of missions. In the preaching of Philip at Samaria and
Peter at Caesarea, we have the case of individual men exer-

cising their function of ministry among those who were not of the Jews, under the leading of the Spirit. In the preaching of the men of Cyprus and Cyrene to the Greeks at Antioch, we have the divine instinct of the Spirit of love and life leading men to open new paths where the leaders of the Church had not yet thought of coming. But this guidance of the Spirit in separating special men was now to become part of the organization of the Church, and the whole community of believers was to be educated to take its share in the work for which the Spirit particularly had come to earth. If Acts 2 is of importance in giving us the enduement of the Church for her Jerusalem work, Acts 13 is of no less importance in the Church's setting apart for definite mission work. We cannot sufficiently praise God for the deepening interest in missions in our day. If our interest is to be permanent and personal; if it is to be a personal enthusiasm of love and devotion to our blessed Lord and the lost He came to save; if it is to be fruitful in raising the work of the Church to the true level of Pentecostal power, we must learn well the lesson of Antioch. Mission work must find its initiative and its power in the distinct and direct acknowledgment of the guidance of the Holy Spirit.

It has often been remarked that true mission work has always been born of a revival of spiritual life in the Church. The Holy Spirit's quickening work stirs us up to new devotion to the blessed Lord whom He reveals, and to the lost to whom He belongs. It is in such a state of mind that the voice of the Spirit is heard, urging the Lord's redeemed to work for Him. It was this way at Antioch. There were certain prophets and teachers at Antioch spending part of their time in ministering to the Lord and fasting. With the public service of God in the church, they combined the spirit of separation from the world and of self-sacrifice. Their Lord was in heaven; they felt the need of close and continued fellowship waiting for His orders; they understood that the Spirit that dwelt in them could not have free and full scope of action except as they maintained direct fellowship with Him as their Master, and entered as much as possible into the fellowship of Christ's crucifixion of the flesh. "They ministered to the Lord and fasted": such were the men, such was their state of mind and their habit of life, when the Holy Spirit revealed to them that He had called two of their number to a special work, and called upon them to be His instruments in separating them, in presence of the whole church, for that work.

The law of the kingdom has not been changed. It is still the Holy Ghost who has charge of all mission work. He will still reveal His will, in the appointment of work and selection of men, to those who are waiting on their Lord in service and separation. When once the Holy Spirit in any age has taught men of faith and prayer to undertake His work, it is easy for others to admire and approve what they do, to see the harmony of their conduct with scripture and to copy their example. And yet the real power of the Spirit's guiding and working, the real personal love and devotion to Jesus as a beloved Lord, may be present to a very small extent. It is because a great deal of interest in the missionary cause is of this nature that there is often so much arguing, begging, and pleading with its supporters. The command of the Lord is known as recorded in a book; the living voice of the Spirit, who reveals the Lord in living presence and power, is not heard. It is not enough that Christians be stirred and urged to take a greater interest in the work, to pray and give more: there is a more urgent need. In the life of the individual, the indwelling of the Holy Spirit and the presence and rule of the Lord of glory which He maintains, must again become the chief mark of the Christian life. In the fellowship of the Church, we must learn to wait more earnestly for the Holy Spirit's guidance in the selection of men and fields of labor; in the awakening of interest and the seeking of support. It is in the mission that is originated in much prayer and waiting on the Spirit that His power can be expected.

Let no one fear, when we speak this way, that we intend to lead Christians away from the real practical work that must be done. There is much that needs to be done and cannot be done without diligent labor. Information must be circulated; readers must be found and kept; funds must be raised; prayermeetings must be kept up; directors must meet, consult, and decide. All this must be done. But it will be done well, and as a service well-pleasing to the Master, only in the measure in which it is done in the power of the Holy Spirit. Oh that the Church, and every member of it, might learn the lesson! The Spirit has come down from heaven to the Spirit of missions, to inspire and empower Christ's disciples to witness for Him to the uttermost parts of the earth.

The origin, the progress, the success of missions are all His. It is He who awakens in the hearts of believers the zeal for the honor of their Lord, the compassion for the souls of the perishing, the faith in His promises, the willing obedience to His commands, by which the mission grows. It is He who draws together in united effort; who calls forth suitable men to go out; who opens the door and prepares the hearts of the heathen to desire or to receive the Word. It is He who at length gives the increase, and, even where Satan's seat is, establishes the cross, and gathers around it the redeemed of the Lord. Missions are the special work of the Holy Spirit. No one may expect to be filled with the Spirit if he is not willing to be used for missions. No one who wishes to work or pray for missions need fear his weakness or poverty. The Holy Spirit is the power that can fit him to take his divinely appointed place in the work. Let every one who prays for missions, and longs for more of a missionary spirit in the Church, pray first that in every believer personally, and in the Church and its work and worship, the power of the indwelling Spirit may have full sway.[1]

"Then when they had fasted and prayed, they sent them away. So they, being sent forth by the Holy Ghost, went down to Seleucia." The sending forth was equally the work of the Church and of the Spirit. This is the normal relation. There are men sent forth by the Holy Spirit alone; amid the opposition or indifference of the Church, the Spirit does His work. There are men sent forth by the Church alone; it thinks the work ought to be done, and does it, but with little of the fasting and praying that recognizes the need of the Spirit and refuses to work without Him. Blessed is the Church and blessed the mission which the Spirit originates, where He is allowed to guide, and where the direction is waited for from himself alone. Ten days' praying and waiting on earth, and the Spirit's descent in fire: this was the birth of the Church at Jerusalem. Ministering and fasting; then again fasting and praying; the Spirit sending forth Barnabas and Saul: this was, at Antioch, the consecration of the Church to be a mission church. Through waiting and prayer on earth; through the power of the Spirit from the Lord in heaven, is the strength, joy, and blessing of the church of Christ and its missions.

May I say to any missionary who reads this in his far-off home, "Be of good cheer, brother! The Holy Spirit, who is the mighty power of God, who is the presence of Jesus within you, the Holy Spirit is with you and in you. The work is His: depend on Him, yield to Him, wait for Him; the work is His, He will do it. May I say to every Christian, whether he be a director, supporter, contributor, helper in prayer or in any other way in the great work of hastening the coming of the Kingdom, "Be of good cheer." From the time of waiting before the throne and the baptism there received, the first disciples went forth until they reached Antioch. There they paused, prayed, fasted, and then passed on to Rome and the region beyond. Let us from these, our brethren, learn the secret of power. Let us call on every Christian, who would be a friend of missions or a mission worker, to come with us and be filled with the Spirit, whose work is the work of missions. Let us lift up a clear testimony, that the need of the Church and the world is believers who can testify to an indwelling Christ by the Spirit and prove it. Let us gather such together in the antechamber of the King's presence— the waiting at Jerusalem, the ministering and fasting at Antioch. The Spirit does still come as of old in power, He does still move and send forth; He is still mighty to convince of sin and reveal Jesus, and to make thousands fall at His feet. He waits for us: let us wait on Him, let us welcome Him.

O God, Thou didst send Thy Son to be the Saviour of the world. Thou didst give Him power over all flesh, that He should give eternal life to as many as Thou hast given Him. And Thou didst pour out Thy Spirit upon all flesh, commissioning as many as received Him to make known and pass on the wondrous blessing. In the love and power in which Thy Spirit was sent forth, He likewise sends forth those who yield themselves to Him to be the instruments of His power in glorifying Thy Son. We bless Thee for this divine and most glorious salvation.

O our God, we stand amazed, and abased, at the sloth and neglect of Thy Church in not fulfilling her divine commission. We are humbled at our slowness of heart to perceive and believe what Thy Son did promise, to obey His will and finish His work. We cry to Thee, our God! Visit Thy Church and let Thy Spirit, the Spirit of divine sending, fill all her children.

O my Father, I dedicate myself afresh to Thee to live and labor, to pray and travail, to sacrifice and suffer for Thy Kingdom. I accept anew in faith the wonderful gift of the Holy Spirit, the very Spirit of Christ, and yield myself to His indwelling. I humbly plead with Thee to allow me and all Thy children to be so mightily strengthened by the Holy Spirit that Christ may possess heart and life, and our one desire be that the whole earth may be filled with His glory. Amen.

SUMMARY

1. "Sent forth by the Holy Ghost." The Holy Ghost was himself *sent* by the Son from the Father to continue His work on earth. He does it by sending forth men for the work. The mission of the Spirit was meant of God to give the Church the Spirit of missions. His outpouring is upon all flesh. He cannot rest till all have heard of Christ.

2. A missionary spirit! What is this but Christ's Spirit—the pure flame of His love for souls burning brightly enough in us to make us first willing, then longing to go anywhere, and to suffer any privations, in order to seek and find the lost in the distant mountains and trackless deserts of the earth.

3. Is it true that we belong to Christ at all? "If any man have not the Spirit of Christ, he is none of his." We know that the Spirit of the Saviour was that of self-sacrifice for the salvation of the world. We must apply the test to our own hearts.

4. Jesus sent down the Holy Spirit to take possession of our hearts for Him that He might live there and work in and through us, even as the Father worked in and through Him. Let me accept this afresh in faith. I will wait on my Lord till my whole soul is filled with the assurance that the Spirit dwells in me, the very presence of himself. To this Spirit I yield myself, even as the disciples did of old. They saw with

Christ's eyes, they felt with His heart, they worked with His energies; for they had His Spirit. And I have His Spirit too.

5. On the second to his last birthday, Livingstone wrote: "My Jesus, my king, my life, my all. I again dedicate my whole self to thee." He died on his knees, with his face buried in his hands, praying.

Note

1. See Note 11, p. 256.

17

THE NEWNESS OF THE SPIRIT

> But now we are delivered from the law, that being dead wherein we were held; that we should serve in newness of spirit, and not in the oldness of the letter.—Rom. 7:6
> But if ye be led of the Spirit, ye are not under the law.—Gal. 5:18

The work of the indwelling Spirit is to glorify Christ and reveal Him within us. Corresponding to Christ's threefold office of prophet, priest, and king, we find that the work of the indwelling Spirit in the believer is set before us in three aspects: enlightening, sanctifying, and strengthening. Of the enlightening, Christ particularly speaks in His farewell discourse, when He promises the Spirit as the Spirit of truth, who will bear witness of Him, will guide into all truth, will take of Christ's and declare it unto us. In the Epistles to the Romans and Galatians His work of sanctifying is especially prominent: this was what was needed in churches just brought out of the depths of heathenism. In the Epistles to the Corinthians, where wisdom was so sought and prized, the two aspects are combined; they are taught that the Spirit can only enlighten as He sanctifies (1 Cor. 2, 3:1-3, 16; 2 Cor. 3). In the Acts of the Apostles, as we might expect, His

strengthening for work is in the foreground; as the promised
Spirit of power He equips for a bold and blessed testimony
in the midst of persecution and difficulty.

In the Epistle to the church at Rome, the capital of the
world, Paul was called of God to give a full and systematic
exposition of His gospel and the plan of redemption. In this
the work of the Holy Spirit must have an important place.
In giving his text or theme (Rom. 1:17), "The righteous shall
live by faith," he paves the way for what he was to expound—that through faith both righteousness and life
would come. In the first part of his argument (v. 11), he
teaches what the righteousness of faith is. He then proceeds
(vv. 12-21) to prove how this righteousness is rooted in our
living connection with the second Adam and in a justification of life. In the individual (6:1-13) this life comes through
the believing acceptance of Christ's death to sin and His life
to God as ours, and the willing surrender (6:14-23) to be servants of God and of righteousness. Proceeding to show that
in Christ we are not only dead to sin, but to the law also, as
the strength of sin, he comes naturally to the new law which
His gospel brings to take the place of the old, the law of the
Spirit of life in Christ Jesus.

We all know how an impression is heightened by the
force of contrast. Just as the apostle had contrasted
(6:13-23) the service of sin and of righteousness, so he here
(7:4) contrasts, to bring out fully what the power and work
of the Spirit is, the service in the oldness of the letter in bondage to the law with the service in newness of the Spirit in
the liberty and power which Jesus through the Spirit gives.
In the following passage, Rom. 7:14-25 and Rom. 8:1-16, we
have the contrast worked out; it is in the light of that contrast alone that the two conditions can be rightly understood. Each state has its key-word, indicating the character
of the life it describes. In Romans 7 we find the word law
twenty times, and the word Spirit only once. In Romans 8,
on the contrary, we find in its first sixteen verses the word
Spirit sixteen times. The contrast is between the Christian
life in the law and in the Spirit. Paul had very boldly said,
not only are you dead to sin and made free from sin that you
might become servants to righteousness and to God (Rom.
6), but also, "We were made dead to the law, so that, having

died to that wherein we were held, we serve in newness of spirit, and not in oldness of the letter." We have here, then, a double advance on the teaching of Romans 6. There it was the death to sin and freedom from it, here it is death to the law and freedom from it. There it was "newness of life" (Rom. 6:4), as an objective reality secured to us in Christ; here it is "newness of spirit" (Rom. 7:6), as a subjective experience made ours by the indwelling of the Spirit. He that would fully know and enjoy the life in the Spirit must know what life in the law is, and how complete the freedom from it with which he is made free by the Spirit.

In the description Paul gives of the life of a believer, who is still held in bondage to the law, and seeks to fulfill that law, there are three expressions in which the characteristic marks of that state are summed up. The first is the word flesh. "I am carnal (fleshly), sold under sin. In me, that is, in my flesh, dwelleth no good thing" (7:14, 18). If we want to understand the word "carnal," we must refer to Paul's exposition of it in 1 Cor. 3:1-3. He uses it there of Christians, who, though regenerate, have not yielded themselves to the Spirit entirely, so as to become spiritual.[1] They have the Spirit, but allow the flesh to prevail. There is therefore, a difference between Christians carnal or spiritual by the element that is strongest in them. As long as they have the Spirit, but, owing to whatever cause, do not accept fully His mighty deliverance, and so strive in their own strength, they do not and cannot become spiritual. St. Paul here describes the regenerate man, as he is in himself. He lives by the Spirit, but, according to Gal. 5:25, does not walk by the Spirit. He has the new spirit within him, according to Ezek. 36:26, but he has not intelligently and practically accepted God's own Spirit to dwell and rule within that spirit, as the life of His life. He is still carnal.

The second expression we find in verse 18: "To will is present with me, but how to do that which is good is not." In every possible variety of expression, Paul (7:15-21) attempts to make clear the painful state of utter impotence in which the law, and the effort to fulfill it, leaves a man: "The good which I would, I do not; but the evil which I would not, that I practice." Willing, but not doing: such is the service of God in the oldness of the letter, in the life before Pentecost (see

Matt. 26:41). The renewed spirit of the man has accepted and consented to the will of God; but the secret of power to do, the Spirit of God, as indwelling, is not yet known. In those, on the contrary, who know what the life in the Spirit is, God works both to will and to do; the Christian testifies, "I can do all things through Him that strengtheneth me." But this is only possible through faith and the Holy Spirit. As long as the believer has not consciously been made free from the law, with its "he that doeth these things shall live through them," continual failure will attend his efforts to do the will of God. He may even delight in the law of God after the inward man, but the power is lacking. It is only when he submits to the law of faith—"he that liveth shall do these things," because he knows that he has been made free from the law, that he may be joined to another, to the living Jesus, working in him through His Holy Spirit—that he will indeed bring forth fruit unto God (see Rom 7:4).

The third expression we must note is in verse 23: "I see a different law in my members, bringing me into captivity under the law of sin which is in my members." This word captivity or sold under sin, suggests the idea of slaves sold into bondage, without the liberty or the power to do as they will. It points back to what he had said in the beginning of the chapter, that we have been made free from the law; here is evidently one who does not yet know that liberty. And it points forward to what he says in chapter 8:2: "The law of the Spirit of life in Christ Jesus hath made me free from the law of sin and death." The freedom with which we have been made free in Christ, as offered according to our faith, cannot be fully accepted or experienced as long as there is a trace of a legal spirit. It is only by the Spirit of Christ within us that the full liberation is effected. As in the oldness of the letter, so in the newness of the Spirit, a twofold relationship exists: the objective and the personal. There is the law over me and outside of me, and there is the law of sin in my members, deriving its strength from the first. Likewise, in being made free from the law, there is the objective liberty in Christ offered according to my faith. There is the subjective personal possession of that liberty, in its fullness and power, to be had alone through the Spirit dwelling and ruling in my members, even as the law of sin had done. This alone can change the cry of the captive: "Oh, wretched man that I am, who shall deliver me from the bondage of this death?" into the song of the ransomed: "I thank God through Jesus Christ our Lord. The law of the Spirit made me free."

How shall we regard the two conditions set before us in Rom. 7:14-23 and 8:1-16? Are they interchangeable, successive, or simultaneous?

Many have thought that they are a description of the varying experience of the believer's life. Although often by the grace of God he is able to do what is good and to live well-pleasing to God, and thus experience the grace of chapter 8, the consciousness of sin or shortcomings plunges him again into the hopelessness of chapter 7. Though sometimes the one and then the other experience may be more prominent, each day brings the experience of both.

Others have felt that this is not the life of a believer as God would have it, or the life that the provision of God's grace has placed within his reach. As they saw that a life in the freedom with which Christ makes us free, when the Holy Spirit dwells within us is within our reach, and as they entered on it, it was to them as if now and forever they had left the experience of Romans 7 far behind, and they cannot but look upon it as Israel's wilderness life, a life never more to be returned to. There are many who can testify what enlightenment and blessing has come to them as they saw what the blessed transition was from the bondage of the law to the liberty of the Spirit.

And yet, however large the measure of truth to this view, it does not fully satisfy. The believer feels that there is not a day that he gets beyond the words, "In me, that is, in my flesh, dwelleth no good thing." Even when kept joyously in the will of God, and strengthened not only to will but also to do His will, he knows that it is not he, but the grace of God: "in *me* dwelleth no good." So the believer comes to see that, not the two experiences, but the two conditions are simultaneous, and that even when his experience is most fully that of the law of the Spirit of life in Christ Jesus making him free, he still bears about with him the body of sin and death.[2] The "making free" which is by the Spirit and the deliverance from the power of sin and the song of thanks to God is the continuous experience of the power of the endless life, as maintained by the Spirit of Christ. As I am led of the Spirit, I am not under the law. Its spirit of bondage, its weakness through the flesh, and the sense of condemnation and hopelessness it works are cast out by the liberty of the Spirit.

If there is one lesson the believer needs to learn, who would enjoy the full indwelling of the Spirit, it is the one taught so forcefully in this passage: that the law, the flesh, and self-effort are all utterly useless in enabling us to serve God. It is the Spirit within, taking the place of the law without, that leads us into the liberty whereby Christ has made us free. "Where the Spirit of the Lord is, there is liberty."

Beloved Lord Jesus, I humbly ask Thee to make clear to me the blessed secret of the life of the Spirit. Teach me what it means to become dead to the law, so that our service to God is no longer in the oldness of the letter that we are joined to another, even to thyself, the risen one, through whom we bring forth fruit unto God, serving in the newness of the Spirit.

Blessed Lord, with deep shame do I confess the sin of my nature, that "in me, that is, in my flesh, dwelleth no good thing," that "I am carnal, sold under sin." I do bless Thee, that in answer to the cry, "Who shall deliver me from the body of this death?" Thou hast taught me to answer, "I thank God through Jesus Christ our Lord. The law of the Spirit of life in Christ Jesus made me free from the law of sin and death."

Blessed Master, teach me now to serve Thee in newness of life and liberty, the ever-fresh gladness of the Spirit. Teach me to yield myself in full and wholehearted faith to the Holy Spirit, that my life may indeed be in the glorious liberty of the children of God, in the power of an indwelling Saviour working in me both to will and to do, even as the Father worked in Him. Amen.

SUMMARY

1. It is not enough that we know that there are two masters to serve, God and sin (Rom. 6:15-22), and yield ourselves to God alone. We must see that in serving God as the only Master, there are two ways of doing so: the oldness of the letter and the newness of the Spirit (Rom. 7:1-6). Until a soul understands the difference, confesses its danger and

uselessness as pictured in Rom. 7:14-25, and utterly forsakes it, it cannot fully know what service in newness and gladness of the Spirit is. It is only after the death of the old life and confidence in the flesh, that the new can arise.

2. In every Catechism each question has its appropriate answer. There are many who never cease repeating the question, "O wretched man that I am, who shall deliver me from the body of this death?" who seldom give the triumphant answer, "I thank God, through Jesus Christ our Lord. The law of the Spirit of life in Christ Jesus made me free." Of that answer, chap. 8:1-16 is the exposition. Never ask the question without giving the answer.

3. The word law is used in two senses. It means the inner rule, according to which all in nature acts and is used to indicate that power, or it is used with regard to an external rule, according to which one must be taught to act who does not do so spontaneously. The external is always the proof that the inner one is lacking. When the inner law prevails, the outer is not needed. "If ye are led of the Spirit, ye are not under the law." The indwelling Spirit makes free from the law.

4. The whole secret of sanctification lies in the promise of the new covenant: "I will put my law in their inward parts, and write it in their heart." Just as each plant in its growth spontaneously obeys the law put into its inmost parts by God, so the believer, who accepts the new covenant promise in its fullness, walks in the power of that inner law. The Spirit within frees from the law without.

Notes

1. See chapter 23. There is a small difference, that of one letter, between the word used there and here in the Greek, but not such as to affect the application of the text.

2. Mark the difference between a state and an experience. As a state, bearing about in his body (Rom. 6:6, 8:13) the flesh that is enmity against God, no believer ever gets beyond Romans 7. As an experience no believer need abide in it, because the life of the Spirit gives from moment to moment the deliverance and the victory.

18

THE LIBERTY OF THE SPIRIT

The law of the Spirit of life in Christ Jesus hath made me free from the law of sin and death. . . . If ye through the Spirit do mortify the deeds of the body, ye shall live.—Rom. 8:2, 13.

In the sixth chapter of Romans Paul speaks (vv. 18, 22) of our having been made free from sin in Christ Jesus. Our death to sin in Christ had freed us from its dominion: being made free from sin as a power, as a master, when we accepted Christ in faith, we became servants to righteousness and to God. In the seventh chapter (vv. 1-6) he speaks of our being made free from the law. "The strength of sin is the law": deliverance from sin and the law go together. Being made free from the law, we are united to the living Christ, that, in union with Him, we might now serve in newness of the Spirit (7:4-6). Paul, in these two passages (6 and 7:1-6), presents being made free from sin and the law, in its objective reality, as a life prepared in Christ to be accepted and maintained by faith. According to the law of a gradual growth in the Christian life, the believer must in the power of the Spirit with which he has been sealed by faith enter into this union and walk in it. As a matter of experience, almost all believers can testify that, even after they have seen and accepted this teaching, their life is not what they had hoped it would be. They have found the descent into the experience of the second half of Romans 7 most real and painful. It is because there is, as a rule, no other way to learn the two great lessons. The first is the uselessness of the human will, by the law urging it to obedience, ever to work out a divine righteousness in man's life. The second is the need of the conscious and full indwelling of the Holy Spirit as the only sufficient power for the life of a child of God.

In the first half of Romans 8, we have set forth this second truth. In the divine exposition of the Christian life in this Epistle, and its growth in the believer, there is a distinct advance from step to step. The eighth chapter— in introducing the Holy Spirit for the first time in the unfolding of the life of faith, as we have it in chapters 6-8— teaches us that it is only as the Spirit definitely motivates our life and walk, and as He is distinctly known and accepted to do this, that we can fully possess and enjoy the riches of grace that are ours in Christ. Let everyone who would know what it is to be dead to sin and alive to God, to be free from sin and the law, and joined to Him who is raised from the dead, come to find the strength he needs in that Spirit, through whom the union with Christ can be maintained as a divine experience, and His life be lived within us in power and truth.

Of the first half of this eighth chapter, the second verse is the center. It reveals the wonderful secret of how our freedom from sin and the law may become a living and abiding experience. A believer may know that he is free, and yet have to admit that his experience is that of a hopeless captive. The freedom is so entirely *in* Christ Jesus, and the maintenance of the living union with Him is so distinctly and entirely a work of divine power, that it is only as we see that the divine Spirit dwells within us for this very purpose, and know how to accept and yield to His working it, that we can really stand perfect and complete in the liberty with which Christ has made us free. The life and the liberty of Rom. 6 and 7:1-6 are only fully ours as we can say, "The law of the Spirit of the life that is in Christ Jesus made me free from the law of sin and death." Through the whole Christian life, this principle rules: "According to your faith be it unto you." As the Holy Spirit, the Spirit of faith, reveals the greatness of God's resurrection power working in us, and as faith in the indwelling Spirit yields to receive that power to the fullest, all that is available to us in Christ Jesus becomes manifest in our daily personal experience. When we perceive the difference between this and the previous teaching (Rom. 6-7:6); when we see what a distinct advantage there is in it; the unique and most glorious place which the Holy Spirit, as God, holds in the plan of redemption and the life of faith, will open up to us. We learn with this, that as divinely perfect as the life of liberty in Christ Jesus is, so also is the power of that life enabling us to walk in that liberty in the Holy Spirit. The living assurance and experience of the Holy Spirit's indwelling will become to us the very first necessity of the new life, inseparable from the person and presence of Jesus Christ our Lord.

"The law of the Spirit of Life in Christ Jesus made us free from the law of sin and death." Paul here contrasts the two opposing laws: the one of sin and death in the members, the other of the Spirit of life ruling and quickening even the mortal body. Under the former we have seen the believer sighing as a hopeless captive. In the second half of Romans 6, Paul addresses him as made free from sin, and by voluntary surrender become a servant to God and to righteousness. He has forsaken the service of sin, and yet it often masters him. The promise, "Sin shall not"—shall never for a moment—"have dominion over you," has not been realized. To will is present, but how to perform he knows not. "O wretched man that I am, who shall deliver me from the body of this death?" is the cry of futility amid all his efforts to keep the law. "I thank God, through Christ Jesus our Lord," is the answer of faith that claims the deliverance in Christ from this power that has held him captive. From the law— the dominion of sin and death in the members—and its actual power in motivating sin, there is deliverance. That deliverance is a new law, a mightier force, an actual power making free from sin. As real as was the energy of sin working in our members, and more mighty, is the energy of the Spirit dwelling in our bodies. It is the Spirit of life that is in Christ. Out of that life, when filled as it was in the resurrection and ascension with the mighty energy of God's power (Eph. 1:17, 21), and admitted on the throne to the omnipotence of God as the eternal Spirit—out of that life there descended the Holy Spirit, himself God. The law, the power, the dominion of the life in Christ Jesus made me free from the law, the dominion of sin and death in my members, with a freedom as real as was the slavery. From the very first beginnings of the new life, it was the Spirit who breathed faith in Christ. When we first entered into justification, it was He who shed abroad the love of God in our hearts. It was He who led us to see Christ as our life as well as our righteousness. But all of this was in most cases still accompanied with a lack of knowledge of His presence and of the great need for a supply of His almighty power. As the believer in Rom. 7:14-23 is brought to the discovery of the deep-rooted legality of the old nature and its absolute impotence, the truth of the Holy Spirit and of the mighty power with which He does, in a practical sense, make us free from the power of sin and death is understood as never before. Our text becomes a declaration of the highest faith and experience combined: "The law of the Spirit of life made me free from the law of sin and death." As real, mighty, and spontaneous as the law of sin in the members was, so likewise is the law of the Spirit of life in those members.

The believer, who wants to live fully in this liberty of life in Christ Jesus, will easily understand what the path is in which he will learn to walk. Romans 8 is the goal to which Romans 6 and 7 lead up. In faith, he will first have to study and accept all that is taught in these two earlier chapters of his being in Christ Jesus; dead to sin and alive to God, free from sin and the law, and joined to Christ. "If ye abide in my word, ye shall know the truth, and the truth shall make you free." Let the Word of God, as it teaches you of your union with Christ, be the life-soil in which your faith and life daily roots; abide, dwell in it, and let it abide in you. To meditate, to hold fast, to hide in the heart the word of this gospel, to assimilate it in faith and patience, is the way to rise and reach each higher truth that the Scripture teaches. If the passage through the experience of carnality and captivity, to which the attempts to fulfill the law bring us, appears to be anything but progress, let us remember that it is in the utter despair of self that entire surrender to the Spirit is born and strengthened. To cease from all hope through the flesh and the law is the entrance into the liberty of the Spirit.

To walk in the paths of this new life it will be particularly needful to remember what is meant by the expression the word so distinctly uses, "walk *after* the Spirit." The Spirit is to lead, to decide and show the path. This implies surrender, obedience, waiting to be guided. He is to be the ruling power; we are in all things to live and act under the law, the legislation, and the dominion of the Spirit. A holy fear of grieving Him, tender watchfulness to know His leading, a daily faith in His hidden presence, humble adoration of Him as God—all must be the mark of such a life. The words which Paul uses toward the close of this section are to express our one aim: "If ye, through the Spirit, make to die the deeds of the body, ye shall live." The Holy Spirit possessing, inspiring, motivating all the powers of our spirit and soul; entering even into the body, and enabling us to die to the deeds of the body, this is what we may count upon: "The law of the Spirit of the life in Christ Jesus made me free from the law of sin and death." This is the "salvation in sanctification of the Spirit" to which we have been called.

"We walk by faith": this is what we particularly need to remember in regard to a "walk after the Spirit." The visible manifestation of Christ to us and His work is so much more intelligible than the revelation of the Spirit within us, that it is here, above all, in seeking the leading of the Spirit, that faith is called for. The almighty power of the Spirit hides himself away in such a real union with our weakness that we need patient perseverance in believing and obeying to come into the full consciousness of His indwelling, and of His having undertaken to do all our living for us. We need the direct, fresh anointing day by day from the holy one, in fellowship with Christ, the anointed, while waiting upon the Father. Here, if ever, the word is needed, "Only believe!" Believe in the Father and His promise! Believe in the Son and His life as yours: "Our life is hid with Christ in God." Believe in the Spirit, as the bearer, communicator, and maintainer of the life and presence of Jesus! Believe in Him as already within you! Believe in His power and faithfulness to work in you in a way that is divine and beyond your comprehension. Believe, "The law of the Spirit of life in Christ Jesus hath made me free from the law of sin and death." Bow in deep silence of soul before God, waiting on Him to work mightily in you by His Spirit. As self is humbled, He will do His blessed and beloved work. He will reveal, will impart, will make and keep divinely present Jesus Christ as the life of your Spirit.

Ever blessed God and Father, we do praise Thee for the wonderful gift of Thy Holy Spirit, in whom Thou with Thy Son come to make abode in us. We do bless Thee for that wonderful gift of eternal life, which Thy beloved Son brought us, and which we have in Jesus himself, as His own life given to us. And we thank Thee that the law of the Spirit of the life in Christ Jesus now makes us free from the law of sin and death.

Our Father, we humbly pray Thee to reveal to us in full and blessed experience what this perfect law of liberty is. Teach us how it is the law of an inner life that in joyful and spontaneous power grows up into its blessed destiny. Teach us that *the law* is none other than that of the eternal life, in its power of continuous and unfading existence. Teach us that it is the law of *the life* of Christ Jesus, the living Saviour himself, living and maintaining it in us. Teach us that it is the law of *the Spirit* of life in Christ Jesus, the Holy Spirit revealing and glorifying Christ in us as an indwelling presence. O Father, open our eyes and strengthen our faith that we may believe that the law of the Spirit is indeed mightier than the law of sin in our members, and make free from it, so that through the Spirit we die to the deeds of the body and indeed live the life of Christ.

O Father, teach this to all Thy children. Amen.

SUMMARY

1. Let us pause a moment here, and ask if this is our experience. "From the law of sin and death" in my members, as it made me groan for deliverance, "the Law of the Spirit of life in Christ Jesus hath made me free." Am I living in this blessed liberty?

2. Let everyone who would do so remember the path as set before us in the gospel of Christ by Paul. You were reconciled to God by the death of His Son; you are now to be saved by His life (Rom. 5:10). By faith you know that that life is yours in all its power (6:1, 11). In the strength of it you gave yourself to be a servant of God (6:15-22). But the service was to be in no legal spirit under the law, but in newness of spirit (7:1-6). Because you did not understand this, you sought in the power of the new life to fulfill the law you delighted in, and yet utterly failed (7:14, 25). Listen. This is where the Holy Spirit comes in (8:1-16). Faith in Jesus and His life leads the way to the life of the Spirit in you. The Holy Spirit frees from the law, and maintains the life of Christ in the power of His living presence. Rom. 8:2 is the key to the blessed life.

3. "As Adam's life is reproduced in the entire human family, so the *new life* of the God-man flows ever to all His people: our life is the reproduction of Christ's spiritual life in His people. The new birth connects us with the second man, who, by the Holy Spirit, gathers His people under Him by a self-communicating act."—Smeaton

4. Would you live that life? Remember our one great lesson as we go along. Acknowledge the Holy Spirit dwelling in you. Study above everything to be full of the faith of His presence as the revealer of Christ and His life in you. Surrender to Him to rule; be ready to wait on Him and "to walk after Him." The law of the Spirit, the force or power of an inward life, the law of the Spirit of life in Christ Jesus, made me free from the law of sin and death.

19

THE LEADING OF THE SPIRIT

For as many as are led by the Spirit of God, they are sons of God.—Rom. 8:14

The leading of the Spirit, by very many Christians, is chiefly thought of as a suggestion of thoughts for our guidance. In the decision of questions of opinion or of obligation, in the choice of words to use from Scripture, or the distinct direction in the performance of some Christian work, they would be glad for some intimation from the Spirit of what the right choice is. They long and ask for it in vain. When at times they think they have it, it does not bring the assurance, or the comfort, or the success, which they think ought to be the seal of what is really from the Spirit. And so the precious truth of the Spirit's leading, instead of being an end of all controversy, and the solution of all difficulty, a source of comfort and of strength, itself becomes a cause of perplexity, and the greatest difficulty of all.

The error comes from not accepting the truth that we

have covered here more than once—that the teaching and the leading of the Spirit is first given in the life, not in the mind. The life is stirred and strengthened; the life becomes the light. As the conformity to this world and its spirit is crucified and dies, as we deliberately deny and keep down the life of nature and the will of the flesh, we *are renewed in the spirit* of our mind, and so the mind becomes able to *prove and know* the good and perfect and acceptable will of God (Rom. 12:2).

This connection between the practical sanctifying work of the Spirit in our inner life, and His leading, comes out very clearly in our context. "If ye through the Spirit do mortify the deeds of the body, ye shall live," we read in 8:13. Then follows immediately, "*For* as many as are led by the Spirit of God they are sons of God." That is, as many as allow themselves to be led by Him in this mortifying of the deeds of the body, these are the sons of God. The Holy Spirit is the Spirit of the holy life which there was and is in Christ Jesus, and which works in us as a divine life-power. He is the Spirit of holiness, and only in holiness will He lead. Through Him God works in us both to will and to do of His good pleasure; through Him God makes us perfect in every good work to do His will, working in us that which is well-pleasing in His sight. To be led of the Spirit implies in the first place the surrender to His work as He convinces of sin, and cleanses soul and body for His temple. It is as the indwelling Spirit, filling, sanctifying, and ruling the heart and life, that He enlightens and leads.[1]

In the study of what the leading of the Spirit means, it is of the first importance to grasp this thought in all its significance. Only the spiritual mind can discern spiritual things and receive the leadings of the Spirit. The mind must first become spiritual to become capable of spiritual guidance. Paul said to the Corinthians, that because, though born again, they were still carnal, as babes in Christ, he had not been able to teach them spiritual truth. If this holds of the teaching that comes through man, how much more of that direct teaching of the Spirit, by which He leads into all truth! The deepest mysteries of Scripture, as far as they are apprehended by human thought, can be studied and accepted and even taught by the unsanctified mind. But the leading of the Spirit—and we cannot repeat it too often—does not begin in the region of thought or feeling. Deeper down, in the life itself, in the hidden laboratory of the inner life, from which issues the power that molds the will and fashions the character in our spirits, there the Holy Spirit takes up His abode, there He breathes and moves and impels.

He leads by inspiring us with a life and disposition out of which right purposes and decisions come forth. "That ye may be filled with the knowledge of his will in all wisdom and spiritual understanding": that prayer teaches us that it is only to a spiritual understanding that the knowledge of God's will can be given. And the spiritual understanding only comes with the growth of the spiritual man, and faithfulness to the spiritual life. He that would have the leading of the Spirit must yield himself to have his life wholly possessed and filled by the Spirit. It was when Christ had been baptized with the Spirit that, "being full of the Spirit, he was led by the Spirit in the wilderness" (Luke 4:1), "that he returned in the power of the Spirit into Galilee" (4:14), and began His ministry in Nazareth with the words, "The Spirit of the Lord is upon me."

It is easy to understand that to enjoy the leading of the Spirit demands a very teachable, servant's mind. The Spirit is not only hindered by the flesh, as the power that commits sin, but still more by the flesh, as the power that seeks to serve God. To be able to discern the Spirit's teaching, Scripture tells us that the ear must be circumcised, in a circumcision not made with hands—in the putting off of the body of the flesh, in the circumcision of Christ. The will and wisdom of the flesh must be feared, and crucified, and denied. The ear must be closed to all that the flesh and its wisdom, whether in self or in men around us, has to say. In all our thoughts of God or our study of His Word, in all our efforts to worship, and in all our work for Him, there must be a continued distrust and abnegation of self, and a very definite waiting on God by the Holy Spirit to teach and lead us. The soul that daily and hourly waits for a divine leading, for the light of knowledge and of duty, will surely receive it. If you would be led of the Spirit, give up, day by day, not only your will and wisdom, but your whole life and being. The fire will descend and consume the sacrifice.

The leading of the Spirit must very particularly be a thing of faith, and that in two senses. The beginning of the leading will come when we learn in holy fear to cultivate and act upon the confidence: The Holy Spirit is in me and is doing His work. The Spirit's indwelling is the crowning piece of God's redemption work: the most spiritual and mysterious part of the mystery of godliness. Here, if anywhere, faith is needed. Faith is the faculty of the soul which recognizes the unseen, the divine; which receives the impression of the divine presence when God draws near; which in its measure accepts of what the divine being brings and gives to us. In the Holy Spirit is the most intimate communication of the divine life; here faith may not judge by what it feels or understands, but simply submits to God to let Him do what He has said. It meditates and worships, it prays and trusts ever afresh, it yields the whole soul in adoring acceptance and thanksgiving to the Saviour's word, "He shall be in you." It rejoices in the assurance: the Holy Spirit, the mighty power of God, dwells within in His own way; I may depend upon it. He will lead me.

Then, beyond a general faith of the indwelling of the Spirit, faith has also to be exercised in regard to each part of the leading. When there is a question I have laid before the Lord, and my soul has in simplicity and emptiness waited for Him to reveal and apply what word or providence has placed before me, I must in faith trust my God that His guidance will not be withheld. As we have said before, we cannot expect the ordinary leading of the Spirit in sudden impulses or strong impressions, or in heavenly voices and remarkable interpositions. There are souls to whom such leading undoubtedly is given; the time may come, as our nature becomes more spiritual and lives more in direct contact with the invisible, that our very thoughts and feelings may become the conscious vehicles of His blessed voice. But this we must leave to Him, and the growth of our spiritual capacity. The lower steps of the ladder are low enough for the weakest to reach; God means every child of His to be led by the Spirit every day. Begin the path of following the Spirit's leading by *believing*, not only that the Spirit is within you, but that He, if you have not before sought or enjoyed the wondrous blessing, does now at once undertake the work for which you ask and trust Him. Yield yourself to God in undivided surrender: believe with implicit confidence that God's acceptance of the surrender means that you are under the control of the Spirit. Through Him Jesus guides and rules and saves you.

But are we not in danger of being led away by the imaginings of our own hearts, and counting as leading of the Spirit what really is a delusion of the flesh? And if so, where is our safeguard against such error? The answer ordinarily given to this last question is, the Word of God. And yet that answer is only half the truth. Far too many have used the Word of God to oppose the danger of fanaticism, but as interpreted by human reason or by the Church, and have erred no less than those they sought to oppose. The answer is: The Word of God as taught by the Spirit of God. It is in the perfect harmony of the two that our safety is to be found. Let us on the one hand remember, that as all the Word of God is given by the Spirit of God, so each word must be interpreted to us by that same Spirit. That this interpretation comes alone from the indwelling Spirit we need hardly repeat; it is only the spiritual man, whose inner life is under the dominion of the Spirit, who can discern the spiritual meaning of the word. Let us on the other hand hold fast, that as all the Word is given by the Spirit, so His great work is to honor that Word, and to unfold the fullness of divine truth treasured there. Not in the Spirit without the Word; not in the Word without the Spirit; but in the Word and Spirit both dwelling richly within us, and both yielded to implicit obedience—this is our assurance of safety in the path of the Spirit's guidance.

This brings us back to the lesson we stressed at the beginning: the leading of the Spirit as inseparable from the sanctifying of the Spirit. Let each one who would be led of the Spirit begin by giving himself to be led of the Word as far as he knows it. Begin at the beginning: obey the commandments. "He that will do, shall know," said Jesus. "Keep my commandments, and the Father will send you the Spirit." Give up every sin. Yield in everything to the voice of conscience. Yield everything to God and let Him have His way. Through the Spirit, mortify the deeds of the body (v. 13). As a son of God place yourself at the entire disposal of the Spirit, to follow where He leads (v. 14). And the Spirit himself, this same Spirit, through whom you mortify sin, and yield yourself to be led as a son, will bear witness with your spirit, in a joy and power before unknown, that you are indeed a child of God, enjoying all a child's privileges in his Father's love and guidance.

Blessed Father, I thank Thee for the message that as many as are led by the Spirit of God, they are the children of God. Thou wouldest not have Thy children guided by any one less than Thy own Holy Spirit. As He dwelt in Thy Son, and led Him, so He leads us too with a divine and most blessed leading.

Father, Thou knowest how by reason of our not fully knowing and not perfectly following this holy guidance, we are often unable to know His voice, and the thought of the leading of the Spirit is more a burden than a joy. Father, forgive us. Be pleased to quicken our faith in the simplicity and certainty of the leading of the Spirit that with our whole heart we may yield ourselves henceforth to walk in it.

Father, here I do yield myself to Thee as Thy child, in everything to be led of Thy Spirit. My own wisdom, my own will, my own way I forsake. Daily would I wait in deep dependence on a guidance from above. May my spirit ever be hushed in silence before Thy holy presence, while I wait to let Him rule within. As I through the Spirit die to the deeds of the body, may I be transformed by the renewing of my mind to know Thy good and perfect will. May my whole being so be under the rule of the indwelling, sanctifying Spirit, that the spiritual understanding of Thy will may indeed be the rule of my life. Amen.

SUMMARY

1. Note very carefully the order of the three verses: Rom. 8:13. The making dead of the deeds of the body through the indwelling Spirit precedes the leading of the Spirit (v. 14). And these two again prepare the way for 15, 16, the abiding witness to our sonship in the living power of the Holy Ghost.

2. "If, ye through the Spirit, mortify the deeds of the body, ye shall live"—one of the deepest teachings of the word in regard to sanctification. The temptation to sin re-

mains to the end. The deeds of the body, each sin as it rises up, can be put to death. It is the presence and life of Christ, through the Holy Spirit, that does this. Through the Spirit, the believer who yields to Him does it. Sin can, without ceasing, be put to death. To do this we must simply be full of the Spirit of life in Christ Jesus. The life of Christ in us brings with it the death of sin.

3. The mortifying of sin has a threefold reference. When a believer has fallen into an actual sin, the Spirit, by the application of the blood, nullifies it. When one fears the evil tendency that may come up and betray him, the Holy Spirit is able to keep that one from sin by the power of Christ's death. But, let us remember, it is by revealing Jesus in the power of His death and life, and filling the soul with Him, that the deeds of the body are made to die through the Spirit. It is on this life in the Spirit that the leading of the Spirit depends.

4. "There can be no safe guidance that is not perpetual. The advantage of a year may be lost in an hour. If we act independently of the Spirit in little things, we shall look for Him in vain in great things."—Bowen

Note

1. In this book there is no separate chapter on the sanctification of the Spirit, on Him as the Spirit of holiness. The reason is that this work is a continuation of a previous volume, *Holy in Christ*, in which there was occasion to speak of what is meant by holiness both as the attribute and the work of the Holy Spirit.

20

THE SPIRIT OF PRAYER

Likewise the Spirit also helpeth our infirmities: for we know not what we should pray for as we ought: but the Spirit itself maketh intercession for us with groanings which cannot be uttered. And he that searcheth the hearts knoweth what is the mind of the

Spirit, because he maketh intercession for the saints
according to the will of God.—Rom. 8:26, 27

Of the offices of the Holy Spirit, the one that leads us
most deeply into the understanding of His place in the divine economy of grace, and into the mystery of the holy
Trinity, is the work He does as the Spirit of prayer. We have
the Father to whom we pray, and who hears prayer. We have
the Son, through whom we pray, and through whom we receive and really appropriate the answer because of our union
with Him. And we have the Holy Spirit in whom we pray,
who prays in us according to the will of God, with such deeply hidden, unutterable sighings that God has to search the
hearts to know what is the mind of the Spirit. Just as wonderful and real as is the divine work of God on the throne,
graciously hearing and effectually answering prayer; just as
divine as is the work of the Son interceding, securing and
transmitting the answer from above, is the work of the Holy
Spirit in us, in the prayer which waits and obtains the answer. The intercession within is as divine as the intercession
above. Let us try to understand why this should be so and
what it teaches.

In the creation of the world we see how it was the work of
the Spirit to put himself into contact with the dark and life-
less matter of chaos, and by His quickening energy to impart to it the power of life and fruitfulness. It was only after
it had been thus vitalized by Him that the Word of God gave
it form and called forth all the different types of life and
beauty we now see. Likewise, in the creation of man it was
the Spirit that was breathed into the body, that had been
formed from the ground, and that thus united itself with
what would otherwise be dead matter. Even so, in the person of Jesus it is the Spirit through whose work a body was
prepared for Him. Through the Spirit His body again was
quickened from the grave, and it is through Him that our
bodies are the temples of God—the very members of our
body the members of Christ. We think of the Spirit in connection with the spiritual nature of the divine being, far removed from the vileness and frailty of matter. We forget
that it is the very work of the Spirit to unite himself particularly with what is material, to lift it up into His own Spirit-

nature, and so develop the highest form of perfection—a spiritual body.

This view of the Spirit's work is essential to the understanding of the place He takes in the divine work of redemption. In each part of that work there is a special place assigned to each of the three persons of the holy Trintiy. In the Father we have the unseen God, the author of all. In the Son of God we have the form of God revealed, made manifest, and brought nigh. In the Spirit of God we have the power of God dwelling in the human body and working in it what the Father and the Son have for us. Not only in the individual, but in the Church as a whole, what the Father has purposed, and the Son has procured, can be appropriated and take effect in the body of Christ only through the continual intervention and active operation of the holy Spirit.

This is especially true of intercessory prayer. The coming of the kingdom of God, the increase of grace, knowledge, and holiness in believers, their growing devotion to God's work, the effectual working of God's power on the unconverted through the means of grace—all this awaits us from God through Christ. But it cannot come unless it is looked for and desired, asked for and expected, believed and hoped for. This is now the wonderful position the Holy Ghost occupies—to Him has been assigned the task of preparing the body of Christ to reach out, receive, and hold fast what has been provided in the fullness of Christ, our head. For the communication of the Father's love and blessing, both the Son and the Spirit must work. The Son receives from the Father, reveals and brings nigh; the Spirit from within awakens the soul to meet its Lord. As indispensable as the unceasing intercession of Christ asking and receiving from the Father above is the unceasing intercession of the Spirit within, asking and accepting from the Son what the Father gives.

The light that is cast upon this holy mystery by the words of our text is wonderful. In the life of faith and prayer there are operations of the Spirit in which the Word of God is made clear to our understanding, and our faith knows how to express what it needs and asks. But there are also operations of the Spirit, deeper than thoughts or feelings, where He works desires and yearnings in our spirit, in the secret springs of life and being, which only God can discover and understand. In our spirits is the real thirst for God himself, the living God. There is the longing to know the love "that passeth knowledge" and to be "filled with all the fullness of God," the hope in Him "who is able to do exceeding abundantly above all we can ask or think," even "what hath not entered the heart of man to conceive." When these aspirations indeed take possession of us, we begin to pray for what cannot be expressed, and our only comfort is that then the Spirit prays with unutterable yearnings in a language which he alone knows and understands.

To the Corinthians Paul says, "I will pray with the spirit, and I will pray with the understanding also." Under the influence of the moving of the Holy Spirit and His miraculous gifts, the danger was to neglect the understanding. The danger in these latter days is the opposite: to pray with the understanding is easy and universal. We need to be reminded that, with the prayer of understanding, there must also come prayer with the Spirit—the "praying in the Holy Spirit" (Jude, v. 20; Eph. 6:18). We need to give due place to each of the twofold operations of the Spirit. God's Word must dwell in us richly; our faith must seek to hold it clearly and intelligently, and to plead it in prayer. To have the words of Christ abiding in us, filling the life and conduct, is one of the secrets of acceptable prayer. And yet we must always remember that in the inner sanctuary of our being, in the area of the unutterable and inconceivable (1 Cor. 2:6), the Spirit prays for us what we do not know and cannot express. As we grow in the apprehension of the divinity of the Holy Spirit, and the reality of His indwelling, we shall recognize how infinitely beyond the conception of our mind is the divine hunger with which He draws us heavenward. We shall feel the need of cultivating the activity of faith, which seeks to grasp and obey God's Word, and from that learn to pray. As we pray we shall remember how infinitely above our conception is God and the spirit-world which we enter by prayer. Let us believe and rejoice that where heart and flesh fail, God is the strength of our heart; His Holy Spirit within the innermost sanctuary of our spirit does His unceasing work of intercession, and prays according to God's will within us. As we pray, let us worship in holy stillness, and yield ourselves to that blessed paraclete, who alone, and truly is, the Spirit of supplication.[1]

"Because he maketh intercession for the saints." Why doesn't the apostle say for us, as he had said, "We know not how to pray as we ought"? The expression "the saints" is a favorite one with Paul, where he thinks of the Church, either in one country or throughout the world. It is the special work of the Spirit, as dwelling in every member, to make the body realize its unity. As selfishness disappears, and the believer becomes more truly spiritual-minded, and he feels himself more identified with the body as a whole, he sees how its health and prosperity will be his own, and he learns what it is to "pray at all seasons in the Spirit, watching thereunto in all perseverance for all saints." It is as we yield ourselves to this work, with a heart large enough to take in all the church of God, that the Spirit will have free scope and will delight to do His work of intercession for the saints in us. It is particularly in intercessory prayer that we may count upon the deep, unutterable, but all-prevailing intercession of the Spirit.

What a privilege to be the temple out of which the Holy Spirit cries to the Father His unceasing Abba and offers His unutterable intercession, too deep for words. What blessedness that as the eternal Son dwelt in the flesh in Jesus of Nazareth, and prayed to the Father as man, even so the eternal Spirit should dwell in us—sinful flesh—to train us to speak with the Father even as the Son did. Who would not yield himself to this blessed Spirit to be made fit to take a share in that mighty intercession work through which alone the kingdom of God can be revealed? The path is open and invites all. Let the Holy Spirit have full control. Let Him fill you. Let Him be your life. Believe in the possibility of His making your very personality and consciousness the place of His indwelling. Believe in the certainty of His working and praying in you in a way that no human mind can apprehend. Believe that in the secret, quiet, steadiness of that work, His divine almighty power is perfecting the divine purpose and the divine oneness with your blessed Lord. Live as one in whom the things that pass all understanding have become truth and life, in whom the intercession of the Spirit is part of your daily life in Christ.

Most Holy God, once more I bow in lowly adoration in Thy presence, to thank Thee for the precious privilege of prayer. Especially would I thank Thee for the grace that has given us, in Thy Son, the Intercessor above, and also Thy Spirit, the Intercessor within.

O my Father, Thou knowest that I can scarcely take in the wondrous thought that Thy Holy Spirit actually dwells in me and prays through my frail prayers. I do beseech Thee, reveal to me all that hinders His taking full possession of me, and filling me with the consciousness of His presence. Let my inmost being and my outward life both be so under His leading, that I may have the spiritual understanding that knows how to ask according to Thy will, and the living faith that receives what it asks. When I know not what or how to pray, O Father, teach me to bow in silent worship, and keep waiting before Thee, knowing that He breathes the wordless prayer which Thou alone canst understand.

Blessed God, I am a temple of the Holy Spirit. I yield myself for Him to use me as the spirit of intercession. May my whole heart be so filled with the longing for Christ's honor, and His love for the lost, that my life may become one unutterable cry for the coming of Thy kingdom. Amen.

SUMMARY

1. Now we can understand how the Lord, in the last night, could give us those wonderful prayer-promises, with their oft-repeated "What ye will." He meant for us to have the Holy Spirit praying in us, guiding our desires and strengthening our faith. He expected us to give our whole being to the indwelling of the Spirit that He might have free course to pray in us according to God's will. Let us take up the holy calling and give ourselves to the Holy Spirit to pray in us.

2. "We know not what to pray as we ought": how often this has been a burden and a sorrow! Let it from now on be a comfort. Because we do not know, we may stand aside and give place to one who does know. We may believe that in our stammering, or even sighs, the mighty intercessor is pleading. Let us not be afraid to believe that within our ignorance and weakness the Holy Spirit is hidden, doing His work.

3. "As we ought." The great *ought* of prayer is faith. The Spirit is the Spirit of faith, deeper than thought. Let us be of good courage; our faith is in the keeping of the Spirit.

4. Here, as elsewhere, all leads up to one point: the Holy Spirit's indwelling must be our one aim. In faith that holds the promise, in tender watchfulness that waits for and follows His leading, in the entire surrender of the flesh to death, that He alone may rule and lead, let us yield to our beloved Lord to fill us with His Spirit. The Spirit will do His work.

Note

1. "Mystics will, on the one hand, take their stand on the incomprehensible intercession of the Spirit, without admitting to anything that could be apprehended by faith. Intellectuals on the other hand, depend too much on that which has been reduced to logical definitions, and obscure to themselves their dim perception of the incomprehensible, by putting over it the veil of their multifarious definitions. Paul keeps the balance between that which we may know by faith and that which transcends all knowledge, when the Spirit alone, in accordance with the inmost purport of creation, knows what we pray. Both that which we utter in words of faith, which we understand, and the unutterable things of the Spirit, must co-exist in the heart, if the heart is to be established.'— Steinhofer on Rom. 8:26.

21

THE HOLY SPIRIT AND CONSCIENCE

I say the truth in Christ, I lie not, my conscience also bearing me witness in the Holy Ghost.—Rom. 9:1
The Spirit itself beareth witness with our spirit. —Rom. 8:16

God's highest glory is *His holiness*, in virtue of which He hates and destroys evil; loves and works good. In man, conscience has the same work. It condemns sin and approves the right. Conscience is the remains of God's image in man, the nearest approach to the divine in him, the guardian of God's honor amid the ruin of the Fall. As a consequence, God's work of redemption must always begin with conscience. The Spirit of God is the Spirit of His holiness; conscience is a spark of the divine holiness. Harmony between the work of the Holy Spirit in renewing and sanctifying man and the work of conscience is most intimate and essential. The believer who would be filled with the Holy Spirit and experience to the fullest the blessings He has to give must in the first place see to it that he yields to conscience the place and the honor which belong to it. Faithfulness to conscience is the first step in the path of restoration to the holiness of God. Intense conscientiousness will be the groundwork and characteristic of true spirituality. As it is the work of conscience to witness to a correct response toward the sense of duty and toward God, and as it is the work of the Spirit to witness to God's acceptance of our faith in Christ and our obedience to Him, so as the Christian life progresses, these become increasingly identical. We shall feel the need and the joy of saying with Paul, with regard to all our conduct: "My conscience also bearing me witness in the Holy Ghost."

Conscience can be compared to the window of a room, through which the light of heaven shines, and through which we can see heaven with all that its light shines on. The heart is the chamber in which our life dwells, our ego, or soul, with its powers and affections. On the walls of that chamber there is written the law of God. Even in the heathen it is still partly legible, though sadly darkened and defaced. In the believer the law is written anew by the Holy Spirit, in letters of light, which often at first are dim but grow clearer and glow brighter as they are freely exposed to the action of the light without. With every sin I commit, the light that shines in makes it manifest and condemns it. If the sin is not confessed and forsaken, the stain remains, and conscience becomes defiled, because the mind refused the teaching of the light (Titus 1:15). And so with one sin after another the window gets darker and darker until the light can hardly shine through at all and the Christian can sin undisturbed with a conscience to a large extent blinded and without feeling. In His work of renewal the Holy Spirit does not create new faculties: He renews and sanctifies those already existing. Conscience is the work of the Spirit of God, the creator; as

the Spirit of God, the redeemer, His first care is to restore
what sin has defiled. It is only by restoring conscience to full
and healthy action, and revealing in it the wonderful grace
of Christ, "the Spirit bearing witness with our spirit," that
He enables the believer to live a life in the full light of God's
favor. It is as the window of the heart that looks heavenward
is cleansed and kept clean that we can walk in the light.

The work of the Spirit on conscience is a threefold one.
Through conscience the Spirit causes *the light of God's holy
law* to shine into the heart. A room may have its curtains
drawn, and even its shutters closed: this cannot prevent the
lightning flash from time to time shining into the darkness.
Conscience may be so sin-stained and seared that the strong
man within dwells in perfect peace. When the lightning
from Sinai flashes into the heart, conscience awakens and is
at once ready to admit and sustain the condemnation. Both
the law and the gospel, with their call to repentance and
their conviction of sin, appeal to conscience. And it is not
until conscience has said Amen to the charge of transgression and unbelief that deliverance can truly come.

It is through the conscience that the Spirit likewise
causes *the light of mercy* to shine. When the windows of a
house are stained, they need to be washed. "How much
more shall the blood of Christ cleanse your conscience." The
whole aim of the precious blood of Christ is to reach the
conscience, to silence its accusations, and cleanse it, until it
can testify: Every stain is removed; the love of the Father
allows Christ, in unclouded brightness, into my soul. "A
heart sprinkled from an evil conscience . . . having no more
conscience of sin" (Heb. 9:14, 10:2, 22) is meant to be the
privilege of every believer. It becomes so when conscience
learns to say Amen to God's message of the power of Jesus'
blood.

The conscience that has been cleansed in the blood must
be kept clean by a walk in the obedience of faith, with *the
light of God's favor* shining on it. To the promise of the indwelling Spirit, and His undertaking to lead in all of God's
will, conscience must say its Amen and then testify that He
does it. The believer is called to walk in humility and watchfulness, lest in anything conscience should accuse him of not
having done what he knew to be right, or having done what

was not of faith. He may be content with nothing less than
Paul's joyful testimony, "Our glorying is this, the testimony
of our conscience, that in holiness and godly sincerity, by
the grace of God, we behaved ourselves in the world" (2 Cor.
1:12. Comp. Acts 23:1, 24:16; 2 Tim. 1:3). Let us note these
words well: "Our glorying is this, the testimony of our conscience." It is as the window is kept clean and bright by our
abiding in the light that we can have fellowship with the
Father and the Son, the love of heaven shining in unclouded, and our love rising up in childlike trustfulness. "Beloved, if our heart condemn us not, we have boldness toward
God, because we keep his commandments, and do those
things that are pleasing in his sight" (1 John 3:21, 22).

The maintenance of a good conscience toward God from
day to day is essential to the life of faith. The believer must
aim at and must be satisfied with nothing less than this. He
may be assured that it is within his reach. The believers in
the Old Testament by faith had the witness that they
pleased God (Heb. 11:4, 5, 6, 39). In the New Testament it is
set before us, not only as a command to be obeyed, but also
as a grace to be wrought by God himself. "That ye might
walk worthy of the Lord unto all well-pleasing, strengthened
with all might according to his glorious power. May God fulfill all the good pleasure of his goodness, and the work of
faith with power. Working in us that which is well-pleasing
in his sight" (Col. 1:10, 11; 2 Thess. 1:11; 1 Thess. 4:1; Heb.
12:28, 13:21). The more we seek this testimony of conscience— that we are doing what is well-pleasing to God—
the more we shall feel the liberty, with every failure that
overtakes us, to look at once to the blood that ever cleanses.
The blood that has sprinkled the conscience abides and acts
in the power of the eternal life that knows no intermission,
and of the unchangeable priesthood that saves completely.
"If we walk in the light, as he is in the light, we have fellowship one with another, and the blood of Jesus Christ cleans-
eth us from all sin." [1]

The cause of the weakness of our faith is the lack of a
clean conscience. Mark well how closely Paul connects them
in I Timothy: "Love out of a pure heart, and a *good conscience*, and *faith unfeigned*" (1:5). "Holding *faith* and a
good conscience, which some having thrust from them, have

made shipwreck of the faith" (1:19). And especially (3:9), "Holding the mystery of *the faith* in a *pure conscience.*" *The conscience is the seat of faith.* He that would grow strong in faith, and have boldness with God must know that he is pleasing Him (1 John 3:21, 22). Jesus said most distinctly that it is for those who love Him and keep His commandments that the promise of the Spirit—with the indwelling of the Father and Son—is meant. How can we confidently claim these promises unless in childlike simplicity our conscience can testify that we fulfill the conditions? Until the Church can rise to the height of her holy calling as intercessor, and claim these unlimited promises as actually within her reach, believers will draw nigh to their Father, glorying, like Paul, in the testimony of their conscience—that by the grace of God they are walking in holiness and godly sincerity. We must see that this is the deepest humility and brings the most glory to God's free grace—the giving up of man's ideas of what we can attain, and accepting God's declaration of what He desires and promises, as the only standard of what we are to be.

How is this blessed life to be attained in which we can daily appeal to God and men with Paul: "I say the truth in Christ, my conscience bearing me witness in the Holy Ghost"? The first step is: Humble yourself under the reproofs of conscience. Don't be content with the general confession that there is a great deal wrong. Beware of confounding actual transgression with temptation to sin. If we are to die to sin by the indwelling Spirit (Rom. 8:13), we must first deal with the practice of sin. Begin with some single sin, and give conscience time in silent submission and humiliation to reprove and condemn. Say to your Father that in this one thing you are, by His grace, going to obey. Accept anew Christ's wonderful offer to take entire possession of your heart, to dwell in you as Lord and keeper. Trust Him by His Holy Spirit to do this even when you feel weak and helpless. Remember that obedience, the taking and keeping of Christ's words in your will and life, is the only way to prove the reality of your surrender to Him, or your interest in His work and grace. Vow in faith that by God's grace you will seek to *always* have a conscience void of offence toward God and toward man.

When you have taken these steps with one sin, proceed with others, step by step. As you are faithful in keeping your conscience pure, the light will shine more brightly from heaven into the heart, discovering sin you had not noticed before, bringing out distinctly the law written by the Spirit you had not been able to read. Be willing to be taught; be trustfully sure that the Spirit will teach. Every honest effort to keep the blood-cleansed conscience clean, in the light of God, will be met with the aid of the Spirit. Only yield yourself heartily and entirely to God's will and to the power of His Holy Spirit.

As you bow to the reproofs of conscience and give yourself wholly to do God's will, your courage will grow strong that it is possible to have a conscience void of offence. The witness of conscience, as to what you are doing and will do by grace, will be met by the witness of the Spirit as to what Christ is doing and will do. In childlike simplicity you will seek to begin each day with the simple prayer: Father, there is nothing now between Thee and Thy child. My conscience, divinely cleansed in the blood, bears witness. Father, let not even the shadow of a cloud intervene this day. In everything would I do Thy will: Thy Spirit dwells in me, and leads me, and makes me strong in Christ. You will enter upon that life which glories in free grace alone when it says at the close of each day, "Our glorying is this, the testimony of our conscience, that in holiness and godly sincerity, by the grace of God, we have behaved ourselves in the world: My conscience bearing me witness in the Holy Ghost."

Gracious God, I thank Thee for the voice Thou hast given in our heart to testify whether or not we are pleasing to Thee. I thank Thee that when that witness condemned me, with its terrible Amen to the curse of Thy law, Thou didst give the blood of Thy Son to cleanse the conscience. I thank Thee that at this moment my conscience can say Amen to the voice of the blood, and that I may look up to Thee in full assurance, with a heart cleansed from the evil conscience.

I thank Thee, too, for the witness from heaven to what Jesus has done and is doing for me and in me. I thank Thee that He glorifies Christ in me, gives me His presence and His power, and transforms me into His likeness. I thank

Thee that the presence and the work of Thy Spirit in my heart, my conscience can likewise say, Amen.

O my Father, I desire this day to walk before Thee with a good conscience, to do nothing that might grieve Thee or my blessed Lord Jesus. I ask Thee, may, in the power of the Holy Spirit, the cleansing in the blood be a living, continual, and most effectual deliverance from the power of sin, binding and strengthening me to thy perfect service. And may my whole walk with Thee be in the joy of the united witness of conscience and Thy Spirit that I am well-pleasing to Thee. Amen.

SUMMARY

1. In a well-ordered house the windows are kept clean, especially where the owner loves to rest and look out on some beautiful view. Oh, see to it every day that the windows are kept clean, that not the shadow of a cloud obstruct the light from above shining on you, or your look of love as it seeks the Father's face above. Involuntary sin is at once cleansed by the blood if faith claims it. Let every failure be at once confessed and cleansed too. Be content with nothing less than walking in the light of His countenance all the day.

2. "Thou hast been faithful over a few things, I will set thee over many things." Faithfulness to conscience as the lesser light is the only way to the enjoyment of the Spirit as the greater light. If we are unfaithful to the witness we have, how can God commit to us the true witness? We cannot say it too earnestly: Tender conscientiousness is the only way to true spirituality.

3. Is not the preaching of conscience, and to conscience, in connection with the preaching of the blood what is needed in the Church? Some preach conscience and say little of the blood. Some preach the blood and say little of conscience. This is one of God's wonderful words, "How much more shall the blood of Christ cleanse your conscience, to serve the living God!" Conscience is the power that pleads for duty, the doing of right. And the object and effect of the blood, when preached and believed as God would have it, is to restore conscience to its full power and action. "The blood shall cleanse your conscience, to serve the living God." The

power of holiness lies in the insight into, and the careful maintenance of, the wonderful harmony of the two.

Note

1. See Note 12, p. 259.

22

THE REVELATION OF THE SPIRIT

And my speech and my preaching was not with enticing words of man's wisdom, but in demonstration of the Spirit and of power: that your faith should not stand in the wisdom of men, but in the power of God. Howbeit we speak wisdom among them that are perfect: yet not the wisdom of this world, nor of the princes of this world, that come to naught: but we speak the wisdom of God in a mystery, even the hidden wisdom, which God ordained before the world unto our glory: which none of the princes of this world knew. . . . But God hath revealed them unto us by his Spirit: . . . Now we have received, not the spirit of the world, but the spirit which is of God; that we might know the things that are freely given to us of God. Which things also we speak, not in the words which man's wisdom teacheth, but which the Holy Ghost teacheth. . . . But the natural man receiveth not the things of the Spirit of God: for they are foolishness unto him. . . . But he that is spiritual judgeth all things.—1 Cor. 2:4-8, 10, 12-15.

In this passage Paul contrasts the spirit of the world and the Spirit of God. The point in which the contrast particularly comes out is in the wisdom or knowledge of the truth. It was in seeking knowledge that man fell. It was in the pride of knowledge that heathenism had its origin: "professing themselves to be wise, they became fools" (Rom. 1:22). It was in wisdom, philosophy, and the search after truth that the Greeks sought their glory. It was in the knowledge of God's will: "the form of the knowledge and of the truth in the law" (Rom. 2:17-20) that the Jew made his boast. And yet when Christ, the wisdom of God, appeared on earth, Jew and Greek combined to reject Him. Man's wisdom, whether or not in possession of a revelation, is utterly insufficient for comprehending God or His wisdom. As his heart is alienated from God, so that he does not love or do His will, so his mind is darkened that he cannot know Him aright. Even when in Christ, the light of God in its divine love, shone upon men, they knew it not and saw no beauty in it.[1]

In the Epistle to the Romans, Paul had dealt with man's trust in his own righteousness and its insufficiency. To the Corinthians, especially in the first three chapters, he exposes the insufficiency of man's wisdom. Not merely when it was a question of discovering God's truth and will, as with the Greeks; but even where God had revealed it, as with the Jews, man was incapable of seeing it without a divine illumination—the light of the Holy Spirit. The rulers of this world, Jew and Gentile, had crucified the Lord of glory because they knew not the wisdom of God. In writing to believers at Corinth, and warning them against the wisdom of the world, Paul is not dealing with any heresy, Jewish or heathen. He is speaking to believers who had fully accepted his gospel of a crucified Christ, but who were in danger, in preaching or hearing the truth, to deal with it in the power of human wisdom. He reminds them that the truth of God, as a hidden spiritual mystery, can be apprehended only by a spiritual revelation. The rejection of Christ by the Jews had been the great proof of the utter incapacity of human wisdom to grasp a divine revelation, without the spiritual, internal illumination of the Holy Spirit.

The Jews prided themselves on their attachment to God's Word, their study of it, their conformity to it in life and conduct. The issue proved that, without their being conscious of it, they utterly misunderstood it and rejected the very Messiah whom they thought they were waiting for and trusting in. Divine revelation, as Paul expounds it in this chapter, means three things: God must make known in

His Word what He thinks and does. Every preacher who is to communicate the message must not only be in possession of the truth, but continually be taught by the Spirit how to speak it. And every hearer needs the inward illumination: it is only as he is a spiritual man, with his life under the rule of the Spirit, that his mind can take in spiritual truth.[2] As we have the mind, the disposition of Christ, we can discern the truth as it is in Christ Jesus.

This teaching is what the Church in our day, and each believer in particular, needs. With the Reformation the insufficiency of man's righteousness, of his power really to fulfill God's law, obtained universal recognition in the Reformed churches, and in theory at least is everywhere accepted among evangelical Christians. The insufficiency of man's wisdom has by no means obtained as clear a recognition. While the need of the Holy Spirit's teaching is in general willingly admitted, we find that neither in the teaching of the Church nor in the lives of believers does this blessed truth have practical and all-embracing supremacy—without which the wisdom and the spirit of this world will still assert their power.

The proof of what we have said will be found in what Paul says of his own preaching: "Our preaching was *not* in man's wisdom, *but* in the Spirit; that your faith might *not* stand in the wisdom of men, *but* in the power of God." He is not writing, as to the Galatians, of two gospels, but of two ways of preaching the one gospel of Christ's cross. He says that to preach it in persuasive words of man's wisdom produces a faith that will bear the mark of its origin—a faith in the wisdom of man. As long as it is nourished by men and means, it may stand and flourish. But it cannot stand alone or in the day of trial. A man may, with such preaching, become a believer, but will be a weak believer. The faith, on the other hand, received as a result of preaching in the Spirit and power, stands in the power of God. The believer is led by the preaching, by the Holy Spirit himself, beyond man, into direct contact with the living God; his faith stands in the power of God. As long as the great majority of our church members, even though there be an abundance of the means of grace, are in a weak and sickly state, with little of the faith that stands in the power of God, we must fear that it is because too much of our preaching is more in the wisdom of man than in the demonstration of the power of the Spirit. If a change is to be effected both in the spirit in which our preachers and teachers speak, and our congregations listen and receive, it must begin, I am sure, in the personal life of the individual believer.

We must learn to fear our own wisdom. "Trust in the Lord with thy whole heart, and lean not to thine own understanding." Paul says to believers: "If any man thinketh that he is wise, *let him become a fool*, that he may be wise" (1 Cor. 3:18). When Scripture tells us that "they that are Christ's have crucified the flesh," this includes the understanding of the flesh, the fleshly mind of which Scripture speaks. Just as in the crucifixion of self I give up my own goodness, my own strength, my own will to death because there is no good in it, and look to Christ by the power of His life to give me the goodness and the strength and the will which is pleasing to God, so it must be also with my own wisdom. Man's mind is one of his noblest and most Godlike faculties. But sin rules over it and in it. A man may be truly converted and yet not know to what an extent it is with his natural mind that he is trying to grasp and hold the truth of God. The reason that there is so much Bible reading and teaching, which has no power to elevate and sanctify the life, is simply this: it is not truth which has been revealed and received through the Holy Spirit.

This holds good, too, of truth which has once been taught us by the Holy Spirit, but which, having been lodged in the understanding, is now held simply by the memory. Manna speedily loses its heavenliness when stored up on earth. Truth received from heaven loses its divine freshness unless the anointing with fresh oil is there every day. The believer needs, day by day, hour by hour, to know that there is nothing in which the power of the flesh can assert itself more insidiously than in the activity of the mind or reason in its dealing with the divine word. This will cause him to realize that he must continually seek, in Paul's language, "to become a fool." He needs, each time he deals with God's Word, or thinks of God's truth, in faith and teachableness, to wait for the promised teaching of the Spirit. He needs to ever ask for the circumcised ear—the ear in which the fleshly power of the understanding has been removed and in which the spirit of the life in Christ Jesus within the heart listens in the obedience of the life even as Christ did. To such this word will be fulfilled: "I thank thee, Father, that thou hast hid these things from the wise and prudent, and hast revealed them unto babes."

The lesson for all pastors and teachers, all professors and theologians, all students and readers of the Bible, is one of deep and searching seriousness. Do we know, or have we even sought to know that there must be perfect correspondence between the objective spiritual contents of the revelation and the subjective spiritual apprehension of it on our part? Between our apprehension of it and our communication of it, both in the power of the Holy Spirit? Between our communication of it and the reception by those to whom we bring it? It would be good, if over our theological halls and our training institutes, over the studies of our commentators and writers, our pastors and teachers, there were written those words of Paul: "God hath revealed it unto us by his Holy Spirit." I wish that our pastors could influence and train their congregations to see that it is not the amount, nor the clarity, nor the interesting aspect of Bible knowledge received that will determine the blessing and the power that it brings, but rather the measure of real dependence on the Holy Spirit that accompanies it. "Them that honor me, I will honor." Nowhere will this word be found more true than here. The crucifixion of self and all its wisdom, the coming in weakness and in fear and in much trembling, as Paul did, will most surely be met from above with the demonstration of the Spirit and of power.

Believer, it is not enough that the light of Christ shines on you in the Word; the light of the Spirit must shine in you. Each time you come in contact with the Word in study, in hearing a sermon, or reading a Christian book, there ought to be a definite act of self-denial, denial of your own wisdom, and yielding yourself in faith to the divine teacher. Believe very definitely that He dwells within you. He seeks the control, the sanctification of your inner life, in entire surrender and obedience to Jesus. Rejoice in renewing your surrender to Him. Reject the spirit of the world with its wisdom and self-confidence; come in poverty of spirit, to be led by the

Spirit of God. "Be not fashioned according to the world, with its confidence in the flesh, and self, and its wisdom; but be ye transformed by the renewing of your mind, that ye may prove what is the good, and perfect, and acceptable will of God." It is a transformed, renewed life that wants only to know God's perfect will that will be taught by the Spirit. Cease from your own wisdom; wait for the wisdom in the spirit which God has promised. You will increasingly be able to testify of the things which have not entered into the hearts of men to conceive: "God hath revealed them to us by His Spirit."

O God, I bless Thee for the wondrous revelation of thyself in Christ crucified, the wisdom of God, and the power of God. I bless Thee, that while man's wisdom leaves him helpless in the presence of the power of sin and death, Christ crucified proves that He is the wisdom of God by the mighty redemption He works as the power of God. I bless Thee, that what He wrought and bestows as an Almighty Saviour is revealed within us by the divine light of Thine Own Holy Spirit.

O Lord, we beseech Thee, teach Thy Church that wherever Christ, as the power of God, is not manifested, it is because He is so little known as the wisdom of God, as the indwelling Spirit alone can reveal Him in Thy sight. Oh, teach Thy Church to lead each child of God to the personal teaching and revelation of Christ within!

Show us, O God, that the one great hindrance is our own wisdom, our imagination that we can understand the Word and truth of God. Oh, teach us to become fools that we may be wise! May our whole life become one continual act of faith that the Holy Spirit will surely do His work of teaching, guiding, and leading into the truth. Father, Thou gavest Him that He might reveal Jesus in His glory within us; we wait for this. Amen.

SUMMARY

1. "God chose the foolish things of the world that he might put to shame the wise" (1 Cor. 1:27; Comp. 19, 20, 21; 3:19, 20). Was it only at Corinth that believers needed this teaching? Or is there not in every man a wisdom that is not

of God, and a readiness to think that he can understand the Word, even without direct contact with the living God himself? This wisdom seeks to master even the most spiritual truth, to form a clear conception or image of it, and rejoices in that instead of the living power in which the Spirit reveals it in the life.

2. Jesus had the spirit of wisdom. How did it manifest itself? In His waiting to hear what the Father spoke. "Morning by morning he wakeneth mine ear to hear, as they that are taught." Perfect teachableness was the mark of the Son on earth. This is the mark of the Spirit in us too: "What things soever he shall hear, these shall he speak." The life is the light. As the Spirit finds our life in perfect obedience to Him, He teaches by what He works in us. "I will destroy the wisdom of the wise."

3. It is inconceivable, until God reveals it to us, how a Christian may deceive himself with the semblance of wisdom in beautiful thoughts and affecting sentiments while the *power* of God is wanting. The *wisdom* of man stands in contrast to the power of God. The only true mark of divine wisdom is its power. The kingdom of God is not words, and thoughts, and knowledge, but power. May God open our eyes to see how much of our religion consists in beautiful words, thoughts, and feelings, but *not in the power of God.*

4. Note well that the Spirit of the world and the wisdom of the world are one. The extent to which many Christians yield themselves to the influence of the literature of the age, without fear or caution, is one of the great reasons that the Holy Spirit cannot guide them or reveal Christ in them. "The Spirit, whom the world *cannot* receive, because it knoweth him not. We received *not* the spirit of this world, but the Spirit which is of God."

Notes

1. See Note 13, p. 260.
2. In thus contrasting the Spirit of God and of the world, Paul first describes, in verses 6-9, the hidden wisdom in its divine contents and character: in verses 10-13 he teaches that this divine wisdom must be divinely revealed and its preaching divinely guided by the Spirit; and then, from verse 14 to 3:4, that for its reception on the part of the hearer, the influence of the Spirit is needed: even the Christian, unless he be living a spiritual life, cannot apprehend it.

23

SPIRITUAL OR CARNAL

And I, brethren, could not speak unto you as unto *spiritual*, but as unto *carnal*, even as unto babes in Christ. I fed you with milk, and not with meat: for hitherto ye were not able to bear it, neither yet now are ye able . . . for whereas there is among you envying and strife . . . are ye not carnal, and walk as men?—1 Cor. 3:1-3.

If we live in the Spirit, let us also walk in the Spirit.—Gal. 5:25

In the previous chapter the apostle had contrasted the believer as spiritual, with the unregenerate as the natural (or psychical) man: the man of the Spirit with the man of the soul (1 Cor. 2:14, 15). Here he supplements that teaching. He tells the Corinthians that, though they have the Spirit, he cannot call them spiritual; that title belongs to those who have not only received the Spirit, but have yielded themselves to Him to possess and rule their whole life. Those who have not done this, in whom the power of the flesh is still more manifest than the Spirit, cannot be called spiritual, but fleshly or carnal. There are three states in which a man may be found. The unregenerate is still *the natural man*, not having the Spirit of God. The regenerate, who is still a babe in Christ, either lately converted or standing still, is *the carnal man*, giving way to the power of the flesh. The believer in whom the Spirit has obtained full supremacy is *the spiritual man.* The whole passage contains rich instruction in regard to the life of the Spirit within us.

The young Christian is still carnal. Regeneration is a birth: the center and root of the personality, the spirit, has been renewed and taken possession of by the Spirit of God. But time is needed for its power from that center to extend throughout the whole being. The kingdom of God is like a seed; the life in Christ is a growth; and it would be against the laws of nature and grace alike if we expected from the babe in Christ the strength that can be found only in men, or the rich experience of the fathers. Even where there is great singleness of heart and faith in the young convert, with true love and devotion to the Saviour, time is needed for a deeper knowledge of self and sin, for a spiritual insight into what God's will and grace are. With the young believer it is not unnatural that the emotions are deeply stirred, and that the mind delights in the contemplation of divine truth. With the growth in grace, the will becomes the more important thing; the waiting for the Spirit's power in the life and character means more than the delight in those thoughts and images of life, which the mind alone can give. We need not wonder if the babe in Christ is still carnal.

Many Christians remain carnal. God has not only called us to grow, but has provided all the conditions and powers needful for growth. And yet it is sadly true, that there are many Christians who, like the Corinthians, remain babes in Christ when they ought to be going on to perfection, "attaining unto a full-grown man." In some cases the blame is almost more with the Church and its teaching than with the individuals themselves. When the preaching makes salvation seem to consist only in pardon and peace and the hope of heaven, or when, if a holy life is preached, the truth of Christ our sanctification, our sufficient strength to be holy, and the Holy Spirit's indwelling, is not taught clearly and in the power of the Spirit, growth can hardly be expected. Ignorance, human and defective views of the gospel, as the power of God unto a present salvation in sanctification, are the cause of the error.

In other cases the root of the error is to be found in the unwillingness of the Christian to deny self and crucify the flesh. The call of Jesus to every disciple is, "If any man will come after me, let him deny himself." The Spirit is given only to the obedient. He can do His work only in those who are absolutely willing to yield self to the death. The sin that proved that the Corinthians were carnal was their jealousy and strife. When Christians are not willing to give up the sin of selfishness and temper; when, whether in the home-relationship or in the wider circle of church and public life, they want to retain the liberty of giving way to, or excusing evil feelings, of pronouncing their own judgments, and speaking words that are not in perfect love, then they remain carnal.

With all their knowledge, and their enjoyment of the Christian Sacraments, and their work for God's kingdom, they can still be carnal and not spiritual. They grieve the Holy Spirit of God; they cannot have the testimony that they are pleasing to God.

The carnal Christian cannot appropriate spiritual truth. Paul writes to these Corinthians: "I fed you with milk, and not with meat; for ye were not able to bear it; nay, not even now are ye able." The Corinthians prided themselves on their wisdom; Paul thanked God that they were "enriched in all knowledge." There was nothing in His teaching that they would not have been able to comprehend with their understanding. But real spiritual entrance into the truth in power—so as to possess it and be possessed by it, and so as to have not only the thoughts but the very thing the words speak of—this only the Holy Spirit can give. He gives it only to the spiritually minded man. The teaching and leading of the Spirit is given to the obedient; and is preceded by the dominion of the Spirit in mortifying the deeds of the body (see Rom. 8:13 and 14). Spiritual knowledge is not deep thought but living contact, entering into and being united to the truth as it is in Jesus, a spiritual reality, a substantial existence. "The Spirit teacheth, combining spiritual things with spiritual"; into a spiritual mind He works spiritual truth. It is not the power of intellect, not even the earnest desire to know the truth, that equips a man for the Spirit's teaching. It is a life yielded to Him in dependence and full obedience to be made spiritual that receives the spiritual wisdom and understanding. In the mind (the scriptural meaning of the term) these two elements—the moral and the cognitive—are united; only as the former has precedence and sway can the latter apprehend what God has spoken.[1]

It is easy to understand how a carnal or fleshly life with its walk, and the fleshly mind with its knowledge, act and react on each other. As long as we are yielding to the flesh, we are incapable of receiving spiritual insight into truth. We may "know all mysteries, and have all knowledge," but without love—the love which the Spirit works in the inner life—it is only a knowledge that puffeth up; it profiteth nothing. The carnal life makes the knowledge carnal. And this knowledge again, being thus held in the fleshly mind, strengthens the religion of the flesh, of self-trust and self-effort; the truth so received has no power to renew and make free. No wonder that there is so much Bible teaching and Bible knowledge, with so little real spiritual result in a life of holiness. I pray that His word might sound through His Church: "Whereas there is among you jealousy and strife, are ye not carnal?" Unless we are living spiritual lives—full of humility, love, and self-sacrifice—spiritual truth, the truth of God, cannot enter or profit us.

Every Christian is called of God to be a spiritual man. Paul reproves these Corinthians, who were only a few years since brought out of gross heathenism, that they are not yet spiritual. The object of the great redemption in Christ is the removal of every hindrance that the Spirit of God might be able to make man's heart and life a worthy home for God who is a Spirit. That redemption was no failure; the Holy Spirit came down to inaugurate a new, yet unknown, dispensation of indwelling life and power. The promise and the love of the Father, the power and the glory of the Son, the presence of the Spirit on earth—all are promise and guarantee that it can be. As surely as the natural man can become a regenerate man, so can a regenerate man, who is still carnal, become spiritual.

And why is it not so? The question brings us into the presence of that strange and unfathomable mystery—the choice that God has given men to accept or refuse His offers; to be true or unfaithful to the grace He has given. We have already spoken of that unfaithfulness on the part of the Church, in its defective teaching of the indwelling and the sanctifying power of the Holy Spirit in the believer, and on the part of believers in their unwillingness to forsake all to let the Holy Spirit take full possession, and do a perfect work in them. Let us here rather seek, once again, to look at what Scripture teaches as to the way to become spiritual.

It is the Holy Spirit who makes the spiritual man. He alone can do it. He does it only where the whole man is yielded to Him. To have the whole being pervaded, influenced, sanctified by the Holy Spirit; to have first our spirit, then the soul, with the will, the feelings, the mind, and so even the body, under His control, moved and guided by Him, this makes and marks the spiritual man.

The first step on the way to this is faith. We must seek the deep, living, absorbing conviction that there is a Holy Spirit in us; that He is the mighty power of God dwelling and working within; that He is the representative of Jesus, making Him present within us as our redeemer king, mighty to save. In the union of a holy fear and trembling before the tremendous glory of this truth of an indwelling God, with the childlike joy and trust of knowing Him to be the paraclete, the inbringer of the divine and irrevocable presence of God and of Christ, this thought must become the inspiration of our life: The Holy Spirit has His home within us; in our Spirit is His hidden, blessed dwelling-place.

As we are filled with faith in what He is and will do, we will seek to know the hindrance if it is not done. But, we find that there is an opposing power—the flesh. From Scripture we learn how the flesh has its twofold action: unrighteousness and self-righteousness. Both must be confessed and surrendered to Him whom the Spirit would reveal and enthrone as Lord, our mighty Saviour. All that is carnal and sinful, all the works of the flesh, must be given up and cast out. No less must all that is carnal be rooted out, however religious it appears, and confidence in the flesh—all self-effort and self-struggling. The soul, with its power, must be brought into the captivity and subjection of Jesus Christ. In deep and daily dependence upon God, we must accept, wait for, and follow the Holy Spirit.

Walking in faith and obedience, we may count on the Holy Spirit to do a divine and most blessed work within us. "If we live by the Spirit"—this is the faith that is needed. Then, if we believe that God's Spirit dwells in us, "by the Spirit let us live"; this is the obedience that is required. In the faith of the Holy Spirit who is in us, we know that we have sufficient strength to walk by the Spirit, to yield ourselves to His mighty working to work in us to will and to do all that is pleasing in God's sight.

Gracious God, we humbly pray Thee to teach us all to profit from the deep lessons of this portion of Thy blessed Word.

Fill us with holy fear and trembling lest, with all our knowledge of the truth of Christ and the Spirit, we should be carnal in disposition and conduct, not walking in the love and purity of thy Holy Spirit. May we understand that knowledge only puffs up, unless it be under the rule of the love that builds up.

Give us to hear Thy call to all Thy children to be spiritual. It is Thy purpose, that even as with Thy beloved Son, their whole whole daily life, even in the very least thing, should give evidence of being the fruit of Thy Spirit's indwelling. May we all accept the call, as from thy love, inviting us to our highest blessedness, conformity to thy likeness in Christ Jesus.

Strengthen our faith, blessed Father! that we may be filled with the confidence that the Holy Spirit will do His work to make us spiritual. We desire to cease from self and doubt. We yield ourselves to Jesus our Lord to rule in us, to reveal himself by the Spirit. We bow before thee in the childlike faith that Thy Spirit, the Spirit of God, dwells in us every moment. May our souls increasingly be filled with holy awe and reverence at His presence. And do Thou, O Father, according to the riches of Thy glory, grant that we may be greatly strengthened by Him in the inner man. Then we shall be truly spiritual. Amen.

SUMMARY

1. "Believer! rise from the disciple stage, which savors not the things that be of God, to the spiritual, pentecostal condition."—Saphir

2. To understand the word "carnal" and the life Paul condemns so strongly here, compare Rom. 7:14, "I am carnal, sold under sin," and the description of the hopeless and undelivered state of which that word is the secret. To understand the word "spiritual," compare Rom. 8:6, "to be spiritually-minded is life and peace," with the description of the life of the Spirit in the context (2-16). Compare also Gal. 5:15, 16, 22, 25, 26, and 6:1, to see how the great mark of *carnal* is a lack of love, of *spiritual*, the meekness and love that keeps the new commandment.

3. When a man is first regenerated, the new life within him is only a seed, in the midst of a great body of sin and flesh, with its fleshly wisdom and will. In that seed there is

Christ and His Spirit as an almighty power; but because it is a frail thing, it is easily overlooked or distrusted. Faith knows the mighty power that there is in that small seed to overcome the world, and bring the whole flesh and life into subjection. So the Spirit rules and conquers and causes the deeds of the body to die, and the man becomes truly spiritual.

4. The lesson that true spiritual insight into God's Word depends upon a spiritual life is one of great importance for all pastors and teachers of the Word. Let us pray for all the leaders of the Church that they may be spiritual men. It is not the soundness of the teaching itself, nor the earnestness of the teacher, but the power of the Spirit—making his life and thoughts and words truly spiritual. That, as a rule, secures the blessing.

5. "It is one thing to have the Holy Spirit; it is another to have Him completely possessing us. No one can be regenerated without having Him; but there is the other side of it—when He fills our entire being and has His way with us."—Kelly

Note

1. See Note 14, p. 263.

24

THE TEMPLE OF THE HOLY SPIRIT

Know ye not that ye are the temple of God, and that the Spirit of God dwelleth in you?—1 Cor. 3:16

In using the illustration of the temple as the type of God's dwelling in us by the Holy Spirit, Scripture invites us to study the analogy. The temple was made in all things according to a pattern seen by Moses on the Mount, a shadow cast by the eternal spiritual realities which it was to symbolize. One of these realities—for divine truth is exceeding rich and full and has many and very diverse applications—shadowed forth by the temple is man's threefold nature. Because man was created in the image of God, the temple is not only an example of the mystery of man's approach into the presence of God, but equally of God's way of entering into man, to take up His abode with him.

We are familiar with the division of the temple into three parts. There was its exterior, seen by all men, with the outer court, into which every Israelite might enter, and where all the external religious service was performed. There was the holy place, into which alone the priests might enter, to present to God the blood or the incense, the bread or the oil, that they had brought from without. Although near, they were still not within the veil; into the immediate presence of God they could not come. God dwelled in the holiest of all, in a light inaccessible, where none might venture. The momentary entering of the high priest, once a year, was only to bring into full consciousness the truth that there was no place for man there until the veil was rent and taken away.

Man is God's temple. In him also, there are the three parts. In the body you have the outer court, the external visible life, where all the conduct has to be regulated by God's law, and where all service consists in looking at how things are around us and for us to bring us close to God. Then there is the soul, with its inner life, its power of mind and feeling and will. In the regenerate man this is the holy place, where thoughts and affections and desires move to and fro as the priests of the sanctuary, rendering God their service in the full light of consciousness. Then there is, within the veil, hidden from all human sight and light, the hidden innermost sanctuary, "the secret place of the Most High," where God dwells, and where man may not enter, until the veil is rent at God's own bidding. Man has not only body and soul, but also spirit. Deeper than the soul with its consciousness, there is a spirit-nature linking man with God. So great is sin's power that in some this place dies: they are sensual, not having the Spirit. In others, it is nothing more than a dormant place, a void waiting for the quickening of the Holy Spirit. In the believer it is the inner chamber of the heart, of which the Spirit has taken possession, and out of which He waits to do His glorious work, making soul and body holy unto the Lord.

However, this indwelling, unless it is recognized, yielded to, and humbly maintained in adoration and love, often brings comparatively little blessing. The one great lesson which the truth, that we are God's temple because His Spirit dwells in us, teaches us, is this: to acknowledge the Holy presence that dwells with us. This alone will enable us to regard the whole temple, even to the outmost court, as sacred to His service, and to yield every power of our nature to His leading and will. The most sacred part of the temple, that for which all the rest existed and on which all depended, was the holiest of all. Even though the priests might never enter there, and might never see the glory that dwelled there, all their conduct was regulated, and all their faith motivated, by the thought of the unseen presence there. It was this that gave the sprinkling of the blood and the burning of the incense their value. It was this that made it a privilege to draw nigh and give confidence to go out and bless. It was the most holy, the holiest of all, that made the place of their serving to them a holy place. Their whole life was controlled and inspired by faith in the unseen indwelling glory within the veil.

It is no different with the believer. Until he learns by faith to tremble in the presence of the wondrous mystery that he is God's temple, because God's Spirit dwells in him, he will never yield himself to his high vocation with the holy reverence or the joyful confidence that he should. As long as he looks only into the holy place, into the heart, as far as man can see and know what passes there, he will often search in vain for the Holy Spirit, or only find cause for bitter shame that his workings are so few and frail. Each of us must learn to know that there is a holiest of all in that temple which he himself is; the secret place of the most high within us must become the central truth in our temple worship. This must be to us the meaning of our confession: "I believe in the Holy Ghost."

And how is this deep faith in the hidden indwelling to become ours? Taking our stand upon God's blessed Word, we must accept and appropriate its teaching. We must believe that God means what it says. I am a temple; just such a temple as God commanded to be built of old; He meant for me to see in it what I am meant to be. There the holiest of all was the central point, the essential thing. It was all dark, secret, hidden, until the time of the unveiling came. It demanded and received the faith of the priest and the people. The holiest of all within me, too, is unseen and hidden, a thing for faith alone to know and deal with. Let me, as I approach the holy one, bow before Him in deep and lowly reverence. Let me there say that I believe what He says, that His Holy Spirit, God, one with the Father and the Son, even now makes His abode within me. I will meditate and be still until something of the overwhelming glory of the truth falls upon me and faith begins to realize that I am His temple, and in the secret place He sits upon His throne. As I yield myself in silent meditation and worship day by day, surrendering and opening my whole being to Him, He will in His divine, loving, living power shine into my consciousness the light of His presence.

As this thought fills the heart, the faith of the indwelling, though hidden, presence will influence; the holy place will be ruled from the most holy. The world of consciousness in the soul, with all its thoughts and feelings, its affections and purposes, will come and surrender themselves to the holy power that sits within on the throne. Amid the terrible experience of failure and sin a new hope will dawn. Though I may have earnestly sought to, I could not keep the holy place for God, because He keeps the most holy for himself. If I give Him the glory due to His name, in the holy worship of the inner temple, He will send forth His light and His truth through my whole being, and through mind and will reveal His power to sanctify and to bless. Through the soul, coming ever more securely under His rule, His power will work out even into the body. With passions and appetites within, with every thought brought into subjection, the hidden Holy Spirit will through the soul perpetrate ever deeper into the body. Through the Spirit the deeds of the body will die, and the river of water, that flows from under the throne of God and the Lamb, will go through the body with its cleansing and quickening power.

O brother, do believe that you are the temple of the living God and that the Spirit of God dwells in you! You have been sealed with the Holy Spirit; He is the mark, the living assurance of your sonship and your Father's love. If until now, this has been a thought that has brought you little comfort, see if the reason is not here. You sought for Him in the holy place, amid the powers and services of your inner life which come within your vision. And you could hardly discern Him there. And so you could not appropriate the comfort and strength the Comforter was meant to bring. No, my brother, not there, not there. Deeper down, in the secret place of the most high, there you will find Him. There faith will find Him. And as faith worships in holy reverence before the Father, and the heart trembles at the thought of what it has found, wait in holy stillness on God to grant you the mighty working of His Spirit, wait in holy stillness for the Spirit, and be assured He will, as God, arise and fill His temple with His glory.

And then remember, the veil was but for a time. When the preparation was complete, the veil of the flesh was rent. As you yield your soul's inner life to the inmost life of the Spirit, as the traffic between the most holy and the holy becomes more true and unbroken, the fullness of the time will come in your soul. In the power of Him, in whom the veil was rent that the Spirit might stream forth from His glorified body, there will come to you, too, an experience in which the veil shall be taken away and the most holy and the holy shall be one. The hidden glory of the secret place will stream into your conscious daily life: the service of the holy place will all be in the power of the eternal Spirit.

Brother, let us fall down and worship! "Be silent, all flesh, before the Lord; for he is awakened out of holy habitation."

Most Holy God, in adoring wonder I bow before Thee in the presence of this wondrous mystery of grace: my spirit, soul, and body Thy temple.

In deep silence and worship I accept the blessed revelation, that in me too there is a holiest of all, and that there Thy hidden glory has its abode.

O my God, forgive me that I have known so little of it.

I do now tremblingly accept the blessed truth: God the Spirit, the Holy Spirit, who is God Almighty, dwells in me.

O my Father, reveal within what it means, lest I sin against Thee by saying it and not living it.

Blessed Jesus, to Thee, who sittest upon the throne, I yield my whole being. In Thee I trust to rise up in power and have dominion within me.

In Thee I believe for the full streaming forth of the living waters.

Blessed Spirit, holy teacher, mighty sanctifier! Thou art within me. On Thee do I wait all the day. I belong to Thee. Take entire possession of me for the Father and the Son. Amen.

SUMMARY

1. Spirit here (John 4:24) denotes that deepest element of the human soul by which it can hold communion with the divine world. It is the seat of self-control, the sanctuary wherein the true worship is celebrated (Rom. 1:9). "The God whom I serve in my spirit."—Godet

2. Note how Paul, in appealing to the Corinthians to rise out of their deep carnal state, more than once pleads with them on the ground of their being temples of the Holy Spirit. In our days many think that the indwelling of the Holy Spirit ought to be preached only to advanced Christians. Let us learn here that every believer has the Holy Spirit; that he ought to know it: that knowing it is the most effective tool for rising up out of a low carnal life. Let us labor to bring every believer to a knowledge of this, his heavenly birthright.

3. It is the body that is the the temple of the Holy Spirit (1 Cor. 6:19). If our spirit be filled with the Spirit of God, it will manifest itself in the body too. "If ye, through the Spirit, do put to death the deeds of the body, ye shall live." Let us believe that the divine Spirit is particularly given to pervade, to purify, to strengthen our bodies for His service. It is His indwelling in the body that makes it a living seed that can share in the resurrection of life.

4. Do you know it? Do you know it fully, distinctly, abidingly? Do you know it by faith? Are you pressing on to know it in full experience, so that your deepest self-consciousness shall spontaneously say: Yes, I am a temple of God, the Spirit of God dwells in me, glory to His name?

25

THE MINISTRY OF THE SPIRIT

> But our sufficiency is of God; who hath also made
> us able ministers of the new testament; not of the let-
> ter, but of the spirit: for the letter killeth, but the
> spirit giveth life. But if the ministration of death
> . . . was glorious, . . . How shall not the ministration
> of the spirit be rather glorious?—2 Cor. 3:5-8

In none of his epistles does Paul expound his conception
of the Christian ministry so clearly and fully as in the second epistle to the Corinthians. The need of vindicating his
apostleship against detractors; the consciousness of divine
power and glory working in him in the midst of weakness;
the intense longing of his loving heart to communicate what
he had to impart, stirs his soul to its very depths, and he
lays open to us the inmost secrets of the life that makes one
a true minister of Christ and His Spirit. In our text we have
the central thought: he finds his sufficiency of strength, the
inspiration and rule of all his conduct, in the fact that he has
been made a minister of the Spirit. If we take the different
passages in which mention is made of the Holy Spirit in the
first half of the Epistle,[1] we shall see what, in his view, is the
place and work of the Holy Spirit in the ministry, and what
is the character of a ministry under His leading and in His
power.

In the Epistle, Paul speaks with authority. He begins by
placing himself on a level with his readers. In his first mention of the Spirit he tells them that the Spirit that is in him
is no other than is in them. "Now he which stablisheth us
with you in Christ, and hath anointed us, is God; who hath
also sealed us, and given the earnest of the Spirit in our
hearts" (1:21, 22). The anointing of the believer with the
Spirit, bringing him into fellowship with Christ, the anointed one, and revealing what He is to us; the sealing, marking
Him as God's own, and giving him assurance of it; the earnest of the Spirit, securing at once the foretaste and the fit-
ness for the heavenly inheritance in glory: of all this they are

both partakers together. Whatever there was among the Corinthians that was wrong and unholy, Paul speaks to them, thinks of them, and loves them as one in Christ. "He which stablisheth us with you in Christ, and hath anointed us"— this deep sense of unity fills his soul, comes out throughout the Epistle, and is the secret of his power. See 1:6, 10, 2:3: "My joy is the joy of you all"; 4:5: "ourselves your servants"; 4:10-12: "death worketh in us, life in you"; 4:15: "all things are for your sakes"; 6:11, 7:3: "ye are in our hearts to die and live with you." If the unity of the Spirit, the consciousness of being members one of another, be necessary in all believers, how much more must it be the mark of those who are ministers? The power of the ministry to the saints depends upon the unity of the Spirit; the full recognition of believers as partakers of the anointing. But to this end the minister must himself live as an anointed and sealed one, making manifest that he has the earnest of the Spirit in his heart.

The second passage is 3:3: "Ye are an epistle of Christ, ministered by us, written with the Spirit of the living God; not in tables of stone, but in fleshy tables of the heart." As distinct an act of God as was the writing of the law on the tables of stone, so is the writing of the law of the Spirit in the new covenant, and of the name of Christ on the heart. It is a divine work, in which, as truly as God wrote of old, the Holy Spirit uses the tongue of His minister as His pen. It is this truth that needs to be restored in the ministry, not only that the Holy Spirit is needed, but that He waits to do the work, and will do it, when the right relation to Him is maintained. Paul's own experience at Corinth (Acts 18:5-11; 1 Cor. 2:3) teaches us what conscious weakness, what fear and trembling, what sense of absolute helplessness may be, or rather is needed, if the power of God is to rest upon us. The whole epistle confirms this: it was as a man under sentence of death, bearing about the dying of the Lord Jesus, that the power of Christ worked in him. The Spirit of God stands in contrast to the flesh, the world, the self, with its life and strength; it is as these are broken down, and the flesh has nothing to glory in, that the Spirit will work. Oh that every minister's tongue might be prepared for the Holy Spirit to use it as a pen that He can write with!

Then come the words of our text (3:6, 7), to teach us what the special characteristic is of this new covenant ministry of the Spirit: it "giveth life." The antithesis, "the letter killeth," applies not only to the law of the Old Testament, but, according to the teaching of Scripture, to all knowledge which is not in the quickening power of the Spirit. We cannot insist upon it too earnestly, that, even as the law, though we know it was "spiritual," so the gospel too has its letter. The gospel may be preached most clearly and faithfully; it may exert a strong moral influence; and yet the faith that comes of it may stand in the wisdom of men, and not in the power of God. If there is one thing the Church needs to cry for on behalf of its ministers and students, it is that the ministry of the Spirit may be restored in its full power. Pray that God may teach them what it is to personally live in the sealing, the anointing, the assurance of the indwelling Spirit; what it is to know that the letter kills, but the Spirit actually gives life; and to know, above all, that the personal life is under the ministry of the Spirit so that He can freely work.

Paul now proceeds to contrast the two dispensations, and the different characters of those who live in them.[2] He points out how, as long as the mind is blinded, there is a veil on the heart which can only be taken away as we turn to the Lord. And then he adds (3:17, 18): "Now the Lord is that Spirit; and where the Spirit of the Lord is, there is liberty. But we all, with open face beholding as in a glass the glory of the Lord, are changed into the same image, from glory to glory, even as by the Spirit of the Lord." It is because God "is a Spirit" that He can give the Spirit. It was when our Lord Jesus was exalted into the life of the Spirit that He became "the Spirit of the Lord," could give the New Testament Spirit, and in the Spirit come himself to His people. The disciples knew Jesus long, without knowing Him as the Spirit of the Lord. Paul speaks of this, too, with regard to himself (2 Cor. 5:16). There may in the ministry be a lot of earnest gospel preaching of the Lord Jesus as the crucified one without the preaching of Him as the Spirit of the Lord. It is only as the latter truth is apprehended, and experienced, and then preached, that the double blessing will come that Paul speaks of here: "Where the Spirit of the Lord is, there is liberty." Believers will be led into the glorious liberty of the children of God (Rom. 8:2, Gal. 5:1, 18). Then will He do the work for which He was sent—to reveal the glory of the Lord in us; and as we behold it, we shall be changed from glory to glory. Of the time before Pentecost it was written: "The Spirit was not yet, because Jesus was not yet glorified." But when He had been "justified in the Spirit, and received up in glory," the Spirit came forth from "the excellent glory" into our hearts, that we, with unveiled face beholding the glory of the Lord might be changed into His likeness. What a calling! the ministry of the Spirit! to hold up the glory of the Lord to His redeemed, and to be used by His Spirit in working their transformation into His likeness, from glory to glory. "Therefore, seeing we have this ministry, we faint not." It is as the knowledge and acknowledgment of Christ as the Lord the Spirit, and of the Spirit of Christ as changing believers into His likeness, lives in the Church, that the ministry among believers will be in life and power—in actual deed, a ministry of the Spirit.

The power of the ministry on the divine side is the Spirit; on the human side, faith. The next mention of the Spirit is in 4:13: "Having the same spirit of faith." After having, in chapter 3, set forth the glory of the ministry of the Spirit; in chapter 4:1-6, the glory of the gospel it preached, he turns to the vessels in which this treasure is. He has to vindicate his apparent weakness. But he does far more. Instead of apologizing for it, he expounds its divine meaning and glory. He proves how this situation constituted his power, because in his weakness divine power could work. It has been so ordained, "that the excellency of the power may be of God, and not of us." So his perfect fellowship with Jesus was maintained as he bore about "the putting to death of the Lord Jesus, that the life of Jesus also might be manifested in his mortal body." So there was even in his sufferings something of the vicarious element that marked his Lord's: "So then death worketh in us, but life in you." And then he adds, as the expression of the animating power that sustained him through all endurance and labor: "But having the same Spirit of faith," of which we read in the scripture, "according to that which is written, I believed, and therefore did I speak; we also believe, and therefore we also speak; knowing that he which raised up the Lord Jesus shall raise up us also with Jesus, and shall present us with you."

Faith is the evidence of things not seen. It sees the invisible, and lives in it. Beginning with trust in Jesus, "in whom, though ye see him not, yet believing, ye rejoice," it goes on through the whole of the Christian life. Whatever is of the Spirit is by faith. The great work of God, in opening the heart of His child to receive more of the Spirit, is to school his faith into more perfect freedom from all that is seen, and the more complete rest in God, even to the assurance that God dwells and works mightily in his weakness. For this reason trials and sufferings are sent. Paul uses very remarkable language in regard to his sufferings in the first chapter (v. 9): "But we had the sentence of death in ourselves, that we should not trust in ourselves, but in God which raiseth the dead." Even Paul was in danger of trusting in himself. Nothing is more natural; all life is confident of self; and nature is consistent with itself until it dies. For the mighty work he had to do, he needed a trust in none less than the living God, who raises the dead. To this God led him by giving him, in the affliction which came upon him in Asia, the sentence of death in himself. The trial of his faith was its strength. In our context he returns to this thought: the fellowship of the dying of Jesus is to him the means and the assurance of the experience of the power of Christ's life. In the spirit of this faith he speaks: "Knowing that he which raised up Jesus shall raise up us also."

It was not until Jesus had died that the Spirit of life could break forth from Him. The life of Jesus was born out of the grave: it is a life out of death. It is as we daily die, and bear about the dying of Jesus; as flesh and self are kept crucified and mortified; as we have in ourselves God's sentence of death on all that is of self and nature—that the life and the Spirit of Jesus will be manifest in us. And this is the Spirit of faith, that in the midst of weakness and apparent death, it depends on God who raises the dead. This is the ministry of the Spirit, when faith glories in infirmities, that the power of Christ may rest upon it. As our faith does not stagger at the earthly weakness of the vessel, as it consents to the fact that the excellency of the power shall be not of ourselves, but of God, then the Spirit will work in the power of the living God.

We find the same thought in the two remainding passages. In 5:5, he speaks again of "*the earnest of the Spirit*" in connection with our groaning and being burdened. And then in 6:6, the Spirit is introduced in the midst of the mention of his distresses and labors as the mark of his ministry. "In everything commending ourselves, as the ministers of God, in much patience, in afflictions . . . *in the Holy Ghost* . . . as dying, and yet, behold, we live; as chastened, and not killed; as sorrowful, yet always rejoicing; as poor, yet making many rich." The power of Christ in the Holy Spirit was to Paul such a living reality that the weakness of the flesh only led him to more fully rejoice and trust in it. The Holy Spirit's dwelling and working in Him was consciously the secret spring and the divine power of his ministry.

We may well ask, "Does the Holy Spirit take the place in our ministry that He did in Paul's?" There is not a minister or member of the Church who does not have a vital interest in the answer. The question is not whether we admit to the doctrine of the absolute need of the Holy Spirit's working, but whether or not we give to the securing of His presence and working, that proportion of our time and our life, of our thoughts and faith, which His place, as the Spirit of the Lord Jesus on the throne, demands. Does the Holy Spirit have the place in the Church which our Lord Jesus would want Him to have? When our hearts open to the inconceivably glorious truth that He is the mighty power of God, that in Him the living Christ works through us, that He is the presence with us of the glorified Lord on the throne, we shall feel that the one need of the ministry and the Church is this: to wait at the footstool of the throne without ceasing for the clothing with the power that comes from on high. The Spirit of Christ, in His love and power in His death and life, is the Spirit of the ministry. As the Church grasps this, it will be what the Head of the Church meant it to be, the ministry of the Spirit.

Blessed Father, we thank Thee for the institution of the ministry of the Word as the great means through which our exalted Lord does His saving work by the Holy Spirit. We thank Thee that it is a ministry of the Spirit, and for all the blessing Thou hast wrought through it in the world. Our prayer is, most blessed God, that Thou wouldst increasingly and manifestly make it throughout Thy Church what Thou wouldst have it be—a ministry of the Spirit and of power.

Give Thy servants and people everywhere a deep sense of how much it still comes short of Thy purpose. Reveal how much there is in it of trust in the flesh, of man's zeal and strength, of the wisdom of this world. Teach all Thy true servants the holy secret of giving place to the Spirit of Christ, that He may use them. May the conscious presence of Christ in their hearts by the Holy Spirit give them great boldness of speech. May the power of the Holy Spirit in their life make them fit vessels for Him to use in teaching others. May divine power in the midst of weakness be the mark of their public ministry.

Teach Thy people to wait on their teaching, to receive it, to plead with Thee for it as a ministry of the Spirit. And may the lives of believers increasingly be, in the power of such a ministry, those of men led and sanctified by the Holy Ghost. Amen.

SUMMARY

1. Christ needed to be made perfect through suffering. It was through suffering He entered the glory out of which the Spirit was sent. "He was crucified through weakness, yet He liveth through the power of God." Paul could not exercise his ministry of the Spirit in power without the continual experience of the same weakness. "So death worketh in us, but life in you. We are also weak in him, but shall live with him through the gift of God toward you." With martyrs and missionaries, persecution and tribulation have been the fellowship of Christ's suffering and weakness, His power and Spirit. We may invite neither persecutions nor suffering; how can in our days this fellowship of Christ's suffering and dying, the rending of the flesh, so indispensable to the ministry of the Spirit, be maintained? In a deep entering into the needs and the sorrows of the suffering humanity around us. And in that self-denial which in nothing allows the flesh, the self-life, to have its way, but increasingly seeks in utter weakness to make way for Christ's power to work, and depends upon His Spirit.

2. The standard of the ministry and the standard of the

life of believers will correspond. As in the life of the Church the Spirit is known and honored, the need of a spiritual ministry will be felt. As the ministry becomes more deeply spiritual, the tone of the Church will be raised. The two act and react on each other. But how humbling the thought, that an earnest, intellectual, eloquent ministry is not necessarily a ministry of the Spirit!

3. Let us make the ministry a matter of unceasing prayer. Let us remember how much the Church depends upon it. Let us plead with God for a ministry of the Spirit. When this becomes the demand of the Church, the supply will not be withheld.

4. What will be the mark of a ministry of the Spirit? A sense of something supernatural, a holy fear of God's presence resting on men, the self-evidencing power of the actual presence of the Spirit.

5. "Our abilities lie in our being made instruments, by whom the Holy Ghost is pleased *to communicate himself.*" —Goodwin

Notes

1. To 6:10, where he ends the more general description of his ministry, and returns to personal appeal.

2. Historically, I may be living in the dispensation of the Spirit, and yet practically in that of the letter.

26

THE SPIRIT AND THE FLESH

Are ye so foolish? having begun in the Spirit, are ye now made perfect in the flesh?—Gal. 3:3

For we are the circumcision, which worship God in the spirit, and rejoice in Christ Jesus, and have no confidence in the flesh. Though I might also have confidence in the flesh.—Phil. 3:3, 4

The flesh is the name by which Scripture indicates our

fallen nature—soul and body. The soul at creation was placed between the spiritual or divine and the sensible or worldly, to give to each its due, and guide them into that perfect union which would result in man attaining his destiny—a spiritual body. When the soul yielded to the temptation of the sensible, it broke away from the rule of the Spirit and came under the power of the body—it became flesh. And now the flesh is not only without the Spirit, but even hostile to it: "the flesh lusteth against the Spirit."

In this antagonism of the flesh to the Spirit there are two sides. On the one hand, the flesh lusts against the Spirit in its committing sin and transgressing God's law. On the other hand, its hostility to the Spirit is no less manifested in its seeking to serve God and do His will. In yielding to the flesh, the soul sought itself instead of the God to whom the Spirit linked it; selfishness prevailed over God's will; selfishness became its ruling principle. And now, so subtle and mighty is this spirit of self, that the flesh, not only in sinning against God, but even when the soul learns to serve God, still asserts its power, refuses to let the Spirit alone lead, and, in its efforts to be religious, is still the great enemy that ever hinders and quenches the Spirit. It is because of this deceitfulness of the flesh that there often takes place what Paul speaks of to the Galatians: "Having begun in the Spirit, are ye now made perfect in the flesh?" Unless the surrender to the Spirit is complete, and the holy waiting upon Him be continued in dependence and humility, what has been begun in the Spirit, very early and very quickly passes over into the confidence in the flesh.

And the remarkable thing is, what at first sight might appear a paradox—as soon as the flesh seeks to serve God, it then becomes the strength of sin. Do we not know how the Pharisees, with their self-righteousness and carnal religion, fell into pride and selfishness and became the servants of sin? Was it not among the Galatians that Paul asked the question about "perfecting in the flesh what was begun in the Spirit," and didn't he warn them against the righteousness of works, because the works of the flesh were so manifest that they were in danger of devouring one another? Satan has no more crafty device for keeping souls in bondage than inciting them to a religion in the flesh. He knows that the power of the flesh can never please God or conquer sin, and that in due time the flesh that has gained supremacy over the Spirit in the service of God, will assert and maintain that same supremacy in the service of sin. It is only where the Spirit truly and unceasingly has the entire lead and rule in the life of worship, that it will have the power to lead and rule in the life of practical obedience. If I am to deny self in my relationships with fellowmen, to conquer selfishness and temper and lack of love, I must first learn to deny self in my relationship with God. *There* the soul, the seat of self, must learn to bow to the Spirit, where God dwells.

The contrast between the worship in the Spirit and trusting in the flesh is very beautifully expressed in Paul's description of the true circumcision—the circumcision of the heart—whose praise is not of men, but of God: "Who worship by the Spirit of God, and glory in Christ Jesus, and have no confidence in the flesh." Placing the glorying in Christ Jesus in the center, as the very essence of the Christian faith and life, he calls attention on the one hand to the great danger by which it is beset, and on the other, the safeguard by which its full enjoyment is secured. Confidence in the flesh is the one thing above all others that renders the glorying in Christ Jesus of none effect, and worship by the Spirit the one thing that alone can make it indeed life and truth. May the Spirit reveal to us what it means to glory in Christ Jesus!

There is a glorying in Christ Jesus that is accompanied by much confidence in the flesh, that all history and experience teach us. Among the Galatians it was so. The teachers whom Paul opposed so earnestly were all preachers of Christ and His cross. But they preached it, not as men taught by the Spirit to know what the infinite and all-pervading influence of that cross must be, but as those who, having had the beginnings of God's Spirit, had then allowed their own wisdom and their own thoughts to say what that cross meant, and so had reconciled it with a religion which to a very large extent was legal and carnal. The story of the Galatian church is repeated to this day even in the churches that are most confidently assured that they are free from the Galatian error. Just notice how often the doctrine of justification by faith is spoken of, as if that were the chief teaching of the Epistle, and the doctrine of the Holy Spirit's indwelling, as received by faith, and our walking by the Spirit, is hardly mentioned.

Christ crucified is the wisdom of God. The confidence in the flesh, in connection with the glorying in Christ, is seen as confidence in its own wisdom. Scripture is studied, and preached, and heard, and believed in, very much in the power of the natural mind, with little insistence upon the absolute need of the Spirit's personal teaching. It is seen in the absolute confidence with which men know that they have the truth, though they have it far more from human than divine teaching, and in the absence of that teachableness that waits for God to reveal His truth in His own light.

Christ, through the Holy Spirit, is not only the wisdom but the power of God. The confidence in the flesh, along with much glorying in Christ Jesus, is to be seen and felt in so much of the work of the Christian Church in which human effort and human arrangement take a much larger place than the waiting on the power that comes from on high. In the larger ecclesiastical organizations, in individual churches and circles, in the inner life of the spirit and prayer, we see how much unsuccessful effort, how much often repeated failure is to be traced to this one evil! There is no lack of acknowledging Christ, His person and work as our only hope, no lack of giving Him the glory, and yet so much confidence in the flesh, rendering it of none effect.

Let me here ask again, whether there are not many who are striving earnestly for a life in the fullness of consecration and the fullness of blessing, who will find here the secret of failure. To help such as these has been one of my first objectives and most earnest prayers in writing this book. When in a message, book, conversation, or private prayer, the fullness of Jesus was opened up to them, with the possibility of a holy life in Him, the soul felt it was all so beautiful and so simple that nothing could any longer keep it back. And perhaps, as that soul accepted what was seen to be so sure and so near, it entered into an enjoyment and experienced a power before unknown. But it did not last. There was a worm at its root. Vain was the search for what the cause of the falling away was, or the way of restoration. Frequently the only answer that could be found was that the surrender was not complete or faith's acceptance not perfect. And yet the soul felt sure that it was ready, as far as it knew, to give up all, and it did long to let Jesus have all and to trust Him for all. The soul could almost despair of an impossible perfection—if perfect consecration and perfect faith were to be the condition of the blessing. And the promise had been that it would all be so simple—just the life for the poor and weak.

Listen, my brother, to the blessed teaching of God's Word today. It was the confidence in the flesh that spoiled your glorying in Christ Jesus. It was self doing what the Spirit alone can do; it was the soul taking the lead, in the hope that the Spirit would second its efforts, instead of trusting the Holy Spirit to lead and do all, and then waiting on Him. It was following Jesus without the denial of self. This was the problem. Come and listen to Paul as he tells of the only safeguard against this danger: "We are the circumcision, who worship by the Spirit of God, and glory in Christ Jesus, and have no confidence in the flesh." Here are the two elements of spiritual worship. The Spirit exalts Jesus, and abases the flesh. If we would truly glory in Jesus, and have Him glorified in us; if we would know the glory of Jesus in personal and unchanging experience free from the impotence which always marks the efforts of the flesh—we must simply learn what this worship of God by the Spirit is.

I can only repeat, once again, that it is the purpose of this whole book to set forth as God's truth from His blessed word: Glory in Christ Jesus. Glory in Him as the glorified one who baptizes with the Holy Spirit. In great simplicity and restfulness believe in Him as having given His own Spirit within you. Believe in that gift; believe in the Holy Spirit dwelling within you. Accept this as the secret of the life of Christ in you: the Holy Spirit is dwelling in the hidden recesses of your spirit. Meditate on it, believe Jesus and His word concerning it, until your soul bows with holy fear and awe before God under the glory of the truth: the Holy Spirit of God is indeed dwelling in me.

Yield yourself to His leading. We have learned that His leading is not just in the mind or thoughts, but in the life and disposition. Yield yourself to God to be guided by the Holy Spirit in all your conduct. He is promised to those who love Jesus and obey Him; confess that He knows you love and obey Him with your whole heart. Remember, then, what the one central object of His coming was: to restore the departed Lord Jesus to His disciples. "I will not leave you orphans," said Jesus; "I will come again to you." I cannot glory in a distant Jesus, from whom I am separated. When I try to do it, it takes effort; I must have the help of the flesh to do it. I can only truly glory in a present Saviour, whom the Holy Spirit glorifies, and reveals within me. As He does this, the flesh is abased, and kept in its place of crucifixion as an accursed thing: as He does it, the deeds of the flesh are made to die. And my whole religion will be: no confidence in the flesh; glorying in Christ Jesus; worship by the Spirit of God.

Beloved believer, having begun in the Spirit, continue, go on, persevere in the Spirit. Beware of, for one single moment, continuing or perfecting the work of the Spirit in the flesh. Let "no confidence in the flesh" be your battle-cry; let a deep distrust of the flesh and fear of grieving the Spirit by walking after the flesh keep you humble before God. Pray to God for the spirit of revelation that you may see that Jesus is all and does all, and how by the Holy Spirit a divine life actually takes the place of your life, and Jesus is enthroned as the keeper and guide and life of the soul.

Blessed God and Father, we thank Thee for the wondrous provision Thou hast made for Thy children's drawing nigh to Thee, glorying in Christ Jesus, and worshipping by the Spirit. Grant, we pray Thee, that such may be our life and all our religious service.

We feel the need of asking Thee to show us how the one great hindrance to such a life is the power of the flesh and the efforts of the self-life. Open our eyes, we pray Thee, to this snare of Satan. May we all see how secret and how subtle is the temptation to have confidence in the flesh, and how easily we are led to perfect in the flesh what has been begun in the Spirit. May we learn to trust Thee to work in us by Thy Holy Spirit, both to will and to do.

Teach us, too, we pray Thee, to know how the flesh can be conquered and its power broken. In the death of Thy beloved Son our old man has been crucified. May we count all things but loss to be made conformable to that death, and have the old nature kept in the place of death. We do yield ourselves to the leading and rule of Thy Holy Spirit. We do believe that through the Spirit Christ is our life, so that instead of the life of effort and work, an entirely new life works within us. Our Father, in faith we yield all to Thy Spirit to be our life in us. Amen.

SUMMARY

1. Christ is the wisdom and the power of God. The root of all trust in our own strength is trust in our own wisdom, the idea that we know how to serve God, because we have His Word. This wisdom of man, in his accepting God's Word, is the greatest danger of the Church, because it is a hidden, subtle form by which we are led to perfect in the flesh what was begun in the Spirit.

2. Our only safety here is the Holy Spirit. A great willingness to be taught by Him, a holy fear of in the least thing walking after the flesh, a loving surrender in everything to the obedience to which Christ promises the Spirit, and with all this, the living faith that the Spirit will in divine power possess our life and live it for us—this is the path of safety.

3. Let us try and realize fully that there are these two motivating principles of man's life. In most Christians there is a mixed life, yielding now to the one, and then to the other. God's will is that we walk "not"—never, not for a moment—"after the flesh, but after the Spirit." Let us accept God's will. The Holy Spirit has been given to bring our life into conformity with it. May God show us how entirely the Holy Spirit can dispossess the life of the flesh, and himself become an entirely new life in us, revealing Christ as our life. Then we can say, "It is no longer I that live, but Christ that liveth in me."

4. The Church must learn from this Epistle that justification by faith is only the means to an end, the entrance to a life of walking by the Spirit of God. We must return to the preaching of John the Baptist—Christ who bears the sin of the world, Christ who baptizes with the Holy Ghost.

5. "Why is it that people lay stress, almost exclusively, with a view to faith in Jesus, on this, that He bears the sin of

the world, and neglect so much the other point, that He is able to baptize with the Holy Ghost? The prophets and apostles, on the contrary, lay stress on this gift of the Spirit as the source of a new life, a new disposition and walk, in which both the impression and the expression of God's law is to be seen. Prophets and apostles treat the matter in its ethical aspect, whereas the traditional treatment represents the gift of the Spirit chiefly as a seal of forgiveness and adoption, and holds that from the joy of gratitude for this— that is, from a mere psychological factor—the new life and strength for good are to spring. This view we find in our best authors. The Scriptures, on the contrary, lay stress on the new creating and satisfying power of the Holy Ghost as the principle of all Christian disposition and personal activity (Rom. 8:2). Christ's sin-bearing only prepares the way for the coming of the Spirit (John 7:39; Gal. 3:13, 14); it is the foundation, but not the whole."—Beck, *Pastorallehren*

27

THE SPIRIT THROUGH FAITH

Christ hath redeemed us from the curse . . . that the blessing of Abraham might come on the Gentiles through Jesus Christ; that we might receive the promise of the Spirit through faith.—Gal. 3:13,14

The word faith is used the first time in Scripture in connection with Abraham. His highest praise, the secret of his strength for obedience, and what made him so pleasing to God, was that he *believed* God; and so he became the father of all them that believe, and the great example of the blessing which the divine favor bestows, and the path by which it comes. Just as God proved himself to Abraham, the God who quickens the dead, He does to us also, in fuller measure, by giving us the Spirit of His own divine life to dwell in us. And just as this quickening power came to Abraham through faith, so the blessing of Abraham, as now made manifest in Christ, even the promise of the Spirit, is made ours by faith. All the lessons of Abraham's life center in this: "We receive the promise of the Spirit through faith." If we want to know what the faith is through which the Spirit is received, how that faith comes and grows, we must study what God has taught us of it in Abraham's story.

In Abraham's life we see what faith is: the spiritual sense by which man recognizes and accepts the revelation of his god, a spiritual sense called forth and awakened by that revelation. It was because God had chosen Abraham, and determined to reveal himself, that Abraham became a man of faith. Each new revelation was an act of the divine will; it is the divine will, and the revelation by which it carries out its purpose, that is the cause and the life of faith. The more distinct the revelation or contact with God, the deeper is faith stirred in the soul. Paul speaks of "trust in the living God": it is only as the living one, in the quickening power of the divine life, draws nigh andtouches the soul, that living faith will be called forth. Faith is not an independent act, by which in our own strength we take what God says. Nor is it an entirely passive state, in which we only allow God to do to us what He will. But it is that receptivity of soul in which, as God comes near, and as His living power speaks to us and touches us, we yield ourselves and accept His word and His working.

It is thus very evident that faith has two things to deal with:the presence and the word of the Lord. It is only the living presence that makes the living word, so that it comes not in word only but in power. It is because of this that there is so much reading and preaching of the Word that bears so little fruit; so much straining and praying for faith, with so little result. Men deal with the Word more than with the living God. Faith has very truly been defined as ,"Taking God at His word." To many this means, "Taking the word as God's"; they didn't see the force of the thought, *"Taking God* at His word." A key or a door handle has no value until I use it for the lock and the door I want to open; it is only in direct and living contact with God himself that the Word will open the heart to believe. Faith *takes God* at His word; it can only do this when and as He gives himself. I may have in God's book all His precious promises most clear and full; I may have learned perfectly how I need only to trust the promise to have it fulfilled, and yet utterly fail to find the longed-for blessing. The faith that enters into the inheritance is the attitude of soul which waits for God himself, first to speak His word to me, and then to do the thing He has spoken. Faith is fellowship with God; faith is surrender to God; the impression made by his drawing high, the possession *He takes* of the soul by His word, holding and preparing it for His work. When once it has been awakened, it watches for every appearing of the divine will; it listens for and accepts every indication of the divine presence; it looks for and expects the fulfillment of every divine promise.

Such was the faith through which Abraham inherited the promises. Such is the faith by which the blessing of Abraham comes upon the Gentiles in Christ Jesus, and by which we thus receive the promise of the Spirit. In all our study of the work of the Holy Spirit, and of the way in which He comes, from His first sealing us, to His full indwelling and streaming forth, let us hold fast this word:"We receive the promise of the Spirit by faith." Whether the believer is striving for the full consciousness that the Spirit dwells within, for a deeper assurance of His shedding abroad of God's love in the heart, for a larger growth of all His fruits, for the clearer experience of His guiding into all truth, or for the enduement of power to labor and to bless, let him remember that the law of faith, on which the whole economy of grace is grounded, here demands its fullest application: "According to your faith be it unto you. We receive the promise of the Spirit by faith." Let us seek for Abraham's blessing in Abraham's faith.

Let, in this matter, our faith begin where his began: in meeting God and waiting on God. "The Lord appeared unto Abraham. . . . And Abraham fell on his face: and God talked with him." Let us look up to our God and Father as the living God, who is himself, by His omnipotent quickening power, to do this wonderful thing for us: to fill us with His Holy Spirit. The blessing He has for us is the same He gave to Abraham—only larger, fuller, more wonderful. To Abraham, both when his own body was as dead, and later on, when his son was already bound on the altar, the prey of death, He came as the life-giving God. "He believed God, who quickeneth the dead. He offered up Isaac, accounting God able to raise him up." To us He comes, offering to fill spirit, soul, and body with the power of a divine life through the Holy Spirit dwelling in us. Let us be like Abraham. "Looking at the promise of God, he wavered not through unbelief, but waxed strong through faith, giving glory to God, and being fully assured that what he had promised, *he* was able also to perform." Let us have our souls filled with the faith of Him who has promised, our hearts fixed on Him who is able to perform. It is faith *in God* that opens the heart for God and prepares to submit to and receive His divine working. God waits on us to fill us with His Spirit. Oh, let us wait on Him. It is God who must do it all with a divine doing, most mighty and most blessed. Let us wait on Him. To read and think, to long and pray, to consecrate ourselves and grasp the promise, to hold fast the blessed truth that the Spirit dwells within us; all this is good in its place, but does not bring the blessing. The one thing needful is to have the heart filled with faith in the living God; in that faith to abide in living contact with Him; in that faith to wait and worship before His holy presence. In such fellowship with God, the Holy Spirit fills the heart.

When we have taken up this position, let us remain in it; we are then in the right condition for the Spirit, in such measure as He already has had access to us, further revealing what God has prepared for us.[1] As we then think of some special manifestation of the Spirit, by which a conviction of need has been revealed or go to the promises of the Word to be led into all the will of God concerning the life of the Spirit in us, we shall be kept in that humble sense of dependence out of which childlike trust is most surely begotten. We shall be preserved from that life of strain and effort which has so often led to failure, because in the very attempt to serve God in the Spirit we were having or seeking confidence in the flesh, in something we felt, or did, or wished to do. The deep undergirding of our life—in listening to the Word or asking God to listen to us, in silent meditation or public worship, in work for God or daily business—will be the assurance that supersedes every other certainty: "How much more will the heavenly Father give," has He given, and will He always be giving, "the Holy Spirit to them that ask him."

Such a faith will be not be without its trials. Isaac—the God-given, faith-accepted life of Issac—had to be given up to death, that it might be received back in resurrection-type, as life from the dead. The God-given experience of the Spirit's working many times passes away, and leaves the soul apparently dull and dead. This is only until the double lesson has been fully learned—that a living faith can rejoice in a living God—even when all feeling and experience appear to contradict the promise; and that the divine life only enters as the life of the flesh is given over to death. The life of Christ is revealed as His death works in us, and as in weakness and nothingness we look to Him. We receive the promise of the Spirit through faith. As faith grows larger and broader, the receiving of the promised Spirit will be fuller and deeper. Each new revelation of God to Abraham made his faith stronger and his acquaintance with God more intimate. When his God drew near, he knew what to expect; he knew to trust Him even in the most unlikely appearances as when asked the death of his son. It is the faith that waits every day on the living God to reveal himself; the faith that in ever-increasing tenderness of ear and readiness of service yields fully to Him and His presence; the faith that knows that only as He wills to reveal himself can the blessing come; but He himself loves to receive. It will surely come— this faith receives the promise of the Spirit.

It was in God's presence that this faith was awakened and strengthened in Abraham and the saints of old. It was in Jesus' presence on earth that unbelief was cast out, and that weak faith became strong. It was in the presence of the glorified one that faith received the blessing of Pentecost. The throne of God is now opened to us in Christ; it is become the throne of God and the Lamb: as we tarry in humble worship, and walk in loving service before the throne, the river of the water of life that flows form under it will flow into us, and through us, and out of us. "He that believeth, rivers of water shall flow out of him."

Ever-blessed God, who does in Thy divine love and power reveal thyself to each of Thy children, increase within us, we pray Thee, the faith through which alone we can know or receive Thee. Whether Thou comest as the Almighty, or the redeeming, or the indwelling God, it is ever faith Thou seekest, and according to faith we receive. O Father, convince us deeply that we have just as much of the Spirit as we have of faith!

Our Holy God, we know that it is Thy presence awakens and works the faith in the soul that yields to Thee. Draw us mightily, we pray Thee, even irresistibly into Thy holy presence, and keep us waiting there. Oh, deliver us from the terrible fascination of the world and the flesh that Thy divine glory may be our all-consuming desire, and our whole heart emptied to receive the Holy Spirit's revelation of Christ within. We desire to take Thy words and let them dwell richly in us. We desire in stillness of soul to be silent unto God and wait for Him; to trust and believe that the Father hath given us His Spirit within us, and is in secret working to reveal His Son. O God, we do live the life of faith; we do believe in the Holy Spirit. Amen.

SUMMARY

1. Faith is the one thing that pleases God. In all worship and work that is acceptable to God in Christ Jesus, it is faith that receives the testimony that we are well-pleasing to Him. Why? Because faith goes beyond self, gives God alone the glory, looks only to God's Son, and is receptive of God's Spirit. Faith is not merely the positive conviction that God's word or promise is true; there may be this confidence even in the power of the flesh. Faith is the spiritual organ of the soul, through which it waits on the living God, listens *to Him*, takes His words *from himself*, has communion with Him. It is as this habit of soul is cultivated, as we live our whole life by faith, that the Spirit can enter fully and flow freely. "He that believeth, rivers shall flow out of him."

2. "The Spirit is called (1 Pet. 1:23) the incorruptible seed, because He is cast into the soul with the Word, as its prolific virtue: the Word is the seed materially, but the Spirit is the seed virtually."—Goodwin

3. You long for the power of the Holy Spirit to keep you ever looking to Jesus, to reveal Jesus as the ever-present Saviour from sin—"only believe." Begin each day with a

quiet act of meditation and faith. In quiet confidence turn inwardly, not to see the work the Holy Spirit does, but to yield your spirit to Him who dwells there in secret. Say in deep humility: "I have within me, small and hidden, the seed of the kingdom, the seed of eternal life. I have found the seed of the living word, the seed of God, within me. I know now where it dwells." Bow before God in fear and trembling, because He works in you, and let faith take time before Him to become confident and fully conscious of the fact: I have the Holy Spirit within me this day.

4. "His seed abideth in him and he cannot sin." Go out into daily life in the strength of the faith that the Holy Spirit dwells within, and that the Father will grant that He works effectually to keep you from sinning. Pause frequently, in holy self-recollection, to let the Spirit remind you that you are God's holy temple. Say with holy trembling: "I bear within me the living seed of the life of God."

5. As individual believers enter into this life of faith and walk in it, there will be power to pray for the Spirit to come in power upon all flesh.

Note

1. See Note 14, p. 263.

28

WALKING BY THE SPIRIT

Walk in the Spirit, and ye shall not fulfil the lust of the flesh. And they that are Christ's have crucified the flesh with the affections and lusts. If we live in the Spirit, let us also walk in the Spirit.—Gal. 5:16, 24, 25

"If we live in the Spirit, let us also walk in the Spirit." These words suggest to us very clearly the difference between the sickly and the healthy Christian life. In the former the Christian is content to "live in the Spirit"; he is satisfied with knowing that he has the new life, but he does not walk in the Spirit. The true believer, on the contrary, is not content without having his whole walk and conversation in the power of the Spirit. He walks by the Spirit, and so does not fulfill the lusts of the flesh.

As the Christian strives to walk worthily of God and well-pleasing to Him in all things, he is often deeply troubled by the power of sin, and seeks the cause for which he so often fails to conquer it. He usually feels that it is due to his lack of faith or faithfulness, his natural weakness, or the mighty power of Satan. But he must not rest content with this solution. It would be better to press on to find the deeper reason why all these things, from which Christ secured deliverance, still can overcome us. One of the deepest secrets of the Christian life is the knowledge that the one great power that keeps the Spirit of God from ruling is the flesh. He who knows what *the flesh* is, how it works and how it must be dealt with, will be the conqueror.

We know that it was because of their ignorance of this that the Galatians so sadly failed. It was this that led them to attempt to perfect in the flesh what was begun in the Spirit (3:3). It was this that made them a prey to those who desired "to make a fair show in the flesh" that they might "glory in the flesh" (6:12, 13). They didn't know how incorrigibly corrupt the flesh was. They didn't know that, as sinful as our nature is when fulfilling its own lusts, as sinful as it is when making "a fair show in the flesh"; it apparently yields itself to the service of God, and undertakes to perfect what the Spirit had begun. Because they didn't know this, they were unable to check the flesh in its passions and lusts; these obtained the victory over them, so that they did what they did not wish. They didn't know that, as long as the flesh, self-effort, and self-will had any influence in serving God, it would remain strong to serve sin, and that the only way to render it impotent to do evil was to render it impotent in its attempts to do good.

It is to discover the truth of God concerning the flesh, both in its service to God and to sin, that this Epistle was written. Paul wanted to teach them how the Spirit, and the Spirit alone, is the power of the Christian life, and how this cannot be unless the flesh, with all that it means, is utterly and entirely set aside. In answer to the question of how this can be, he gives the wonderful answer which is one of the central thoughts of God's revelation. The crucifixion and death of Christ is the revelation not only of an atonement for sin, but also of a power which frees from the actual dominion of sin, as it is rooted in the flesh. When Paul in the midst of his teaching about the walk in the Spirit (16-26) tells us, "They that are Christ's have *crucified* the flesh with its passions and lusts," he tells us the only way by which deliverance from the flesh is to be found. To understand these words, "crucified the flesh," and experience it, is the secret of walking not after the flesh but after the Spirit. Let each one who longs to walk by the Spirit try to grasp its meaning.

"The flesh"—in Scripture this expression means the whole of our human nature in its present condition under the power of sin. It includes our whole being—spirit, soul, and body. After the Fall, God said, "Man is flesh" (Gen. 6:3). All his powers, intellect, emotions, and will are under the power of the flesh. Scripture speaks of the will of the flesh, of the mind of the flesh (fleshly mind), of the passions and lusts of the flesh. It tells us that in our flesh no good dwells. The mind of the flesh is at enmity against God. On this ground it teaches that nothing that is of the flesh, nothing that the fleshly mind or will thinks or does, however fair the show it makes, and however much men may glory in it, can have any value in the sight of God. It warns us that our greatest danger in religion, the cause of our weakness and failure, is our having confidence in the flesh, its wisdom and its work. It tells us that, to be pleasing to God, this flesh, with its self-will and self-effort, must be entirely given up, to make way for the willing and the working of another, even the Spirit of God. The only way to be made free from the power of the flesh, and have it put out of the way, is to have it crucified and given over to death.

"They that are of Christ Jesus *have crucified* the flesh." Men often speak of crucifying the flesh as a thing that has to be done. Scripture always speaks of it as a thing that has been done, an accomplished fact. "Knowing this, that our old man *was crucified* with him. *I have been crucified* with Christ. They that are of Christ Jesus *have crucified* the flesh. The cross of our Lord Jesus Christ, through which the world *hath been crucified* unto me, and I unto the world."

What Christ did, through the eternal Spirit, on the cross, He did not as an individual, but in the name of human nature which, as its head, He had taken upon himself. Everyone who accepts Christ receives Him as the crucified one, receives not only the merit, but the power of His crucifixion, is united and identified with Him, and is called on intelligently and voluntarily to realize and maintain that identification. "They that are of Christ Jesus" have, in virtue of their accepting the crucified Christ as their life, given up their flesh to the cross which is of the very essence of the person and character of Christ as He now lives in heaven; they "have crucified the flesh with its passions and lusts." [1]

But what does this mean: "They have *crucified* the flesh"? Some are content with this general truth: the cross takes away the curse which was upon flesh. Others think they must cause the flesh pain and suffering; they must deny and mortify it. Others think of the moral influence the thought of the cross will exercise. In each of these views there is an element of truth. But if they are to be realized in power, we must go to the root-thought: to crucify the flesh is to give it over to the curse. The cross and the curse are inseparable (Deut. 21:23; Gal. 3:13). To say, "Our old man has been crucified with him, I have been crucified with Christ," means something very serious and awesome. It means this: I have seen that my old nature, my self, deserves the curse; that there is no way of getting rid of it but by death: I voluntarily give it over to death. I have accepted as my life the Christ who came to give himself, His flesh, to the cursed death of the cross; who received His new life only because of that death and in virtue of it: I give my old man, my flesh, self, with its will and work, as a sinful, accursed thing, to the cross. It is nailed there—in Christ I am dead to it, and free from it.

The power of this truth depends upon its being known, accepted, and acted upon. If I only know the cross in its substitution, but not, as Paul gloried in it, in its fellowship (Gal. 6:14), I can never experience its power to sanctify. As the blessed truth of its fellowship dawns upon me, I see how by faith I enter into and live in spiritual communion with Jesus who, as my head and leader, made and proved the cross the only ladder to the throne. This spiritual union, maintained by faith, becomes a moral one. I have the same mind or disposition that was in Christ Jesus. I regard the flesh as sinful, and only fit for the curse. I accept the cross, with its death to what is flesh, secured to me in Jesus, as the only way to become free from the power of self, and to walk in new life by the Spirit of Christ.

The way in which this faith in the power of the cross is a revelation and at the same time the removal of the curse and the power of the flesh is a very simple truth, and yet a deep one. I begin to understand that my one danger in living by the Spirit is yielding to the flesh or self in its attempt to serve God. This renders the cross of Christ of none effect (1 Cor. 1:17; Gal. 3:3, 5:12, 13; Phil. 3:3, 4; Col. 2:18-23). I see how all that was of man and nature, of law and human effort, was forever judged by God on Calvary. There flesh proved that, with all its wisdom and all its religion, it hated and rejected the Son of God. There God proved that the only way to deliver from the flesh was to give it over to death as an accursed thing. I begin to understand that the one thing I need is to look upon the flesh as God does; to accept the death-warrant that the cross brings to everything in me that is of the flesh; to look upon it, and all that comes from it, as an accursed thing. As this habit of soul grows on me, I learn to fear nothing so much as myself. I tremble at the thought of allowing the flesh, my natural mind and will, to usurp the place of the Holy Spirit. My whole attitude towards Christ is that of lowly fear, in the consciousness of having within me that accursed thing that is ever ready, as an angel of light, to intrude itself in the holiest of all, and lead me astray to serve God, not in the Spirit of Christ, but in the power that is of nature. It is in such a lowly fear that the believer is taught to believe fully the need, but also the provision, of the Holy Spirit to take entirely the place which the flesh once had, and day by day to glory in the cross, of which he can say, "By it I have been crucified to the world."

We often seek for the cause of failure in the Christian life. We often think that because we are sound on what the Galatians did not understand—justification by faith alone—their danger was not ours. Oh, that we knew to what an extent we have allowed the flesh to work in our religion! Let us pray God for grace to know it as our bitterest enemy, and the enemy of Christ. Free grace does not only mean the pardon of sin; it means the power of the new life through the Holy Spirit. Let us consent to what God says of the flesh, and all that comes of it: that it is sinful, condemned, accursed. Let us fear nothing so much as the secret workings of our flesh. Let us accept the teaching of God's word: "In my flesh dwelleth no good thing; the carnal mind is enmity against God." Let us ask God to show us to what extent the Spirit must possess us if we are to be pleasing to Him in all things. Let us believe that as we daily glory in the cross, and, in prayer and obedience, yield the flesh to the death of the cross, Christ will accept our surrender, and will, by His divine power, maintain mightily in us the life of the Spirit. We shall learn not only to live by the Spirit, but, as those who are made free from the power of the flesh, by its crucifixion, preserved by faith, to walk by the Spirit in every daily task.

Blessed God, I beseech Thee to reveal to me the full meaning of what Thy word has been teaching me, that it is as one who has crucified the flesh with its passions and lusts that I can walk by the Spirit.

O my Father, teach me to see that all that is of nature and of self is of the flesh; that the flesh has been tested by Thee and found wanting, worthy of nothing but the curse and death. Teach me that my Lord Jesus led the way, and acknowledged the justice of Thy curse, that I too might be willing and have the power to give it up to the cross as an accursed thing. Oh, give me grace day by day greatly to fear before Thee, lest I allow the flesh to intrude into the work of the Spirit, and to grieve Him. And teach me that the Holy Spirit has indeed been given to be the life of my life, and to fill my whole being with the power of the death and the life of my blessed Lord living in me.

Blessed Lord Jesus, who didst send Thy Holy Spirit to secure the uninterrupted enjoyment of Thy presence and Thy saving power within us, I yield myself to be entirely Thine, to live wholly and only under His leading. I do with my whole heart desire to regard the flesh as crucified and accursed. I solemnly consent to live as a crucified one. Saviour, Thou dost accept my surrender; I trust in Thee to keep me this day walking through the Spirit. Amen.

SUMMARY

1. The power of Christ's life cannot work in me apart from the power of His death. His death alone deals effectually with the flesh, with self, with the natural life, to make way for the new life, the Holy Spirit. We must pray to see how entirely the flesh must die, how actually and entirely the Holy Spirit must cast out your self-life, if He is to reveal in you the Christ-life.

2. Many will say that calling the flesh, the natural man, the life of self—an accursed thing, is a hard saying. Oh, it is easy to encircle the cross with flowers, and say a thousand beautiful things about it. But what God says of it is this: The cross is a curse. The Son of God on the cross "was made a curse." If my flesh is crucified, it can only be because it is accursed. It is a blessed moment in a life when a man gets a sight of what a cursed thing sin is. It is a still more blessed thing, and may work a deeper humiliation, when God shows a man what an accursed thing the flesh is, and how he has cherished it, and for its sake grieved the Holy Spirit of God.

3. The flesh and the Spirit are the two powers. Under the rule of either, every act is done. Let our every step be a walk after and through the Spirit.

4. The death of Christ led to the glory where He received and gave the Holy Spirit. It is a life where death to the flesh is the ruling principle in which the power of the Spirit can be revealed.

5. "And the Church, walking in the fear of the Lord, and in the comfort of the Holy Ghost, was multiplied." A deep, lowly fear of the holy presence within, a fear of listening to self instead of Him, is one secret of walking in the comfort of the Holy Ghost. "Be, then, in the fear of the Lord all the day long."

Note

1. In *The Law of Liberty in the Spiritual Life*, by Rev. E. H. Hopkins, there is a singularly clear and scriptural exposition of the life of faith. The chapters on conformity to the death of Christ and on conflict are most helpful to the right understanding of the relation of the believer to the flesh and the Spirit.

29

THE SPIRIT OF LOVE

But the fruit of the Spirit is love. . . .—Gal. 5:22
I beseech you . . . for the love of the Spirit.—Rom. 15:30
Who also declared unto us your love in the Spirit. —Col. 1:8

Our subject in this chapter leads us up into the very center of the inner sanctuary. We are to think of the love of the Spirit. We must learn that love is not only one of the graces of the Spirit, nor is it only the chief among them, but the Spirit is nothing less than the divine love itself come down to dwell in us, and we have only as much of the Spirit as we have of love.

God is a Spirit: God is love. In these two words we have the only attempt that Scripture makes to give us, in human language, what may be called a definition of God.[1] As a Spirit, He has life in himself, is independent of all around Him, and has power over all to enter into it, to penetrate it with His own life, to communicate himself to it. It is through the Spirit that God is the Father of spirits, that He is the God of creation, that He is the God and redeemer of man. Everything owes its life to the Spirit of God. And this is so because God is love. Within himself He is love, as seen in the Father giving all He has to the Son, and the Son seeking all He has in the Father. In this life of love between the Father and the Son, the Spirit is the bond of fellowship. The Father is the loving one, the fountain; the Son, the beloved one, the great reservoir of love, ever receiving and ever giving back; the Spirit, the living love that makes them one. In Him the divine life of love has its ceaseless flow and overflowing. The same love with which the Father loves the Son rests on us and seeks to fill us also. It is through the Spirit that this love of God is revealed and communicated to us. In Jesus it was the Spirit that led Him to the work of love for which He was anointed—to preach glad tidings to the poor and deliverance to the captives. Through that same Spirit

He offered himself as a sacrifice for us. The Spirit comes to us laden with all the love of God and of Jesus. The Spirit is the love of God.

When that Spirit enters us, His first work is, "The love of God is shed abroad in our hearts by the Holy Ghost which was given unto us." What He gives is not only the faith or the experience of how greatly God loves, but something infinitely more glorious. The love of God, as a spiritual existence, as a living power, enters our hearts. It cannot be otherwise, for the love of God exists in the Spirit; the outpouring of the Spirit is the inpouring of love. This love now possesses the heart—the same love with which God loves Jesus, ourselves, and all His children; the love which overflows to all the world is within us, and if we know it and trust it and yield to it, it is the power to live in love. The Spirit is the life of the love of God; the Spirit in us is the love of God taking up abode within us.

Such is the relation between the Spirit and the love of God; let us now consider the relation between our spirit and love. We must here again refer to what has been said of man's threefold nature—body, soul, and spirit, as constituted in creation and disorganized by the Fall![2] We saw how the soul, as the seat of self-consciousness, was to be subject to the spirit, the seat of God-consciousness. We have seen how sin is simply self-assertion—the soul refusing the rule of the spirit in order to gratify itself in the lust of the body. The fruit of that sin was that self ascended the throne of the soul—to rule there instead of God in our spirits. Selfishness thus became the ruling power in man's life. The self that had refused God His right, at the same time refused fellowman his due, and the terrible story of sin in the world is simply the history of the origin, the growth, the power, and the reign of self. It is only when the original order is restored, when the soul gives the spirit the precedence it claims, the self is denied to make way for God, that selfishness will be conquered, and love toward our brother flow from our love toward God. In other words, as the renewed spirit becomes the abode of the Spirit of God and His love, and as the regenerate man yields himself to let the Spirit have complete sway, that love will again become our life and our joy. To every disciple the Master says here again, "Let him deny self, and follow me." Many have sought in vain to follow Jesus in His life of love, but could not because they have neglected what is so indispensable—self-denial. Self following Jesus always fails, because it cannot love as He loves.

If we understand this, we are prepared to admit the claim that Jesus makes, *and that the world makes,* that the proof of discipleship is *love.* The change we have undergone is so divine, the deliverance from the power of self and sin so complete, the indwelling of the Spirit of God's love so real and true, the provision thus made to enable us to live so sufficiently that love (or the new commandment as the fulfilling of the law) ought to be the natural outflow of the new life in every believer. If it is not so, it is simply another proof of how little believers understand their calling to walk after the Spirit—to be spiritual men. The complaints or confessions that are made by ourselves or others, of tempers unconquered, selfishness, harsh judgments, unkind words, the lack of a Christlike meekness, patience and gentleness, or of the little that is being done by the majority of Christians in the way of self-sacrifice for the perishing—all this is simply the proof that we do not yet understand that to be a Christian means to have the Spirit of Christ. It means to have His love, to have been made by Him a fountain of love springing up and flowing out in streams of living water. We don't know what the Spirit is meant to be in us, because we have not accepted Him for what the Master meant Him to be in us. We are more carnal than spiritual.

It was thus with the Corinthians. In them, we see the remarkable phenomenon of a church, "in everything enriched in Christ, in all utterance, and all knowledge, coming behind in no gift, abounding in everything in faith, and utterance, and knowledge," and yet so sadly lacking in love. The sad spectacle teaches us how, under the first movings of the Holy Spirit, the natural powers of the soul—knowledge, faith, utterance—may be greatly affected, without self being yet fully surrendered; and how thus many of the gifts of the Spirit may be seen, while the chief of all, love, is sadly lacking. It teaches us how to be truly spiritual. It is not enough for the Spirit to take hold of these natural soul-endowments and arouse them to action in God's service. Something more is needed. He has entered the soul, that through it He may obtain a firm and undivided sway in both soul and spirit, that with self deposed God may reign. The sign that self is deposed and that God does reign will be love—the surrender and the power to count nothing life but love, a life in the love of the Spirit.

The state of the Galatians was not very different, to whom the words, "The fruit of the Spirit is love," were addressed. Though their error was not that of the Corinthians—boasting of gifts and knowledge, but seeking after and trusting in carnal observances and ordinances—the result in both was the same—the Spirit's full dominion was not accepted in the inner life of love, and so the flesh ruled in them, causing bitterness and envy and enmity. Even today it is still in much of what bears the name of the Christian Church. On the one hand, there is the trust in gifts and knowledge, in soundness of creed and earnestness of work; on the other hand, the satisfaction in forms and services leaves the flesh in full vigor—not crucified with Christ—and so the Spirit is not free to work out true holiness or a life in the power of Christ's love. Let us learn the lesson and pray very fervently that God will teach it to His people, that a church or a Christian professing to have the Holy Spirit must prove it, in the first place, by the exhibition of a Christ like love. Both in its gentleness in bearing wrong and in its life of self-sacrifice to overcome wrong—to save all who are under its power—the life of Christ must be repeated in His members. The Spirit is indeed the love of God come down to us.

As searching and sacred as this truth is in this aspect, likewise it is comforting and encouraging in another. The Spirit is the love of God come down to us. We have that love within our reach; it is indeed dwelling within us. Since the day when, by believing, we were sealed with the Holy Ghost, the love of God has been shed abroad in our hearts. "The love of God hath been shed abroad in our hearts, through the Holy Ghost which was given unto us." Though there may have been little of it seen in our lives, though we ourselves may hardly have felt or known it, though the blessing may have been unrecognized, there it was—with the Holy Spirit came down the love of God into our hearts—the two could never be separated. If we would come now to the experience of the blessing, we must begin by a very simple faith in what the Word says. The Word is Spirit-breathed, the divinely prepared organ through which the Spirit reveals what He is and does. As we take that Word as divine truth, the Spirit will make it truth in us. Let us believe that the Holy Spirit, possessor and bearer to us of all of God's love, has been within our heart with all of that love ever since we became God's children. Because the veil of the flesh has never been rent in us, the outpouring and power of that love has been weak and hidden from our consciousness. Let us believe that He dwells within us to reveal within us, as the power of our life, the love of God.

In the faith that the love-shedding Spirit is within us, let us look up to the Father in earnest prayer, to plead for His mighty working in our inner man; that Christ may dwell in our hearts; that we may be rooted and grounded in love; that our whole life may have its strength and nourishment in love. As the answer comes, the Spirit will first reveal to us the love of God—the love of the Father to Christ, the same as His love to us; the love of Christ to us, the same with which the Father loved Him. Through the same Spirit this love then rises and returns to its source, as our love to God and Christ. Because that Spirit has revealed that same love to all God's children, our experience of it coming from God or returning to God, is equal with our love to the brethren. As the water descending in rain, flowing out as fountains or streams, and rising up to heaven again as vapor is all one, so is the love of God in its threefold form—His love to us, our love to Him, and our love to our brethren. The love of God is within you by the Holy Spirit. Believe it, rejoice in it; yield yourself to it as a divine fire consuming the sacrifice and lifting it heavenward. Exercise and practice it in fellowship with everyone on earth. Then you shall understand and prove that the Spirit of God is the love of God.

Blessed Lord Jesus, in holy reverence I bow before Thee as love incarnate. The Father's love gave thyself. Thy coming was a mission of love. Thy whole life was love; Thy death its divine seal. The one commandment Thou gavest Thy disciples was love. Thy one prayer before the throne is that Thy disciples may be one, as Thou with the Father, and that

His Love may be in them. The one chief trait of Thy likeness that Thou longest to see in us, is that we love even as Thou lovest. The one irresistible proof to the world of Thy Divine mission will be the love of Thy disciples to each other. And the Spirit that comes from Thee to us is the very Spirit of Thy self-sacrificing love, teaching Thy saints to live and die for others, as Thou didst.

Holy Lord Jesus, look upon Thy Church, look upon our hearts. And wherever Thou seest that there is not love like Thine, oh, make haste and deliver Thy saints from all that is still selfish and unloving! Teach them to yield that self, which cannot love, to the accursed cross, to await the fate it deserves. Teach us to believe that we can love, because the Holy Spirit hath been given us. Teach us to begin to love and serve, to sacrifice self and live for others, that love in action may learn its power, may be increased and perfected. Oh, teach us to believe that because Thou livest in us, Thy love is in us too, and we can love as Thou dost. Lord Jesus, Thou love of God! Thine own Spirit is within us; oh, let Him break through, and fill our whole life with love! Amen.

SUMMARY

1. The way whereby the Spirit works any grace in the believer is by stirring them up to act upon it. The Spirit of God does not effectually work love, or give strength to love, until we act upon it; because all inward graces are discerned by their acts, as seed in the ground is by its springing up. We cannot see or feel any such thing as love to God or man in our hearts before we act upon it. We do not know our spiritual strength, except as we use and exercise it.

2. "The love of God," the fount from which flows love to men, "hath been shed abroad in our hearts through the Holy Ghost which was given unto us." The love is there, but we may remain ignorant of it, unless we begin in the faith that we have the power to obey the command, and to love God and man with our whole heart. Faith and obedience ever precede the conscious enjoyment and experience of the Spirit's power. As God is love to you, be love to all around you. "I beseech you, by the love of the Spirit."

3. Let us now seek to keep the two sides of the truth in

harmony. On the one hand, wait often in God's holy presence for the quickening of your faith and consciousness that the love-shedding Holy Spirit does dwell in you; does fill you. On the other hand, give yourself, apart from what you feel, to a whole-hearted obedience to the command of love, and act out in your life the gentleness and forebearance, the kindliness and helpfulness, the self-sacrifice and benevolence of Christ Jesus. Live in the love of Jesus, and you will be a messenger of His love to every disciple of His you meet, to everyone who does not yet know Him. The more intimate your communion with Jesus, and the more the life of heaven is through the Holy Spirit, the more accurate will be your translation of that life into the relationships of daily life.

4. "No man hath beheld God at any time! If we love one another, God abideth in us!" The compensation for not beholding God is this: we have one another to love! If we do this, God abideth in us! We don't need to ask if our brother is worthy: God's love to us and to him is love to the unworthy. It is with this love, the divine love, that the Holy Spirit fills us, teaching us to love the brethren with it.

Notes

1. The third expression of the same sort—God is light—is a figurative one.
2. See Note 3, p. 227.
3. See Note 16, p. 278.

30

THE UNITY OF THE SPIRIT

. . . that ye walk . . . with all lowliness and meekness, with longsuffering, forbearing one another in love; endeavoring to keep the unity of the Spirit in the bond of peace. There is one body, and one Spirit.—Eph. 4:1-4

198

> Now there are diversities of gifts, but the same
> Spirit. . . . All these worketh that one and the self-
> same Spirit, dividing to every man severally even as
> He will. For by one Spirit are we all baptized into one
> body; and have been all made to drink into one Spir-
> it.—1 Cor. 12:4, 11, 13

We know how, in the first three chapters of Ephesians,
Paul had set forth the glory of Christ Jesus as the head of the
Church, and the glory of God's grace in the Church as the
body of Christ indwelt by the Holy Spirit, growing up into
an habitation of God through the Spirit, and destined to be
filled with all the fullness of God. Having thus lifted the believer to his true place in the heavenlies with his life hidden
in Christ, he comes with him, down to his life on earth, and
in the second half of the epistle teaches how he is to walk
worthily of his calling. The very first lesson he has to give in
regard to this life and walk on earth (Eph. 4:1-4) rests on the
foundation truth that the Holy Spirit has united him not
only to Christ in heaven, but to Christ's body on earth. The
Spirit dwells not only in Christ in heaven and in the believer
on earth, but particularly in Christ's body with all its members; and the full, healthy action of the Spirit can only be
found where the right relation exists between the individual
and the whole body—as far as he knows or comes into contact with it. His first concern in his holy walk must be,
therefore, to endeavor to maintain the unity of the Spirit. If
this unity of the Spirit and body were fully acknowledged,
the principal virtues of the Christian life would be lowliness
and meekness (vv. 2, 3), in which each would deny self for
the sake of others, and all would forbear one another in love
amid all differences and shortcomings. So the new commandment would be kept, and the Spirit of Christ—the
Spirit of love—sacrificing itself wholly for others, would
have free scope to do His blessed work.

The need of such teaching is remarkably illustrated by
the first Epistle to the Corinthians. In that church there
were abundant operations of the workings of the Holy Spirit.
The gifts of the Spirit were strikingly manifested, but the
graces of the Spirit were remarkably absent. They did not
understand that there are diversities of gifts, but the same
Spirit; that amid all differences, one and the same Spirit di-

vides to each severally as He will; that all had been baptized into one Spirit, into one body, and all made to drink of one Spirit. They didn't know the more excellent way—that the chief of all the gifts of the Spirit is the love that seeks not its own, and only finds its life and its happiness in others.

To each believer who would fully yield himself to the leading of the Spirit, as well as to the Church as a whole, in its longings for the experience in power of all that the indwelling of the Spirit implies, the *unity of the Spirit* is a truth filled with rich, spiritual blessing. In previous writings I have more than once made mention of the expression of Pastor Stockmaier: "Have a deep reverence for the work of the Holy Spirit within you." That injunction needs as its complement a second one: Have a deep reverence for the work of the Holy Spirit in your brother. This is no easy thing—even Christians, advanced in other respects, often fail here. The cause is not difficult to discover. In our educational books we are taught that the faculty of discrimination—the observing of differences—is one of the earliest to be developed in children. The power of cooperation—the observing of harmony that exists amid apparent diversity—is a higher one, and comes later; as the power of organization, in its highest action, is found only in true genius. The lesson finds its most striking exemplification in the Christian life and church. We need little grace to know where we differ from other Christians or churches, to contend for our views, or to judge their errors in doctrine or conduct. But this indeed is grace, when amid conduct that tries or grieves us, or teaching that appears to us unscriptural or hurtful, we always give place to the unity of the Spirit, and have faith in the power of love to maintain the living union in the face of apparent separation.

Keep the unity of the Spirit: such is God's command to every believer. It is the new commandment, to love one another, in a new form, tracing the love back to the Spirit by which it has life. If you would obey the command, note carefully that it is the unity of *the Spirit*. There is a unity of creed or custom, of church or choice, in which the bond is more of the flesh than of the Spirit. If you would keep the unity of the Spirit, remember the following things:

First, seek to know that the Spirit in you is the means by

which the unity finds its power of attachment and victory. There is much in you that is of self and of the flesh that can excel in a unity that is of this earth, but that will greatly hinder the unity of the Spirit. Confess that it is not by power or love of your own that you can love; all that is of yourself is selfish and does not promote the true unity of the Spirit. Be humbled by the thought that it is only God in you that can ever unite with what appears displeasing to you. Be thankful for the fact that He is in you—He can conquer self and love even what seems unloving.

Seek to know and appreciate the spirit in your brother, with whom you are to be united. As in you, so also in him, there is but a beginning, a hidden seed of the divine life, surrounded by much that is yet carnal—often trying and displeasing. We need a heart humbled by the fact that we are unworthy, a heart loving and quick to excuse our brother—for so did Jesus on the last night: "the spirit indeed is willing, but the flesh is weak." We need to look persistently at what there is in our brother of the image and Spirit of the Father. Esteem him not by what he is in himself, but by what he is in Christ. As you sense how the same life and Spirit, which you owe to free grace, is in him too, the unity of the Spirit will triumph over the prejudice and lack of love that is of the flesh. The Spirit in you, acknowledging and meeting the Spirit in your brother, will bind you in the unity of a life that is from above.

Keep this unity of the Spirit in active exercise of fellowship. The bond among the members of my own body is most living and real, maintained by the circulation of the blood and the life it carries. "In one Spirit we were all baptized into one body. There is one body and one Spirit." The inner union of life must find expression and be strengthened in the manifested communion of love. Cultivate fellowship not only with those who are of the same way of thinking and worshipping as yourself, lest the unity be more in the flesh than the Spirit. Endeavor, in all your thoughts and judgments of other believers, to exercise the love that thinks no evil. Never say an unkind word of a child of God, nor of others. Love every believer, not for the sake of how he is in agreement with you or pleasing to you, but for the sake of the Spirit of the Father which is in him. Give yourself expressly and of set purpose to love and labor for God's children within your reach, who through ignorance, or weakness, or waywardness, don't know that they have the Spirit, or are grieving Him. The work of the Spirit is to build up habitation for God; yield yourself to the Spirit in you to do the work. Recognize your dependence upon the fellowship of the Spirit in your brother, and his dependence upon you, and seek to grow with him in the unity of love.

Take your part in the united intercession that rises up to God for the unity of His Church. Take up and continue the intercession of the great high priest for all who believe: "that they may be one." The Church is one in the life of Christ and the love of the Spirit. It is not yet one in the manifested unity of the Spirit. Hence the need of the command: Keep the unity. Plead with God for the mighty workings of His Spirit in all lands and churches and circles of believers. When the tide is low, each little pool along the shore with its inhabitants is separated from the other by a rocky barrier. As the tide rises, the barriers are flooded over, and all meet in one great ocean. So it will be with the church of Christ. As the Spirit of God comes, according to the promise—as floods upon the dry ground—each will know the power in himself and in others, and self will disappear as the Spirit is known and honored.

How is this wondrous change to be brought about, and the time hastened that the prayer be fulfilled: "That they all may be one, that the world may know that thou hast sent me, and hast loved them as thou hast loved me"? Let each of us begin with himself. Resolve even now, beloved child of God, that this shall be the one mark of your life, the proof of your sonship—having and knowing the indwelling Spirit. If you are to unite, not with what pleases you, or is in harmony with your way of thinking and acting, but with what the Spirit in you sees and seeks in others, you must give yourself entirely to His way of thinking and acting. And if you are to do this, He must have control of your whole being. You need to abide in the living and never-ceasing consciousness that He dwells within you. You need to pray unceasingly that the Father may grant you, according to the riches of His glory, to be strengthened with might by His Spirit in the inner man. It is in the faith of the Triune God, the Father giving the Spirit and the Spirit dwelling within you; it is in this faith, adoring at the footstool of God's throne; it is in direct contact and fellowship with the Father and the Son, that the Spirit will take full possession and pervade your entire being. The fuller His indwelling and the greater His working is, the more truly spiritual your being becomes, the more self sinks away, and the Spirit of Christ uses you in building up and binding together believers into an habitation of God. Christ's Spirit will be in you the holy anointing, the oil of consecration, to set you apart and fit you to be, as Christ was, a messenger of the Father's love. In the humility of daily life, in the forebearance of love amid differences and difficulties in the Church, in the sympathy and self-sacrifice that finds and helps all who need help, the Spirit in you will prove that He belongs to all the members of the body as much as to you. Through you His love reaches out to all around to teach and to bless.

Blessed Lord Jesus, in Thy last night on earth Thy one prayer for Thy disciples was: "Holy Father, keep them, that they may be one." Thy one desire was to see them a united flock, all gathered and kept together in the one almighty hand of love. Lord Jesus, now Thou art on the throne; we come to Thee with the same plea: Oh, keep us, that we may be one! Pray for us, Thou great high priest, that we may be made perfect in one that the world may know that the Father hath loved us as He loved Thee.

Blessed Lord, we thank Thee for the signs that Thou art awakening in Thy Church the desire for the manifestation to the world of the unity of Thy people. Grant, we pray Thee, to this end, the mighty workings of Thy Holy Spirit. May every believer know the Spirit that is in him and that is in his brother, and in all lowliness and love keep the unity of the Spirit with those with whom he comes into contact. May all the leaders and guides of Thy Church be enlightened from above that the unity of the Spirit may be more to them than all human bonds of union in creed or church order. May all who have put on the Lord Jesus, above all things put on love, the bond of perfectness.

Lord Jesus, we do beseech Thee, draw Thy people in united prayer to the footstool of Thy throne of glory, whence

Thou givest Thy Spirit to reveal Thy presence to each as present in all. Oh, fill us with Thy Spirit, and we shall be one—one Spirit and one body! Amen.

SUMMARY

1. The health of every member, even every particle of my body, depends upon the health of the surrounding portion. Either the healing power of the sound part must expel what is unhealthy, or this will communicate its disease. I am more dependent upon my brother than I know. He is more dependent on me than I know. The Spirit I have is the Spirit of Christ dwelling in my brother also. All I receive is meant for him too. To keep the unity of the Spirit in active exercises, to live in loving fellowship with believers around me, is the life in the Spirit.

2. " 'That they may be made perfect in one.' They approach perfection as they approach unity. Perfection is impossible in a state of separation. My life is not wholly given to me, but a part of it is given to my brother, to be available to me when I abide in him."—Bowen

3. It has taken you time and prayer and faith to know the Spirit of God within you; it will take time and prayer and faith, and much love, to know fully the Spirit of God in your brother.

4. "It is only in the unity of the body that the Spirit of God can fully and mightily display His power, either in the Church or to the world. God speaks to groups of men as He never speaks to individuals; there is a fuller tone, a more intense fervor, in Pentecostal revelations than in private worship, and as we ourselves know, there is a keener joy in communion than can be realized even in the most devout solitude."—*The Paraclete*

31

FILLED WITH THE SPIRIT

Be filled with the Spirit; speaking to yourselves in
psalms and hymns. . . . —Eph. 5:18, 19

These words are a command. They teach us, not what
the state of apostles or ministers ought to be, but what
should be the ordinary, consistent experience of every true-
hearted believer. It is the privilege that every child of God
may claim from his Father—to be filled with the Spirit.
Nothing less will enable him to live the life he has been redeemed for—abiding in Christ, keeping His commandments, and bearing much fruit. And yet, how seldom this
command has been counted among those which all ought to
keep! How seldom it has been thought possible or reason-
able that all should be expected to keep it!

One reason for this is, undoubtedly, that the words have
been misunderstood. Because on the day of Pentecost and
on subsequent occasions, being filled with the Spirit was accompanied with manifest enthusiasm of a supernatural joy
and power, such a state has been looked upon as one of ex-
citement and strain—quite inconsistent with the quiet
course of ordinary life. The suddenness, strength, and outward manifestation of the divine impulse were so linked
with the idea of being filled with the Spirit that it was
thought to be something for special occasions, a blessing
possible to only a very few. Christians felt they could not or
need not venture to fix their hopes so high; as if, were the
blessing given to them, it would be impossible in their circumstances to maintain it or manifest it.

The message I have to bring is that the command is indeed for every believer, and that the promise and power are
as wide as the precept. May God give us grace that our meditation on His word may awaken in our hearts, not only
strong desire, but the firm assurance that the privilege is
meant for us, that the way is not too hard, that the blessing

will actually become our own.

In a country like South Africa, where they often suffer from drought, they have two types of dams or reservoirs made for halting and storing water. On some farms there is a fountain, but a stream too weak to irrigate with. There a reservoir is made for collecting the water, and the filling of the reservoir is the result of the gentle, quiet inflow from the fountain day and night. In other cases, the farm has no fountain at all; the reservoir is built in the bed of a stream or in a hollow where, when rain falls, the water can be collected. In such a place, the filling of the reservoir, with a heavy rainfall is often the work of a very few hours, and is accompained with a rush and violent flow. The noiseless supply of the former farm is, at the same time, the more certain, because the supply, though apparently weak, is permanent. In tracts where the rainfall is uncertain, a reservoir may stand empty for months or years.

We can compare this to the way in which the fullness of the Spirit comes. As on the day of Pentecost, there are times when new beginnings are made—an outpouring of the Spirit of conversion in heathen lands, or of revival among Christian people—suddenly, mightily, manifestly, men are filled with the Holy Ghost. In the enthusiasm and the joy of the newly found salvation, the power of the Spirit is undeniably present. And yet, for those who receive it this way, there are special dangers. The blessing is often greatly dependent on the fellowship with others, or extends only to the upper and more easily reached currents of the soul's life—the sudden is often the superficial, the depths of the will and the inner life have not been reached. There are other Christians who have never been partakers of any such marked experience, but in whom, nevertheless, the fullness of the Spirit is no less distinctly seen in the deep and intense devotion to Jesus; in a walk in the light of His countenance and the consciousness of His holy presence; in the blamelessness of a life of simple trust and obedience, and in the humility of a self-sacrificing love to all around. They are like Barnabas was—"a son of consolation, a good man, and full of the Holy Ghost."

Which of these is the true way of being filled with the Spirit? The answer is easy. There are farms on which both the above-named reservoirs are to be found, auxiliary to each other. There are even reservoirs, where the situation is favorable, in which both methods of filling are used. The regular, quiet, daily inflowing keeps them supplied in time of great drought; in time of rain they are ready to receive and store up large supplies. There are Christians who are only content with special mighty visitations: the rushing mighty wind, floods outpoured, and the baptism of fire—these are their symbols. There are others to whom the fountain springing up from within, and quietly streaming forth, appears to be the true type of the Spirit's work. Happy are they who can recognize God in both, and keep themselves always ready to be blessed in whichever way He comes!

What are the conditions of this fullness of the Spirit? God's Word has one answer—faith. It is faith alone that sees and receives the invisible, that sees and receives God himself. The cleansing from sin and the loving surrender to obedience, which were the conditions of the first reception of the Spirit, are the fruit of the faith that saw what sin is, what the blood is, and what the will and the love of God are. Of this experience we are not speaking here. This word is for believers who have been faithful to obey, but have not yet what they long for. By faith they must discover what there is that needs to be cast out. All filling requires first an emptying. I am not speaking here of the cleansing of sin and the surrender to full obedience. This is always the first essential step. But I speak now of believers who think they have done what God demands and yet fail to receive the blessing. Remember again, the first condition of all filling is emptiness. What is a reservoir but a great hollow—a great emptiness—prepared, waiting, thirsting, crying for the water to come. Any true abiding fullness of the Spirit is preceded by emptying. "I sought the blessing long and earnestly," said one, "and I wondered why it did not come. At last I found it was because there was no room in my heart to receive it." In such emptying there are various elements involved: A deep dissatisfaction with the religion we have until now had. A deep consciousness of how much there has been of the wisdom and the work of the flesh in it. A discovery, confession, and giving up of all in life that had been kept in our own hands and management, in which self had reigned; of all in which we had not thought it necessary or possible, that

Jesus should directly be consulted and pleased. A deep conviction of inability and utter helplessness to grasp or claim what is offered. A surrender, in poverty of spirit, to wait on the Lord in His great mercy and power, "according to the riches of his glory, to strengthen us mightily by his Spirit in the inner man." A great longing, thirsting, waiting, crying—a praying without ceasing for the Father to fulfill His promise in us and take full possession of us within. Such an emptying is the prerequisite to the filling.

Together with this, we need the faith which accepts, receives, and maintains the gift. It is through faith in Christ and in the Father that the divine fullness will flow into us. Of the same Ephesians, to whom the command was given, "Be filled with the Spirit," Paul said, "In Christ, having believed, ye were sealed with the Holy Spirit of promise." The command refers to what they had already received. The fountain was within them but it had to be opened up and a place made for it. It would then spring up and fill their being. Yet this was not to be in their own power. Jesus had said, "He that believeth in me, rivers of living water shall flow out of him." The fullness of the Spirit is so truly in Jesus; the receiving from Him must in reality be in the unbroken continuity of a real life-fellowship. The ceaseless inflow of the sap from Him, the living vine, must so distinctly be met by the ceaseless recipiency of a simple faith that the upspringing of the fountain within can only be as a result of our dependence on Jesus. It is by the faith of Jesus, whose baptism with the Spirit has as distinct a beginning as His cleansing with the blood, but is also maintained by as continuous a renewal, that the inflow will grow ever stronger until it becomes an overflowing.

Faith in Jesus and the constant upspringing of the Spirit will not dispense with faith in the Father's special gift and a prayer for a renewed fulfillment of His promise. For the Ephesians, who had the Spirit within them as the earnest of their inheritance, Paul prays to the Father: "that he would grant you, according to the riches of his glory, that ye may be strengthened with power through his Spirit in the inner man." The verbs both denote not a work, but an act— something done at once. The expression "according to the riches of his glory" indicates a great exhibition of the divine love

and power—something very special. They had the Spirit
indwelling them. He prayed for them that the direct intervention of the Father might give them such mighty workings
of the Spirit, such a fullness of the Spirit, that the indwelling of Christ with His life of love that passeth knowledge
might be their blessed personal experience. At the time of
the flood, the windows of heaven and the fountains of the
great deep were opened together. It is still so in the fulfillment of the promise of the Spirit: "I will pour floods upon
the dry ground." The deeper and clearer the faith in the indwelling Spirit, and the simpler the waiting on Him, the
more abundant will be the renewed outpouring of the Spirit
from the heart of the Father directly into the heart of His
waiting child.

There is one more aspect in which it is essential to remember that this fullness comes by faith. God loves to appear in a lowly and unlikely state, to clothe himself in the
garment of humility which He wants His children to love
and wear. "The kingdom of heaven is like a seed": only faith
can know what glory there is in its smallness. Likewise was
the dwelling of the Son on earth and so the indwelling of the
Spirit in the heart. He asks that we believe in Him when we
see and feel nothing. Believe that the fountain that springs
up and flows forth in living streams is within you, even when
all appears to be dry. Take time to retire into the inner
chamber of the heart, and from there send up praise and offer worship to God in the assurance of the Holy Ghost within. Take time to be still and realize His presence; let the
Spirit himself fill your spirit with this most spiritual and
heavenly of all truths—that He dwells within you. Not first
in the thoughts or feelings but in the life—deeper than
where we can see and feel, is His temple, His hidden dwelling place. When once faith knows that it has what it asks, it
can afford to be patient, and can abound in thanksgiving
even where the flesh would murmur! It can trust the unseen
Jesus and the hidden Spirit. It can believe in that little, unlikely seed—the smallest of all seeds. It can trust and give
glory to Him who is able to do exceeding abundantly above
all it can think, and can mightily strengthen the inner man
just when all appears weak and ready to faint. Believer,
don't expect the fullness of the Spirit to come in a way that

your human reasoning devises but as the coming of the Son of God, without form or comeliness, in a way that is folly to human wisdom. Expect the divine strength in great weakness; humble yourself to receive the divine wisdom which the Spirit teaches; be willing to be nothing, because God chooses "the things that are not to bring to nought the things that are." You will learn not to glory in the flesh but to glory in the Lord. In the deep joy of a life of daily obedience and childlike simplicity, you shall know what it is to be filled with the Spirit.

O my God, Thy fullness of love and glory is like a boundless ocean—infinite and inconceivable! I bless Thee that in revealing Thy Son, it pleased Thee that all the fullness of the Godhead should dwell in Him bodily, that in Him we might see that fullness in human life and weakness. I bless Thee that His Church on earth is even now, in all its weakness, His body, the fullness of Him that filleth all in all; that in Him we are made full; that by the mighty working of Thy Spirit, and the indwelling of Thy Son, and the knowledge of Thy love, we may be filled with all the fullness of God.

Blessed Father, I thank Thee that the Holy Spirit is to us the bearer of the fullness of Jesus, and that in being filled with the Spirit we are made full with that fullness. I thank thee that there have been many men on earth since Pentecost of whom Thou hast said that they were full of the Holy Ghost. O my God, make me full! Let the Holy Spirit take and keep possession of my deepest, inmost life. Let Thy Spirit fill my spirit. Let the fountain flow from Thee through all my soul's affections and powers. Let it overflow my lips, speaking Thy praise and love. Let the very body, by the quickening and sanctifying energy of the Spirit, be Thy temple, full of the divine life. Lord, my God, I believe Thou hearest me. Thou hast given it to me. I accept it as mine.

Oh, grant that throughout Thy Church the fullness of the Spirit may be sought and found, may be known and proved. Lord Jesus, our glorified king, oh, let Thy Church be full of the Holy Ghost. Amen.

SUMMARY

1. Filled with the Spirit. It is not in the emotions, not in conscious light, power, or joy, that the filling of the Spirit must first be sought, but in the hidden, inmost part, deeper than knowledge or feeling—the region to which faith gives access and where we *are* and *have* before we know or feel.

2. Would you know what it is to be filled with the Spirit? See Jesus. Look at Him on the last night: "knowing that the Father had given all things into his hands, and that he was come from God and went to God"—washing the disciples' feet. We know the deep calm of the consciousness that He was of God, in the fullness of the Spirit. Seek it therefore, and in due time it will break out in testimony, in the fellowship of the saints, or the saving of the lost.

3. Notice carefully the connection: "Be filled with the Spirit, speaking to one another." It is only in the fellowship of the body, its building up in love, that the Spirit reveals His presence. Jesus said, "The Spirit shall bear witness, and ye shall bear witness." It is in action on our part—in obedience—that the full consciousness of the Spirit's presence comes. "They were filled with the Holy Ghost, and began to speak." Having the same Spirit of faith, therefore, we speak. The fountain must spring up; the stream must flow. Silence is death.

4. "Grieve not the Holy Spirit of God." This word precedes the other: "Be filled with the Spirit." We cannot cause the life or the growth, but we can remove the hindrance. We can act in obedience; we can turn from the flesh to wait upon God; we can yield to the Spirit as far as we know God's will. *The filling comes from above.* Wait for it, tarry at the footstool of the throne in much prayer. And as you pray, believe that the unseen power has full possession of your whole being.

5. "Be filled with the Spirit." It is the duty, the calling, the privilege of every believer—a divine possibility, in virtue of the command; a divine certainty, in the power of faith. God hasten the day when every believer will believe this!

NOTE 1

The Baptism of the Spirit (Chapter 2)

The blessed promise that our Lord would baptize with the Holy Spirit has given rise to considerable difference of opinion as to the way in which its fulfillment may be expected. This is surely a proof of how much we are lacking its full experience. Where the Spirit is in great power, He would bring His own evidence that we have the baptism and what it includes. There are two diverse views in particular to which much attention has been directed of late. The one maintains that because every believer receives the Holy Spirit in regeneration, there can be no thought of a baptism of the Spirit still to be sought for. The promise was fulfilled to the Church in the gift of Pentecost, and of that heritage of the Church every believer gets his share upon believing in Christ. The opposite view holds that just as Christ's disciples, Philip's converts at Samaria, and the twelve men at Ephesus were true believers, and yet needed to receive the promised Spirit, so now every believer must seek and may expect this baptism subsequent to his conversion. A third view takes a somewhat middle ground, and while agreeing with the first, that the Holy Spirit dwells in every believer, it maintains that the believer may from time to time receive very special conscious renewals of the Spirit's presence and power from on high, and that these may justly be regarded as fresh baptisms of the Spirit. I cannot better compare the two former views than by giving extracts from two representative books: the one, *Be Filled with the Spirit; or, Scriptural Studies about the Holy Ghost*, by Rev. Ernest Boys; the other, *The Baptism of the Holy Ghost*, by Rev. Asa Mahan.

In his book, Mr. Boys goes through the whole of the New Testament noting all the passages that make reference to the Spirit, to find the answer to the question: Whether believers are already possessed by the Spirit in all His fullness and power, as a permanent and abiding presence, or whether they are to look for some particular experience called by some "the Baptism of the Spirit." He thinks that a careful study of the New Testament leads to the conclusion that *every* true believer is called, not to wait to enjoy the fullness of the Holy Spirit, but is entitled to believe that he already has the glorious privilege, and is to act accordingly. "The operations of the Holy Ghost in producing faith and regeneration we believe to be His work *on* rather than *in* the heart. How far they involve His actual entrance into the heart it is beyond our power to determine. But of this we are sure—that when there has resulted that faith which makes one the child of God, then there takes place, *in the case of everyone*, a real entrance into, and a permanent, abiding, indwelling of the Holy Spirit in the heart. Whatever be the believer's attitude and relationship towards the Spirit in matters of the Christian life and experience, he should not spend his time and prayers in seeking *a further indwelling* of the Spirit. This, in all its fullness, is a glorious fact already. But he is to enter more thoroughly into an intelligent and spiritual perception of what at present actually exists."

In speaking of the day of Pentecost, he very strongly urges the thought that in His descent then, He came permanently to dwell on earth. "In Acts 2 we have the personal descent of the Holy Ghost to take up His abode in the Church on earth, and to 'abide with it for every' (John 14:16). As the Son of God became incarnate by union with an actual human body, so there is a sense in which the Holy Ghost became incarnate also at Pentecost, uniting himself with the human bodies of men and women who believed in Christ. He has dwelt in the Church, as the body of Christ, only by dwelling in the heart of each individual who is a real member of that body, and thereby uniting him with Christ as the head. And now, we believe, it is from this earthly dwelling-place, and not, as it were, afresh from heaven, that He communicates himself afresh to each new member of the spiritual body, working also in and through the believers. Each believer is thus not only an agent, through whom the Holy Ghost manifests and carries home the reality of divine truth to others, but is also, in a certain sense, a source from which He personally communicates himself to other hearts" (John 15:26, 27; 7:38, 39).

Speaking of the prayer in Eph. 3:14-21, he writes: "In searching Scripture, we shall find that in no isolated case are believers after Pentecost exhorted to ask for the Holy

Spirit as a gift not yet received; but that the Holy Spirit, already dwelling in them, may carry on with power His various offices in the inner man." And in summing up at the conclusion, he says: "If language means anything at all, we have the constantly repeated assurance of the inspired writers, that the indwelling of the Holy Ghost is a present reality in every one who is a true child of God. . . . It must be confessed, however, that there is very little indication of the Spirit's indwelling to be seen in the lives and conduct of a vast number of professing Christians. In view of things as they are in the Christian Church, it is no surprise that godly people are looking around for a remedy, and that they turn to the Holy Spirit for the answer. But we are surprised that men do not see that the secret is obvious—that the remedy is very near to them; even within them. What we want is that same, simple, childlike faith in the person of the Holy Spirit *within us*, as we have been taught to exercise in all the work of Christ on our behalf. . . . All spiritual experience springs, in the first place, from a simple belief in facts which cannot appear real to our consciousness until we simply believe them, in spite of all feelings and appearances to the contrary. Let us bring this simple and childlike faith to bear upon the truth of the Holy Spirit's indwelling in our hearts, and let us start afresh on a life of surrender to His leadings, and in the realization of the scripture exhortations which have been unfolded in the previous chapters. So shall we find the true secret of happiness, of holiness, of spiritual power—which is, daily and hourly to be filled with the Spirit."

I have purposely quoted quite extensively, both because I wish to emphasize the deep importance of the aspect of truth here presented, and to present how that it is in fact only one side of the truth. In connection with the former subject, I may say that for a conference held in the course of this year, at which some twenty-seven ministers met and spent six days in prayer and study on the work of the Holy Spirit, a copy of Mr. Boys' book had been sent to each member some weeks before. When we met, more than one testified to the blessing that had been received in reading it. There was one passage to which one testified as having been a great blessing to him, and by which others had been impressed as making clear the position we ought to take towards the Holy Spirit, without which our prayers for His workings would be of little avail. Mr. Boys writes: "If we were asked very briefly the true meaning of being 'filled with the Spirit,' we should say that it involved *not our having 'more of the Spirit,' but rather the Spirit having more of us.* There is a vast difference between the two; and many who earnestly seek this fullness of the Spirit fail to see this. They are longing, waiting, praying for God to give them something more; when, in order to be 'filled with the Spirit,' they must *give Him* something more than they have already given." Not many days later a similar testimony was received from one who had not been able to come, but who wrote of the book having been to him like a new revelation, to see that he had all of the Holy Ghost he needed to have or ever could have. I am certain that there are many Christians, and many ministers in Christ's Church, in whom this is the one thing lacking—the living faith that the Spirit is dwelling within them, equal to every emergency, and only waiting to be allowed a more entire possession and a more complete control. In our evangelical preaching we need to have every young convert fully instructed in this truth, that the only living assurance of acceptance, the only power of holiness and fruitfulness, the only possibility of the enjoyment of Christ's presence and indwelling are to be found in the faith of the indwelling Spirit.

Let us now turn to the other side. In Dr. Mahan's book, *The Baptism of the Holy Ghost,* we have an entirely different aspect of God's truth from one who equally desires only to know what the mind of God in Scripture is. A few sentences from the preface to a new edition will make his position clear. Referring to John 14:15-17, he writes: "The Holy Spirit had convinced the disciples of sin, had induced them to believe in Christ, to love Him, and to keep His commandments. From the hour of their conversion He had been with them, and their bodies had been His temples. During the ten days these disciples waited at Jerusalem, awaiting the promise of the Father, the same Spirit was with them still— perfecting their obedience, intensifying their aspirations, unifying their accord, and completing their preparation for the inward enlightenments and enduements of power which were the result from the approaching baptism. All that preceded Pentecost was preparatory to this baptism, but no part of it. Their conversion and subsequent preparation were the work of the Spirit just as much as the baptism, and the former was indispensable to the latter. Had the apostles continued in the preparatory stage of their experience, or had they gone forth to the work prior to the reception of the promise of the Spirit, the world would never have felt their influence. Waiting, on the other hand, 'the promise of the Father,' and going forth as Christ did, 'in the power of the Spirit,' they soon turned the world upside down.

"The same holds true of all believers, the least as well as the greatest, under the present dispensation—the dispensation of the Spirit. As with the apostles and their associates, so with every believer in Jesus. After inducing repentance toward God and faith toward our Lord Jesus Christ, the Spirit abides with and works in him, as He did in them prior to Pentecost, and this for the one purpose, to perfect his love and obedience and inward preparation that 'the Holy Ghost may fall on him as he did on them at the beginning.' If the convert stops short of this consummation, and if he does this particularly under the belief that he did receive the baptism of the Holy Ghost in conversion, he will almost inevitably remain through life in the weakness and darkness of the old dispensation, instead of going forward to his life-work under the enduement of power and spiritual illuminations characteristic of the new dispensation.

"Here this great doctrine is met by the counter one, that every new-born soul does receive the promised baptism of the Spirit, and all accompanying enduements of power at the time of his conversion. In confirmation of this doctrine such passages are presented which affirm that 'all have been baptized into one body,' and that the bodies of all believers are 'temples of the Holy Ghost.' All this, we teach, is true of every convert now, and has been true of every converted person since the Fall. The apostles must have had the Spirit of Christ, or they could not have been His. Yet, in the New Testament sense of the word, 'the Holy Ghost was not yet given,' and they were not 'baptized with the Holy Ghost' until Pentecost had fully come. So, of all converts in this dispensation, they have the Spirit of Christ, and their bodies are His temples. This was true of all the converts in Samaria before Peter and John came there. Yet the Holy Ghost had not fallen upon one of them. How any person can contemplate the revealed results of the baptism of the Holy Ghost, and then affirm in the presence of obvious facts, that every such convert has received the 'enduement of power' included in 'the promise of the Spirit,' is a mystery of mysteries to us. Language is without meaning if 'the promise of the Spirit' does not await the believer after he has entered into a state of justification, and then in a state of 'love and obedience,' and supreme consecration to Christ, 'tarries' before God until he is 'endued with power from on high.' "

In this statement of scriptural truth we have perfect agreement with the previous one on the one great point, that every believer has the Holy Spirit dwelling in him, that he ought to know this, and believe that the Spirit will work in him what he needs for further growth and strength. The difference arises when the question comes to the way in which the believer is to attain the full experience of all that the indwelling of the Spirit implies. While the former answer is: Believe that He is within you, open up and surrender your whole being to Him, He will fill you; the second says, Wait before the throne for this filling as a special, distinct gift, the fulfillment of the Father's promise.

Let me say right now, that if it is maintained, in connection with this second view, that every believer must consciously seek and receive, as a distinct experience, such a baptism, this does not appear to me what the Word of God teaches. But if it be put in this way, that in answer to believing prayer many believers have received, and those who seek it will often receive, such an inflow of the Spirit of God as will to them indeed be nothing less than a new baptism of the Spirit, I cannot but regard it as in harmony with the teaching of Scripture. I have already expressed my deep sense of the truth and value of the positive part of the teaching in Mr. Boys' book, but with the extent to which he goes in denying that we should still pray for the Spirit I can hardly agree, and am anxious to point out how, as it appears to me, there are aspects of the truth in God's Word with which his view must still be supplemented.

There is one truth, which I cannot help but think he has

somewhat lost sight of. In a passage quoted above, he speaks very strongly about the Spirit having come to this earth, and taken up His abode in the body of Christ, the Church; so much so, that all communications of the Spirit to the unconverted come through believers. This is an aspect of truth of utmost importance, and far too little realized. But there is another aspect that we must not lose sight of. The Spirit is the Spirit of God. He is not only in the Church, *but also in the Father and the Son.* The Father, the Son, and His body, the Church: the Spirit is the one life in which these have their fellowship. God has not given His Spirit to believers in the sense of parting with Him; nor has He given to the extent that He need not give anymore.[1] By no means. All divine giving is in the power of eternal life, the power of a continuous life-flow from God through Christ to His people. And it is therefore consistent with the fullest acknowledgment of the Spirit dwelling in us that the believer calls for more. I admit and regret that there is a great deal of prayer in which the presence of the Spirit is forgotten, even ignored, and I deeply feel the loss which the Church suffers as a result of it. And yet it would be falling into the other extreme if, because God has given and we have received the Spirit, we were no longer to pray for more of Him.

It is often said, "But how can you ask for that which you already have?" The answer is a very simple one. The fingers that hold the pen with which I write are as full of blood as can be in perfect health; and yet, if they could speak, would we not continually hear them calling to the heart, "Send in fresh blood, without which we cannot live!" The branch that hangs full of fruit is as full of sap as it can hold, and yet it unceasingly pleads its emptiness and needs to the vine for that unceasing supply, without which the fruit could not be ripened. The lungs are full of breath, and yet call for a fresh supply every moment. And so it is with the believer, who understands that he does not have the Spirit as a power he can use or dispose of, or as a person who renders him independent of the Son. It is the Spirit who brings us into a living connection with Christ and an ever-increasing dependence upon Him. Our whole life of prayer must be in harmony with a faith that acknowledges the Spirit that has been received, and yet always waits for His fuller inflow out of Christ in whom His fullness dwells.

We see this union of having and asking in the life of the Son. He knew that the Father had given Him all things, even that the Father was in Him, and yet He felt the need of prayer. He had had the indwelling Spirit from His birth and yet receiving the Spirit from above at His baptism was an actual divine transaction; as He prayed, the heavens opened and the Spirit descended. We also see this in Paul's Epistles. He reminded the Ephesians that they had been sealed with the Holy Spirit of promise, and then he told them that he prayed for them that God might give them "the Spirit of wisdom and revelation." He not only asks that the Spirit in them may make them wise; he is not afraid to pray for "the Spirit of wisdom." Later on, when he asks that the Father would, "according to the riches of his glory, strengthen them with might by the Spirit," he indicates that it is not enough to know and believe that the Spirit is in us, but that through prayer to the Father the increase of the Spirit's power will come, and we shall be filled with Him. His interchange of the expression, "Give you the Spirit of wisdom," and "Give you to be strengthened with the Spirit," gives us liberty to ask in either way. But we must realize that the Spirit is already in us, and that it is only through the prayer of faith to the Father that the increased inflow of His presence and power can come. The faith that He is in us, the assurance that He wants more of us, and the knowledge that if He has us completely, He will fill us urges us to prayer to our Father, whose power it is to give the Spirit through the Son. It would surely be unfortunate if a believer, having once received the Spirit, were to feel that Christ's word, "How much more shall your heavenly Father give the Holy Spirit to them that ask him," was something he had outgrown, and that for this chief of blessings he could no longer ask. Just as the anointing with fresh oil is a daily need, so it is daily received in living fellowship with the Father through Him in whom the fullness ever abides. Likewise, the thought of Jesus baptizing with the Spirit is not to recall what is now a past thing, done once for all, but a promise of what may be a daily, continuous experience. The faith that we have the Spirit within us, even when it has almost come like a new revelation, and filled us with joy and strength, will lose its freshness and its power unless the inflow is maintained in living fellowship with the Father and the Son. The lesson of

Pentecost holds good for all ages. As our Lord is seated on the throne in glory to give the Spirit, the footstool of the throne remains the place where the Spirit is received. The deeper our faith becomes that we have the Spirit, the more continuous will be our prayer that the Father grant us His mighty workings. It is only in living communion with the Father and the Son, in the worship and prayer of faith, that the Spirit will work mightily.

These remarks may have prepared the way for what appears to me the scriptural light in which the prayer for the baptism of the Spirit may be offered, and an answer expected.

1. To the disciples, the baptism of the Spirit was distinctly not given for regeneration, but the definite communication of the presence in power of their glorified Lord.

2. Of this Spirit, with which the church of Christ was baptized, every believer is made a partaker; he has the Spirit of Christ dwelling in him.

3. Just as there was a twofold operation of the one Spirit in the Old and New Testaments, of which the state of the disciples before and after Pentecost was the most striking illustration, so there may be, and in the great majority of Christians is, a corresponding difference of experience. This difference between the bare knowledge of His presence and His full revelation of the dwelling Christ in His glory, is due either to ignorance or unfaithfulness.

4. When once the full realization of what the indwelling of the Spirit was meant to bring is brought home to the soul, and it is ready to give up all to be made a partaker of it, the believer may ask and expect what may be termed a baptism of the Spirit. Praying to the Father in accordance with the two prayers in Ephesians, and coming to Jesus in the renewed surrender of faith and obedience, he may receive such an inflow of the Holy Spirit as to be consciously lifted to a different level from the one on which he has lived until now.

5. The way in which the baptism comes may vary. To some it comes as a glad and noticeable quickening of their spiritual life. They are so filled with the Spirit that all their feelings are stirred. They can speak of something they have distinctly experienced as a gift from the Father. To others it is given, not to their feelings, but to their faith. It comes as a deep, quiet, but clearer insight into the fullness of the Spirit

in Christ as actually being theirs, and a faith that feels confident that His sufficiency is equal to every emergency that may arise. In the midst of weakness they know that His power is resting on them. In either case they know that the blessing has been given from above, to be maintained through obedience and deep dependence on Him from whom it came.

6. Such a baptism is particularly given as power for service. It may sometimes be received before the believer fully understands his calling to serve, and while he is chiefly occupied with his own sanctification. It cannot be maintained unless the call to witness for the Lord is obeyed. The baptism of Pentecost was distinctly given as preparation for service. The baptism of Cornelius and his praying company, as God's seal to their faith, and their full participation in the blessings of the kingdom of God, immediately opened their mouths to speak. We must beware of laying down fixed rules. God's gifts and love are greater than our hearts. Every believer who desires, with the light he has, to be surrendered fully to the glory of his Lord, may come and claim the fullness of the gift. It will prove its own power to open the mouth and bring forth testimony for God.

7. The preparation for the baptism is still the same as with the first disciples. Having called them to forsake all for Him, our Lord had first kept them three years in His school, training them in the knowledge, love, and obedience to His will. Great personal devotion to Jesus was the first requisite. He had then led them in the fellowship of His death, to give up all hope in themselves or in His outward appearance—all confidence in the flesh. As they were thus taught the utter insufficiency of the flesh, either in their own good purposes or His bodily presence—to conquer sin or give deliverance— the need was awakened for something higher. Last of all, He kept them, first for forty days, and then again for ten days, in waiting anticipation, looking to himself to give them something beyond what they could ask or think. With great diversity of method and degree, every believer will have to pass through some preparation not so different from what the disciples experienced. Blessed are they who allow the master himself to take them into His baptism class, to regulate their course of training, and rest content with nothing less than to be full of the Holy Ghost. To some it comes

without any idea of a baptism at all; in intense devotion to their Lord, they know that He dwells in them, and has full control of them as His own.

Whatever difference there still may be in our way of expressing what we seek, let us remember that our Father understands each of His children better than they do themselves. Let us rejoice, even amid varying methods of expression, that the desire is growing among God's people to have nothing less than what God meant by His promise of a baptism with the Holy Ghost and with fire. Let us be faithful to the Spirit, as He dwells within us. Let us stir up ourselves and each other to wait for, from our God—who is able to do above what we ask or think—an experience of His mighty inworking and His overflowing fullness in all believers, such as we cannot imagine.

---

1. "We are not to think of the 'giving' of the Spirit as an isolated deposit of what, once given, is now locally in possession. The first 'gift' is, as it were, the first step in a series of actions, of which each one may also be expressed as a gift."—Moule on Eph. 1:17

NOTE 2

The Spirit as a Person (Chapter 5)

If we are to understand the place and work of the Holy Spirit in us, we must know something of His place and work in the divine being. He has been given to make us partakers of the divine life and nature, to be in us and to do for us what He is and does in the Father and the Son. The contemplation of what He is as the Spirit of the Father and the Son in the Holy Trinity, of what He was and wrought in the man Christ Jesus on earth, and what His particular relation is to our glorified Lord Jesus, need not divert us from the practical question of what He is to ourselves. Rather it may help us greatly to realize the wondrous glory and mystery of the united gift of the Father and the Son—the Spirit of their personal life—to be the Spirit of our personal life. The following suggested quotations from one of the most deeply scriptural and spiritual theologians, J. T. Beck (in *Vorlesungen über Chr. Glaubenslehre*), may help us in our effort to apprehend what God has revealed to us in His Word. It is a blessed thing when a believer realizes, "The Spirit of God dwelleth in me," and knows that God has given him something divine—even a divine person—as his life. But it becomes a thousand-fold more wonderful to him when he begins to see that it actually is the same Spirit who is the personal life of the Father and the Son, that has now become his own personal life.

"In Christianity, revelation comes not only in the form of an elementary witness for God, as in the revelation of nature; nor only in the Old Testament revelation in the form of special legislative organization and ideal promise; but as a new life-organization of the quickening Spirit. Christianity brings a revelation in which the supernatural—the divine—is spirit and life to us earthly human beings. With this in view, it must be mediated differently than in the previous forms; it must have a higher intermediate for its revelation. If the divine is indeed dynamically and substantially a personal life to be transmitted into the human individuality, the only adequate vehicle for such a mediation would be one in which the revelation, or the divine principle of formation, could make itself personal in a human being. That is, it would not be sufficient for the divine to reveal himself in some man only, by whatever force, through the channel of conscience, any more than it would be, by way of inspiration, be sufficient to develop His power to influence and elevate the life of reason or Spirit, through the means of prophecy. Conscience and inspiration do not suffice as the means of revelation—in a revelation that is to be perfect. What is needed is a mediation, in which God concentrates His own peculiar Spirit and life as a principle in a human individual to be personally appropriated. In a revelation, which actually translates the divine into man's individual personal life, that is, to form men of God, the divine, as a personal life also, must first be embodied in a personality within humanity.

For this reason, wherever something strictly new is concerned, something that in its peculiarity has not yet existed—every new type of life, before it can multiply itself to a

number of specimens—must first have its full contents combined in perfect unity, in an adequate new principle. And
so, for the making personal of the divine among men, the
first thing needed was one in whom the principle of the divine life had become personal. Christianity concentrates the
whole fullness of revelation in the one human personality of
Jesus Christ. He is the mediator—the mediating central
principle of the new divine organism, in its fullness of Spirit
and life, in and for the human, personal life. With the entrance of Christ into the human individual, the divine life
becomes immanent in us, not in its universal world-relation,
but as a personal principle, so that man is not only $\pi o i \eta \mu a$
$\Theta \epsilon o \tilde{v}$, a being made of God, but $\tau \acute{\epsilon} \chi \nu o \nu \ \Theta \acute{\epsilon} o \tilde{v}$, or a being begotten of God. With the growing transformation of the in-
dividual into the life-type of Christ there is perfected the
development of the personal life out of God, in God, and to
God— the development not only of a moral or theocratic
communion, but a communion of nature. With the fall of
man, the divine and human in man had been rent asunder,
and the separation has grown into estrangement and enmity. Man has become an ungodly personality. In opposition to this, both the divine and the human have been reconciled and united in Christ's divine-human personality as the
human manifestation of the otherwise invisible God.

"With regard to the Spirit, it is never said of Him—the
Spirit is God, or the Spirit is Lord; but on the contrary, God
is Spirit, the Lord is the Spirit, 'the quickening Spirit.' It is
thus the Spirit, through whom God and the Lord each is *the
person that He is*, is $\Theta \epsilon \acute{o} \varsigma$, is $K \acute{v} \rho \iota o \varsigma$. But the Spirit does not
on this account belong to the divine being without an inde-
pendent existence.[1] Although He is a separate person from
the Father and the Son; He himself forms the divine personality within the Father and the Son. Outside of God, in the
world and man, He effects an independent revelation of
God, which reaches into the the hidden depths of Deity on
the one side, and on the side of man inwardly communicates
God's very own life, even to the production of a divine Son-
life. The one divine personality of THE FATHER is the all-
inclusive divine central subject, in whom the Son and Spirit, in unity of being, have a self-standing existence. The Son
is revealed as the speaking SELF of the Father, in whom He

reveals himself as in His image; the SPIRIT is revealed as the inner SELF of the Father and the Son, in whom the inner life of God in the power of its personal being, maintains and communicates itself. Because the Spirit is the bearer of the inner life of God, He does not manifest himself externally—there is no personal appearance, as of the Son. Just as in the Son the Phanerosis (manifestation) of the Father took place externally, in His outward self (John 14:19, 12:45), so in the Spirit, the inward self of the Father and the Son belong to the inner life, that the perfected Phanerosis, the manifestation of God to us, may become the Apocalypse, the revelation of God within us.

"What is needed for the redemption of human nature from its bondage to the world and sin, and the revival within of the supernatural—for which it had been destined—is such a union with the divine life, that it should be revealed in man not only as a law or a hope—as the postulate of the will or the desire, an ideal—but as an actual fulfilling of the real need of the personal life—that is, that the divine life should become the real, personal life. In virtue of its absolute worth, because of its very nature, the divine can never be satisfied with being accepted as an element only having a place in our personal thinking, willing and doing. It is not enough that, along with other things that touch and interest us, it too should have a place in our thoughts or actions, and be something from which we gain certain desirable results for our life. Such an apparently moderate or sober view drags the divine down and places it on a line with the objects of this world. Nor does it make any real difference when the divine is spoken of as the highest and most worthy of all objects. *The divine only receives its true acknowledgment when it is accepted as what it really is—the absolute world-principle—and becomes the absolute life-principle of our personal development.* The divine often has, however, no creative personal power over our bondage to the power of the world, with its sin and death. To make the divine become personal in us, under such circumstances, is not what our spiritual power, or reason, can accomplish. We need the formation of a new nature, and to form anew is the work of the Creator—the divine principle of organization in the world. This is that in which revelation finds its perfection—

in the forming of the divine as a living, creative Spirit, "the life-giving Spirit," *so that as a productive life-principle, or as the power of a personal life, it could become immanent in man's moral life. And out of that, in continuous development, the divine could be reproduced in the individual as his personal life. God, in harmony with His idea as the absolute, should be the all-determining life-principle in man*—it is in this that revelation finds its perfect completion.

"Christ as the *personal* word of God, first as the incarnate Son, had to perfectly organize His special witness and mediation before the Holy Spirit could in a new way of working, come forth from God as the Spirit immanent in the Father and the Son. As the divine personal life-principle, and as the person-constituting principle He began His life-begetting work. The divine, personal Spirit, flowing forth from the divine, personal Word, now becomes the highest principle of inspiration, which apprehends the mysteries of the kingdom, as well as the highest personal life-forming principle of a new type of man—the image of the only-begotten Son.

"The personality of Christ has its ground in the individualizing of the Spirit. It was the same in the first creation, when God breathed the Spirit of life into man and he became a living soul—a personality. Likewise in the second creation, regeneration, when through the imparting of the Spirit to man, in his consciousness or conduct, there comes into existence a new man—a new God-like personality."

Dr. Dorner, in his *System of Christian Doctrine*, writes as follows concerning the difference between the revelation of God in Christ, and in the Holy Spirit:

"The character of Christ's substitution is not negative, nor repressive of personality, but productive. He is not content with the existence in himself of the fullness of the spiritual life, into which His people are absorbed by faith. Believers are themselves to live and love as free personalities. Christ's redeeming purpose involves the creation, by the Holy Spirit, of new personalities in whom Christ gains a settled, established being. By this very means God exists in them after a new manner, not only because the power of redemption is God's being in Christ, but new also because, although Christ remains the principle of this life, the life shapes itself in freedom and distinctness from Christ. Only by means of such freedom can the bond between Christ and man become two-sided, and therefore be all the firmer—the reciprocal relationship of love. At the same time, the fullness of the Spirit of light and life, grace and truth, which dwells objectively in Christ, no longer remains merely objective to the world, but lives and unfolds itself in the world, as a living treasure of salvation. Through the Holy Spirit it comes to pass, that Christ's impulse is not simply continued and extended to men, but becomes an indigenous impulse in them, a new focus being formed for naturalized divine powers. As a new divine principle, the Holy Spirit creates, though not substantially new faculties, a new volition, knowledge, feeling; a new consciousness. In brief, He creates a new person, disabling the old union-point of the faculties, and creating a new, pure union of the same. The new personality is formed in inner resemblance to the second Adam, on the same family type, so to speak. Everything by which the new personality, in its independence, makes itself known, is ascribed by Holy Scripture to this third divine principle. Through the Holy Spirit, the believer has the consciousness of himself as a new man in the power and motivation of a holy life that is free in God. He is the Spirit of joy and freedom, as opposed to the *gramma* or letter. Subjection to the divine motivation transforms mere passivity and receptiveness into spontaneity, or productiveness and independence. Through the Holy Spirit, the individual personality is raised to a complete charismatic personality. By all these means the Holy Spirit plants and nurtures the one relatively independent factor—the presupposition of the origin of the Church, namely, the new believing personality."

This thought that the Spirit of God, as the Spirit of the divine personality, becomes the life-principle of our personality, is one of extreme importance and of infinite fruitfulness. The Spirit not only dwells in me as a locality, nor does He only embrace my inmost ego, by which I am conscious of myself, but He becomes the new and divine life-principle of the new personality. The same Spirit that was and is in Christ, His inmost self, becomes my inmost self. What new meaning it gives to the word, "He that is joined to the Lord is *one Spirit* with him!" And what force to the question,

"Know ye that *the Spirit of God* dwelleth in you?" The Holy Spirit is within me as a personal power, with a will and a purpose of His own. As I yield up my personality to His I shall not lose it, but find it renewed and strengthened to its highest capacity. We see how entirely the Spirit takes charge of that which the flesh before had charge of! We thought ourselves free, but were slaves. The Holy Spirit working out His will and purpose in me—teaching me to work it out—makes me free.

---

1. See *Leitfaden der Chr. Glaubenslehre*, p. 229: "The Spirit is so far from being, as with us, something belonging to God, that it is said: God is Spirit, the Lord is the Spirit, so that it really is just the Spirit, *through whom God is the person that He is*. The divine Spirit is not only, as with us, something belonging to and in the Father and the Son, but that very thing through which Father and Son is God; the Spirit is the personal being of God in Father and Son. Therefore He is called the holy and holymaking, the power and the quickener; in Him the very own personal being of the Father and the Son is begotten into man. It is only in the Spirit that the personal life of God is centered; so little can He himself be anything impersonal."

NOTE 3

The Place of the Indwelling (Chapters 6 and 29)

In studying the teaching of Scripture on the indwelling of the Holy Spirit, it is important to see clearly what it tells us about the place where the Spirit dwells, and the manner in which He works. And to this end we need to be particularly careful to seek correct views as to the difference between the soul and the spirit of man, and their mutual relation.

In the history of man's creation we read, "The Lord God formed man of the dust of the ground"—thus was his *body* made—"and breathed into his nostrils the breath" or spirit "of life": thus his *spirit* came from God; "and man became a *living soul*." The Spirit quickening the body made man a living soul, a living person with a consciousness of himself. The soul was the meeting-place, the point of union between body and spirit. Through the *body*, man, the living soul, stood related to the external world of sense; could influence it, or be influenced by it. Through the *spirit*, he stood related to the spiritual world and the Spirit of God, from whom he had his origin. He could be the recipient and the minister of its life and power. Standing midway between two worlds, and belonging to both, the soul had the power of determining itself, of choosing or refusing the objects by which it was surrounded, and to which it stood related.

In the constitution of these three parts of man's nature, the spirit, as linking him with the divine, was the highest; the body, connecting him with the sensible and animal, was the lowest; and the soul stood in an intermediate position, partaker of the nature of the others—the bond that united them—and through which they could interact with each other. Its work, as the central power, was to maintain them in their proper relationship; to keep the body, as the lowest, in subjection to the spirit, and receive from the divine Spirit through the human spirit, that which would perfect it; and so pass down, even to the body, the means by which it could become a spiritual body.

The wondrous gifts with which the soul was endowed, particularly those of consciousness and self-determination, or mind and will, were but the mold or vessel into which the life of the Spirit, the real substance and truth of the divine life, was to be received and assimilated. They were a God-given capacity for making the knowledge and the will of God its own. In doing this, the personal life of the soul would have become filled and possessed with the life of the Spirit—the whole man would have become spiritual. We know how the opposite of this took place. The soul yielded to the solicitations of sense, and became its slave, so that the Spirit no longer ruled, but vainly strove to vindicate for God His place until God said, "My Spirit shall not strive with man for ever, for that he also is flesh," wholly under the power of the flesh. The spirit in man became dormant—a capacity for knowing and serving God which would have to wait its time for deliverance and quickening. The soul ruled instead of the spirit, and the great mark of all religion, even in its most earnest struggles after God, is that it is the soul, man's own energy without the divine Spirit, putting forth its effort to find and to please God.

In regeneration it is this spirit of man which is quickened again and renewed. The word regeneration, or being born again, Scripture uses as that change whereby the soul passes from death to life, effected like the natural birth, at once and once for all. The word renewed is used of that continuous and progressive work by which the life of the Spirit of God enters more fully into our life, and asserts its supremacy through our entire nature.

In the regenerate man the original relation between the soul and the spirit has been restored. The spirit of man has been quickened to become a habitation of God's Spirit, who is now to teach and to lead, by communicating divine life, something substantial and real—the truth, the actual good things which Christ has for us. This divine leading into the truth by the Spirit of God takes place not in our soul or mind, in the first place, but in our spirit, in the inner recesses of a life deeper than mind or will. And it takes place only as the soul, in the confession of how blinded it has become, of how slowly its faculties really become spiritual and divinely enlightened, in the willingness to be foolish and ignorant, and in teachableness to wait on God's Spirit to give His truth in the life, yields itself to that complete supremacy of the Spirit which was its original destiny.

And now comes the most important lesson, not easy to learn, for the sake of which we have at some length spoken of the relation between the soul and spirit. The greatest danger the religion of the Church or the individual has to dread is the inordinate activity of the soul, with its power of mind and will. It has been so long accustomed to rule, that even when in conversion it has surrendered to Jesus, it too easily imagines that it is now its work to carry out that surrender, and serve the King it has accepted. Many a believer has no conception of the reality of the Spirit's indwelling, and of the extent to which *He* must get the mastery of the soul, that is, of our whole self in all our feeling and thinking and willing, so as to purge out all confidence in the flesh, and work that teachableness and submissiveness which is indispensable to the Spirit's doing His work. The call of the Master to hate our own life, not to seek it but to lose it (the word used is *psyche*—soul), is the call to give the soul, with its power of willing and acting, unto death, that it may find its true life again in the quickening and leading of the Spirit. As long as this is not understood, there will not be that fear of self and its wisdom, that absolute dependence and waiting on the Spirit, which is the first condition of the spiritual life.

To those who would be saved from these dangers, who long to return to the normal state in which, and for which, God created man, the way is open, though not always easy. Begin with the prayer that we may *know* the Holy Spirit, His dwelling-place, His way, and His work, and what He claims. Seek a deep impression of the holy mystery and the divine reality of His indwelling. As truly as God dwelt in the flesh of Jesus of Nazareth, so truly, though in a different way, He dwells in you. Have a deep reverence for the holy presence. Be very jealous of anything that would grieve Him. Remember especially that what grieves Him most, next to sin, and what is sometimes more dangerous to ourselves than sin, is the soul repeating the first offence—*following its own thoughts about what is good and wise.* Understand that you have received the Spirit, that now the soul may be entirely under His dominion. Don't think that the fact of your admitting that you need the Spirit's teaching, or that you asked for Him, is enough to secure His working. It is not. It needs a very real giving up of the life of the soul, of all its strength and wisdom day by day, and a very real subjection of the whole mind and will to wait for His quickening and His teaching, if you are indeed to learn to know and worship God in the Spirit.

To sum up what has been said: The spirit is the seat of our God-consciousness; the soul of our self-consciousness; the body of our world-consciousness. In the spirit God dwells; in the soul, self; in the body, sense. As long as the right relationship existed, and the soul with itself was subject to the spirit, and through it to God, all was well. But sin came as the assertion of self in seeking its life through sense and not obedience to the spirit. And so the soul—self, selfishness—became the ruling principle of man's life.

In the regenerate man there is no more subtle temptation than this—that even in the service of God, self still seeks to assert itself in its will and strength to do God's will, instead of waiting in dependence on the Holy Spirit for Him to work, to will, and to do. This is why the Lord Jesus said so distinctly, "Let a man deny himself, and take up his cross"; the life and the power of self must be sacrificed and given up for the Spirit to work. Even so He speaks of our hating and loving our life (*soul*) if we are to find the true life, the life of the Spirit. In the believer there is always going on a secret struggle between the soul and the Spirit. On behalf of God, the Spirit seeks to possess and pervade all. On behalf of self, the soul seeks to take the first place, and to assert the right of independent action. As long as this is the case, and the soul takes the lead, expecting the Spirit to follow, and help and bless what it does, our life and work will be barren of truly spiritual results. Only when the soul, with all its self-willing and running, is daily denied and laid in the dust for the Spirit to work, will the power of God be manifest in our service. Here is the cause of such frequent failure in the spiritual life, of the evanescent character of many of our most precious experiences; our faith stood more in the wisdom of man, in the influence of human teaching and human apprehension, than in the power of God and His Spirit.

This is what is meant in Heb. 4:12: "The word of God is living, and active, and sharper than any two-edged sword, piercing even to the dividing of soul and spirit." Just as in creation the first work of the word was to divide—separating between light and darkness, earth and sea—so the living word, by the Holy Spirit, does its work in us, making the difference between the spirit clear to us. We learn to understand that the renewed spirit is the home of God's Holy Spirit.

"Master, where dwellest thou?" the disciples asked, when first they began to know Jesus. "Come and see," was His answer, and they abode *with Him* that night. "Holy teacher, where dwellest Thou?" is a question we may indeed ask, as we long to know the Spirit. The answer Jesus has given us: "He shall be *in you*." In that inner shrine of our wondrous nature, the spirit—deeper than the soul—with all its life of feeling and thought and will, which God made for himself. In the spirit quickened by His power, *there dwells the Holy Spirit*. There, in the life which He has imparted, there He dwells; that life He leads ever deeper into the truth, the actual possession of the substance of the grace revealed in Christ. It is only the soul that knows that He dwells there, and waits for His teaching there, to whom will be given as much as it needs and can bear of that truth in the intellect—which, without it, is impotent, and even dangerous. Paul writes: "God, whom I serve in my spirit." It is as I know that I have *a spirit*, "the seat of self-collectedness, the inner sanctuary," formed for receiving the communications from the divine world—deeper than thought or feeling—and retire there to wait on God's Spirit, and set it open to Him, that I will learn to know where He dwells. Only when He is acknowledged and honored there, will He come forth from the secret place to manifest His power in the region of the soul and its conscious life. When speaking of the believer as a temple, I shall have occasion again to point out the difference between the holy place, the soul; and the most holy, the spirit (chap . 24).

NOTE 4

Growth in the Knowledge of the Spirit (Chapter 8)

In the following extract from Dr. Saphir's *Christ Crucified: Lectures on 1 Corinthians II*, the thought is put very distinctly, that as a rule the believer in the first stage of the Christian life hardly knows that he owes his faith and the power of the Christian life to the direct working of the Holy Spirit. As a consequence of this ignorance, there very often comes a time of darkness, with the idea of awakening him to seek for the reason of his failure, and the power of restoration and abiding growth. The discovery of the work and indwelling of the third person, the Holy Spirit, is what he needs, to see that all that is in Christ can actually be his in continuous experience. I am sure that clear teaching in regard to this advance in the knowledge of the Christian, and the proclamation to the very weakest of God's children that the indwelling of the Holy Spirit is their privilege and their strength, is just what is needed in the Church in our day, and cannot fail to bring light and blessing to many.

"We read that the Apostle Paul found disciples in Ephesus, whom he asked, 'Have ye received the Holy Ghost since you believed?' And their reply was, 'We have not so much as heard whether there be any Holy Ghost.' As the Lord Jesus said to Philip, 'Have I been so long time with you, and yet hast thou not known me?' so may the Holy Ghost say to some true and sincere believers, 'Have I been so long with you, revealing unto you the truth as it is in Jesus, working in you faith, shedding abroad in your hearts God's love, comforting you in your sorrow for sin, helping your infirmities in prayer, opening to your understanding wonders out of God's Word, *and yet have you not known me?*' This ignorance arises, to some extent, from the fact that the Spirit testifies not of himself, but of the Father and the Son. It is His duty to glorify Christ. As when in the dark night a bright light is concentrated on one point, the light-bearght and blessing to many.

"We read that the Apostle Paul found disciples in Ephesus, whom he asked, 'Have ye received the Holy Ghost since you believed?' And their reply was, 'We have not so much as heard whether there be any Holy Ghost.' As the Lord Jesus said to Philip, 'Have I been so long time with you, and yet hast thou not known me?' so may the Holy Ghost say to some true and sincere believers, 'Have I been so long with you, revealing unto you the truth as it is in Jesus, working in you faith, shedding abroad in your hearts God's love, comforting you in your sorrow for sin, helping your infirmitites in prayer, opening to your understanding wonders out of God's Word, *and yet have you not known me?*' This ignorance arises, to some extent, from the fact that the Spirit testifies not of himself, but of the Father and the Son. It is His duty to glorify Christ. As when in the dark night a bright light is concentrated on one point, the light-bearer himself remains unseen; so the blessed Spirit, unperceived by the awakened sinner, causes all light to fall on the crucified Saviour and the loving Father. The soul exclaims: How great is the love of God! How marvelous is the grace of Jesus! He who has kindled the light, who has opened the eyes of the heart, who has renewed the soul, *is as yet unknown and unobserved.* John the Baptist compared himself with the friend of the bridegroom, who stands and rejoices greatly because of the bridegroom's voice. In like manner does the Spirit direct the soul to Christ, and fills the heart with joy in believing Jesus, *while as yet He does not reveal His own love and work.*

"Another reason why the young believer knows little of the Spirit is because the Holy Ghost is so gentle. His approach is so soft, His adaptation to our peculiarities of character so perfect, His influences so deep and penetrating, that we think our own reason, imagination, will, and conscience, have been acting of their own accord and with perfect spontaneity.

"How little do we realize that the Holy Ghost has been influencing every faculty, every emotion, every mental process; so noiselessly, so quietly, so lovingly, so inwardly has the great Spirit been working—preparing, chiselling, and fitting every stone of the building—as at the building of Solomon's temple no sound was heard. With perfect knowledge and with infinite love the Holy Ghost deals with our spirits, and when the creative decree goes forth, it is usually as the still small voice which came to Elijah after the earthquake, the tempest, and the fire.

"Yet the believer knows that he has experienced divine grace and power. God has revealed Christ to him. God has created him anew. It is a supernatural influence of which he is conscious; and as 'it is unique, so it brings with it the assurance of its truth. There is a testimony within his heart that the true light now shines. 'I know whom I believe.' Now, we ourselves know. Yet 'the reason why we ourselves know is that our knowledge is not of ourselves but of God.' Hereby we know that we know Him, by the Spirit He has given to us. And this light is sweet. There is a blessedness in this knowledge of the Father and the Son, a peace and joy which satisfy the heart and fill the immortal soul, so that there is perfect rest. Why is this? Because the Holy Ghost, who is God, has revealed to us the things which are freely given us of God; because by the Spirit we call the Father Abba, and Jesus, Lord.

"As the believer progresses, and his path becomes more complicated, he is *taught more about the Spirit, for he needs this doctrine increasingly for his comfort and growth.* His faith is not so strong and unwavering as he imagined; the ardor of his love soon vanishes; the power of sin, which at first he imagined was utterly broken, makes itself felt again; prayer becomes languid, and joy seems to have taken flight. In other words, God leads him into the valley, and lest he should make a Christ of his faith, and a well-spring of a cistern, he is taught something of himself. Who does not know of this second stage in the Christian life, at first so painful, so humiliating, and filling the soul with perplexity? *It is thus that we learn that the Spirit who has renewed our hearts must also sustain the new life;* that we depend entirely on divine grace and power, not merely to bring us to Christ, but to keep us in Him.

"Thus, as in all God's dealings, there is progress in ever-increasing, widening, and deepening cycles. The believer experiences again in a more enlarged and profound manner what he was taught at his conversion. He sees now more clearly the guilt and helplessness of man, our utter dependence on a Father to love us, on a Saviour to save us by the shedding of His blood, and on a divine Spirit to quicken and enlighten the soul, and fill it with the love of God. He feels now with deeper humility and truer joy that salvation is of God, that divine grace lays the foundation and performs the good work in us until the day of Christ. *Then he beholds the gift and the indwelling of the Holy Ghost.* Thus was it that the first disciples, after a season of childlike peace and joy in the presence and companionship of Jesus, lost the Saviour, and with Him the garden of the soul; trees and flowers and songs of birds vanished, and all was winter—cold, silent, and dead. And then He returned unto them never to leave them; and on the day of Pentecost, in the person of the Comforter, He descended and made all things new; and it was summer—full of fragrance and brightness. They had to lose Jesus for a while, to long for the Spirit, and to rejoice in His coming.

"The gift of the Holy Ghost is the most precious gift of that love which the Father has towards us for the sake of His dear Son, and because we love Him, and believe that He came from God. *It is the gift in which the purposes of God towards us are fulfilled and consummated.*

"The Messiah and the Spirit always go together; and the gift of the Spirit is the great purpose of the Messiah's coming and the first-fruits of His work."

"I shall never forget the awakening to conscious faith and peace which, in my own experience, came after a decisive and appropriating view of the crucified one as the sinner's sacrifice of peace. It came from a clearer and more intelligent grasp of the personality of that Spirit through whose mercy the soul had seen that blessed vision. It was a new development of insight into the love of God; a new contact with the inner and eternal movements of redeeming mercy; a new discovery of divine resources. Gratitude, love, and adoration found a newly realized reason, and spring, and rest. He who had awakened, who had regenerated, shone before the soul with the smile of a personal and eternal kindness and friendship, standing side by side in union unspeakable—yet not in confusion—with Him who had suffered and redeemed, and with Him who had given His Son, who had laid the eternal plan of grace, and willed its all-merciful success."—H. C. G. Moule

NOTE 5

The Spirit of Truth (Chapter 9)

We are so accustomed to think of the word truth as meaning doctrine—that it is only by a distinct and often-repeated effort that we can realize that it is in a very different and very much higher sense that our Lord uses it. When John speaks of Christ as full of grace and *truth*, and then explains this by saying, "The law came by Moses; grace and *truth* by Jesus Christ," we notice at once that he contrasts the powerless shadows and forms of the law with the living substance and reality of what Christ brought, as the real communication of the eternal life of God from heaven. The following extract from Beck may help us to grasp the thought that truth has indeed a life and kingdom of its own:

"Man's creative power, both spiritual and bodily, can never create any true or real life, unless there is something already given and received to begin with—to work on and to work out. It always results in an objective external creation. Likewise, in nature, we must always have the original matter, with its own resident life-power already formed, before we can, with our powers, obtain any product in the real sense—whether spiritual or physical—we never produce; we only *reproduce*. Nature is an independent kingdom within which we live and work, but in which we call into existence or create *nothing*. Likewise, truth—the spiritual world—is an independent kingdom, which we cannot bring forth out of our spirit, but which must in its self-existence reveal itself to us, that out of it we may receive the substance and elements of real life before we can produce anything spiritually. An actual existence must in its own original power reveal itself to us, and with its creative energy enter into us, before we can produce anything from within. Where is this actual existence—this life kingdom of truth? This question compels every honest thinker to come out of his own isolated self, and in this objective world (it may be the inner one, as far as it has an actual objective existence) to seek for the revelation of truth, that he may open his spirit to it and reproduce what it has set before him. And so faith is the substance of Christian truth, which enters into man as his spiritual property, and in living power becomes immanent within him. As a faith, Christianity is neither idea, nor law, nor feeling—but a life—a deep, penetrating, and all-pervading life."

It is this life kingdom of divine truth, this actual divine life, that Jesus came to earth as the embodiment of. It is of this truth that the Holy Spirit is the motivating principle—the very life. And when He comes out of Christ who has said, "I am the truth," He comes as the bearer of all there is in Christ to make Him truth within us—an actual living possession. It is only as we thus possess Christ, the truth, that our knowledge of the doctrine truth will be living and profitable. The Spirit of truth gives us life-truth within, and from there He leads into truth of conduct and character. Only as we yield to Him in this is the doctrinal truth we hold really the truth of God to us. The Church or the individual has only so much of the truth of God as we have of the Spirit of God.

NOTE 6

The Mission of the Spirit (Chapter 9)

Love Revealed: Meditations on the Parting Words of Jesus with His Disciples in John 13 to 17, by George Bowen. Such is the title of a book from which I will give some extracts. The book clarifies the thought with some force, that many Christians are living on an antepentecostal level, and that the promise of Christ to reveal His power to the world through His people is still awaiting its fulfillment in our experience. To those who are not yet acquainted with this book, I can most confidently recommend it as full of spiritual instruction.

" *'I will love him, and will manifest myself to him.'* (John 14:21).

"If we wish, therefore, to sound the depths of this promise, 'I will manifest myself to him,' we must honor Christ, the Father, and the Spirit by believing in the power of the Spirit. To have faith in Christ and not to have faith in the Spirit seems to be a great contradiction, yet we submit it for the judgment of candid inquirers if this contradiction is not strikingly exhibited in the case of almost all who profess to be followers of Christ. To know the Father we must know the Son; to know Christ we must know the Spirit. 'He shall glorify me,' said Christ. Do you believe this? Is this your conception of Christ's glory—that it is a glory that the Spirit of God can enable you to behold? When the omnipotent Spirit has been allowed by our faith to go to the full extent of His resources in the revelation of Christ, it will be time enough for us to turn away from Him to some more perfect way of bringing Christ near to us.

"Our Lord himself tells us that he that is least in the kingdom of heaven—the kingdom that He came to establish—was greater than any of the prophets that had been in the world before His advent. Greater? Why? Because he is a habitation of God through the Spirit, because that magnificent gift which Christ died to obtain for us has been bestowed.

"Now all these views of the glory of the present dispensation seem to vanish, when we subject them to a comparison with the actual experiences of Christians in general. But we do them a real injustice in this way. We are rather to submit the experiences of Christians to the test of Scripture. When we do so, does it not appear that the Church has fallen back into an ante-pentecostal state? that it has slipped out of its own dispensation? There was a measure, though weak, of spiritual influence enjoyed by the disciples before the death and resurrection of Christ; otherwise they would not have been able to call Jesus Lord; but it was nothing in comparison with what they received on the day of Pentecost. The day of Pentecost was a pattern day; all the days of this dispensation should have been like it, or should have exceeded it. But, no! the Church has fallen to the state in which it was before this blessing had been bestowed, and it is necessary for us to ask Christ to begin over again. We, of course, in respect to knowledge—intellectual knowledge of spiritual things—are far in advance of the point where the disciples were before Pentecost. But it should be borne in mind that when truths have once been fully revealed and been made a part of orthodoxy, the holding of them does not necessarily imply an operation of the Spirit of God. We surely deceive ourselves in this way, imagining that because we have the whole Scripture and are familiar with all its great truths, the Spirit of God is necessarily working in us. We need a baptism of the Spirit as much as the apostles did at the time of Christ's resurrection; we need the unsearchable riches of Christ revealed to us more copiously than they were to Isaiah in the temple.

"We profess to love Him. We profess, therefore—the inference is unavoidable—to desire to enjoy higher and more satisfactory manifestations of Him than have yet been entrusted to us. It follows, then, that we ought to feel very greatly the pressure of the obligation to seek the outpouring of the Holy Spirit. Blessed be God! the Holy Spirit is being poured out in many churches, and many Christians are at this very hour enjoying such views of Christ as fill them with a preternatural joy and love and strength. But we have not yet entered into the fullness of this glorious dispensation. If we love Christ, we will press deeper into it, believing that his omnipotence will find ways of revealing itself in the spiritual world of which we have as yet no conception.

' "Nevertheless I tell you the truth; it is expedient for you that I go away: for if I go not away, the Comforter will not come unto you; but if I depart, I will send him unto you' (John 16:7).

"Strange and scarcely credible though the announcement may appear to you, I nevertheless tell you the simple truth, when I say that it will be to your advantage that I ascend unto the Father and send to you the Holy Ghost, the Comforter, to be your perpetual guide. And when I say that it will be to your advantage, I do not mean that the Holy Spirit is greater than I am, or that He will prove a truer friend to you. In fact, the special office of the Spirit will be to bring you and myself into a more intimate and a more blessed union than has yet been revealed to your consciousness. Though you have journeyed with me during these latter years of my earthly pilgrimage, yet there is no use in disguising the fact that a moral chasm yawns between us. You yourselves must often have felt the deepest pain in reflecting upon the very small amount of influence exerted upon you by the one who is manifestly God in the likeness of men. You have mourned that the words and acts of the one who was proclaimed the Only-Begotten of the Father, who was transfigured before you, was served by angels, who spake unto the winds and the waves and they obeyed Him—you have mourned that the discourse and acts of such a one should have so weakly affected your hearts. The desire for sanctification exists in you, but the new and elevated conception of holiness, which has been introduced into your minds, only makes you more mindful of your great moral deficiencies. If miracles could have given you the victory over your sins, you would now be the holiest of men. Since that hour when one of you fell at my feet, exclaiming, "Depart from me, for I am a sinful man," how many glorious displays of my power have you witnessed! Yet are you still sadly aware that pride, ambition and worldliness still have authority over you?

"Surely you must have admitted to yourselves that if

three and a half years of such stupendous exhibitions of power have left you the unsanctified men that you are, ten years of such displays would not give you the victory over your evil natures. For three and a half years you have listened to one greater than Solomon—to one who spoke as never man spoke, to the wisdom of God; and you have enjoyed such opportunities as never before were enjoyed by mortal man to know the mind of God concerning the way in which He would be served—and what is the result? You yourselves are constrained to admit that the result is very unsatisfactory.

"Oh, if all that man needed were to have a teacher, to have lessons of divine wisdom set before him in the most intelligible and most expressive forms, then you would now be incomparably the holiest of men, proof against all temptation, superior to all earthly influences. But what is true, in fact? Was it not necessary that I should this very evening begin the work of instruction over again, as it were, by washing your feet? Have you not this very evening been disputing among yourselves who shall be the greatest? Are you not this very night to make even the unprofessing world astonished by deserting me in my hour of trial?

"Why do I now dwell upon these things? Simply that you may more easily recognize that my life on earth, however marvelous and glorious it may be as part of the divine system by which God is bringing you to himself, is of itself still unable to effect your spiritual redemption. It is one thing that the image of God should have been placed before you; it is a very different thing that you should be changed into that image. Man foolishly asserts that he only needs to know the true, the good, the beautiful, to be himself the embodiment of truth and goodness and beauty. Heaven has come down to earth; the very king of heaven has tabernacled among men; He whom Isaiah saw in the temple, high and lifted up, adored by seraphim, has come down from His throne, dismissed the seraphim to heaven, and dwelt with the people of Isaiah year after year, yet it is not seen that the men so amazingly distinguished have been rendered seraphic in holiness and love. Something else, then, is necessary that men may not only be made acquainted with the image of God, but changed into the same.

"Not only must you realize that you have little remembered, little learned, little obeyed, of all that I have told you and shown you; you must be keenly aware of the fact that your influence as my servants and the expounders of my gospel is all but nothing. In the presence of a perverse and rebellious race your hearts sink within you, and you ask yourselves, 'How shall we ever be able to bring men over to our views of Christ?' You feel your need of some unknown power by which the minds of men may be rendered obedient to the You find yourselves utterly at a loss to communicate your deepest convictions. You are ready to ask, 'Is there not something beyond miracles?—something beyond the power of a holy life?' Is there not in the resources of God some means of reaching the hearts of men, and subduing that hostility by which they are hindered from receiving the testimony of a holy life and a blessed gospel? There is. I die that you may have life, and that you may have it more abundantly. I ascend on high that the Comforter may come unto you. Then shall you be strengthened with a strength of which you have before now had no consciousness. Rivers of living water, even of the water of life, shall flow forth from you. Then the wilderness shall be glad, the desert shall rejoice and blossom as the rose.

" 'And when he is come, he will reprove the world of sin, and of righteousness, and of judgment' (John 16:8).

" 'When he.' 'He' in the original is emphatic. It might be rendered 'that one.' He it is who, coming, will convince mankind of sin. His very advent will revolutionize their ideas of sin, being a testimony from heaven more striking than that of the voice from heaven at the baptism of Jesus, to the fact that Jesus the crucified is none other than Christ, the glorified. By the simple fact that the world has placed itself in opposition to Jesus, testimony to Jesus will be testimony against the world. Observe that the promise of the Spirit was unto the disciples: 'I will send him unto you'; and the change here intimated to be worked out in the hearts of men, generally was to be in consequence of the descent of the Spirit of God upon the disciples. The gospel is preached to convince men of sin, of righteousness, and of judgment. The disciples of Christ are in the world that they may make known the sin of men, the judgment of God, and the means of escaping that judgment by means of the righteousness of Christ. But here we are told that the work of introducing the new convictions on these subjects into the minds of men is to be accomplished by the Spirit of God. Accordingly the apostles speak of themselves as having preached the gospel with the Holy Ghost sent down from heaven.

"What is here promised, then, is such an outpouring of the Spirit of God as shall not only reveal itself in the consciousness of the disciples, but substantiate itself as an undeniable and wonderful fact to the apprehensions of the onlooking world. And such was the advent of the Spirit on the day of Pentecost. 'He hath shed forth this which ye now see and hear,' said Peter to the multitude. That which they both saw and heard did what all the miracles, the incomparable words, the irreproachable life of Jesus, had failed to do. Let us say that these miracles began now to be seen, those divine words began now to be heard, for the first time. By the outpouring of the Holy Spirit upon the disciples, the people of Jerusalem began to look upward, and see Jesus at the right hand of the majesty on high. They saw their own sin, heinous beyond all conception; saw the righteousness of Him whom they had put to death, the prince of life; saw it to be such a righteousness that in comparison the entire race of man stood out, paralleled in darkest iniquity; and they saw the judgment of God, inevitable and dire, against all who should be found in opposition to Christ. It was as though they had been taken up into heaven, and had seen the judgment seat, the books opened, and their own deeds manifested in the unerring light of that tremendous scene. Sublime arrangements of Him whose wisdom is unsearchable! Are the people of God at all awake to all that is implied in the promise of the Spirit? Is it enough that they languidly recognize their obligation to make known the gospel to their fellowmen, and take various steps to have it preached? Is not the great thing wanted this: that the Spirit of God should be so poured out upon Christ's people that men should be made aware of His presence with them, and of the presence of Christ at the right hand of God? So poured out that there should be a coming together, in some sense, of the blessed God and of the world which has separated itself from Him; that the powers of the world to come should take hold upon men, and constrain them to cry out, 'Men and brethren, what must we do?'

"The Greek is wonderfully apt in that it does not represent the Spirit of God as coming once for all, but as persistently coming. He it is who, coming, shall convince. He comes as the rain from heaven that must still come and come again; as the wind that must still blow and blow again. We are not to look back for our Pentecost. The Pentecost of the Acts is simply given to make the church of Christ acquainted with the privileges belonging to this dispensation. It is only the first step in a ladder of Pentecosts by which the world and the kingdom of Christ are to be brought together! It is the example to accompany the promise, that we may be stirred up to plead the promise with the greatest fervency.

"Oh, it were unpardonable if, in a day when God is doing so much to inspire us with lofty conceptions of the power of the Holy Spirit, we should still refuse to apprehend the glorious unlimitedness of this promise. Consider it. We are to look at the work here assigned to the Holy Spirit, in order that we may obtain a just view of His power. Look abroad upon the earth and see the nations, tribes, and tongues refusing to be convinced by all that God in His providence has taught them during thousands of years; by all that missionaries are teaching them at this eleventh hour, of sin, of righteousness, of judgment. Picture the wickedness which envelopes the earth like a dense and deadly atmosphere, scarcely allowing any of the rays of the Sun of Righteousness to penetrate it. Consider that the Spirit of God, for whose effusion we are taught to pray, is pledged to rain conviction upon the world, and anticipate for a most sublime and blessed end the final judgment by leading men to look to the righteousness of Christ, the Desire of all nations.

" 'These things I have spoken unto you in proverbs: but the time cometh, when I shall no more speak unto you in proverbs, but I shall show you plainly of the Father' (John 16:25).

"When figures are used in speech, there is an outer meaning and an interior meaning. As the shell conceals and yet protects the kernel, so a truth conveyed topically may be unperceived at first. Afterward, when additional light is given, it becomes manifest, and the saying ceases to be a riddle. The gospel is full of parables that could very little be understood until Christ had suffered and entered into His glory. When the Spirit of God was poured out upon His disciples, the veil which had been over the words of Jesus disappeared, and the interior truths shown forth upon them in all their clarity. Christ himself was such a proverb. Once His divine glory had shown forth upon their astonished gaze, but that was by way of anticipation, it very little dissipated the confusion of their minds. Nothing about Christ could produce its legitimate and full effect upon them until they had been brought out of the restricted and depressed valley of Judaism, and placed upon the elevated platform of the new dispensation.

"The Spirit of God inundates the minds of men with truths which previously had no meaning to them. Now it appears that an observation of some importance may be made here. Truths which the Holy Ghost has taught us may be retained in the mind by the mere natural power of memory. Are we not then in danger of deceiving ourselves as to the measure of spiritual power we enjoy? We might have as scanty a measure of the Spirit's influence as the disciples had in the days preceding the death of Christ, and yet be immensely ahead of them in respect to the amount of our knowledge of the way of life. Is it not to be feared that in those portions of the Church which have not yet been visited by a true revival, Christians are to be compared with the first disciples, not as they were on the day of Pentecost, but as they were previously—compared, we mean, with regard to the actual divine influence enjoyed by them? Because they have the truth, they imagine they have the Spirit of truth. Perhaps the word of Christ to them is: 'Tarry ye in Jerusalem until endued with power from on high.' We are baffled, bewildered, confounded, by our utter helplessness to convince men of sin, of righteousness, and of the judgment to come. Is it not that we fail to realize how absolute is our need of the mighty and manifest advent of the Spirit? It is possible for Christ to so cause the Holy Spirit to be seen descending upon us that the world around shall discover, by this fact alone, the heavens opened and the Son of God standing at the right hand of God.

"Many in these days occupy no worthier position than

that first inferior one of the apostles. The apostles were not absolutely without the influence of the Spirit during the time that Jesus dwelt among them, but these influences did little more than make the present darkness visible, and show them in the dim distance the light of the future. Without knowing it, there are thousands of Christians who have a weak and questionable measure of influence which belongs to a different dispensation from this, and shows them to be two thousand years behind their privileges! We have said it, and without shame we say it again. They have, at the same time, knowledge such as the ante-pentecostal church did not have. It is the consciousness of this superior knowledge that tends to keep them ignorant of their spiritual destitution. Their position is appalling, for they are familiar with the inspiring promises, and have no faculty to catch a glimpse of the glorious things proffered in these promises. They actually suppose that these promises have no more exalted interpretation than that which their own emotionless and inglorious experience affords. Blessed be God! We are not limited to one Pentecost under this dispensation. Let us only become aware of the abnormal state in which we are, and take knowledge of the higher experiences to which God is inviting us. Pentecost was not so much a mountain summit as a mountain high path or tableland, along which the Church should have travelled to the New Jerusalem. Let us look steadfastly up, and see among the clouds this highway of holiness, and prove the power of the Saviour to bring us to it."

NOTE 7

The Name Comforter (Chapter 10)

It is admitted on all hands that the word Comforter does not give the full meaning of the Greek word *paracletos*. There is an active form, *paracletor*, of which comforter is the correct translation. The passive form, *paracletos*, just like the Latin *advocatus*, means one who has been *called in* to assist, to take charge of a case, or to plead a cause. Among those who take *advocate* as the correct rendering, there is more than one way of applying the word. Some think of Him as bearing this name because He has been *called in* of Christ to undertake His cause with the disciples and the world; others as one who can be *called in* by the disciples when they are in need of advice or strength. With those who think that the rendering advocate expresses fully what our Lord meant, there is also a diversity of opinion. Owen says, "He is an advocate for the Church—in, with, and against, the world." So also Howe, "The advocate, a great pleader, who undertakes to manage the cause of Christ and Christianity against the world." In this view the work of the Spirit in meeting the personal need of the believer does not come forth clearly. Others think of the Spirit as the advocate for Christ with believers. This is thus expressed by Bowen: "Christ is our advocate with the Father, and the Holy Spirit Christ's advocate with us. As Christ pleads for us at the throne of grace, so the Spirit pleads for Christ in our hearts. The Spirit vindicates Him from our unworthy thoughts, shows Him to be the chief among myriads, and altogether lovely."

These views give only partial aspects of the work of the blessed paraclete. "The word has an incomparably larger meaning than advocate on the one hand, and Comforter on the other. It includes both, but takes in a great deal more than either. It means one who is identified with our interests, one who undertakes all our cause, one who engages to see us through all our difficulties, one who in every way becomes our representative, and the great personal agent that transacts our business for us."—W. Kelly, *The Work of the Spirit*

Even this does not appear to cover all the ground. An advocate is indeed a representative. But the most comprehensive and most precious apsect of the Spirit's work is this, that He was to be the representative of Jesus. He was to make Jesus always present with us. This was the sorrow of the disciples, that they were to lose their Lord. This was the comfort Jesus promised, that they would have one in whom His presence should be restored. And this makes the Spirit the other advocate, that He has been called in and given by

Jesus to represent Him, and make His presence real to them, to reveal and impart all that our Lord is to us. When Jesus, in speaking of *another* paraclete, implies that He is the first, and when He bears that name in John 2:2, we must regard Him as appointed and given by the Father as the medium of intercourse between Him and us, obtaining and communicating His blessing. The word paraclete or advocate covers His whole work and person as He mediates the divine life and love to us, securing for us all the Father has to give, and bringing to the Father all we have to offer. This is the true and full meaning of Christ's work as advocate, of which His intercession is only one aspect. And when He gives us the paraclete as the other advocate, it is that His work should take in, in all its breadth, Christ's own work, to make it life and reality within us. Just as Christ, as advocate, mediates with the Father, so the Spirit mediates with Christ, revealing in our hearts as a present and continuous experience, in the power of the endless life all that Christ's advocacy secures to us. The Holy Spirit is the other advocate, the alter ego in our hearts of Christ in heaven.

It would be difficult to discard the use of the word Comforter in English. It will not be needed if we remember that the sorrow of the disciples was at the loss of Jesus' presence, that the comfort to be given was the restoration, in greater power, of the presence of Him, their divine advocate. It is because the Spirit is the indwelling representative of Jesus as the advocate in heaven, making Him always present in the heart, that He is the other advocate or Comforter.

NOTE 8

The Glory of Christ (Chapter 11)

The glory of God does not consist in His surroundings, or the circumstances wherein He dwells. His glory is the perfection and power of His divine will, the divineness of the method of His being and working. When God glorified Christ in himself, He not only exchanged the circumstances of His earthly life for those of the heavenly world, but entered upon an entirely new form of existence. Instead of being limited by flesh, by time and space, He passed as man into the life of God, who is a Spirit. On earth He could only work on His disciples as men next to himself, and separate from himself through means of words and example, reaching only their mind and affections, but not renewing their very spirit. From heaven He could, as out of His divine glory, in the power of the Spirit, begin and work in them in a very different way, entering their hidden life, and, through Him, coming to dwell in their heart. It is as the glorified one—the one that has exchanged the limited life of external effort and influence for the inner life of power by which He fills all things—that He gives the Spirit, the Spirit of glory. The work of this Spirit is to glorify Jesus. That does not mean to give us some sense of His glory in heaven, but to communicate to us personally that presence and power of Jesus which, in virtue of His divine glory, He can now manifest within us. But it is only the soul wholly yielded to the teaching of the Holy Spirit who knows "the Lord of glory" in this way.

The thought of the Lord of glory being glorified within us by the Spirit of glory looks very simple when once understood. And yet it is a deep spiritual mystery only reached in the way Christ reached His glory—through conformity to His sufferings and the fellowship of His cross. Each new impartation must be according to the riches of God's glory and the mighty strengthening of His Holy Spirit—a most real and direct act of God's ineffable grace continuing and increasing to the soul, the gift of His love.

To understand the way in which this glory works, we must notice carefully the connection between suffering and glory. "Behoved it not the Christ to suffer, and to enter into his glory?"[1] On earth Christ was the Lord of glory (John 1:14; 1 Cor. 2:8), but that glory was hidden under the lowliness of the human manifestation. And so, when the Spirit of the glorified Lord enters us to glorify Him in us, the glory is hidden amid the weakness and humiliation of our nature. And it is often only as we suffer in the flesh that the quickening of the Spirit is experienced.

The fatal error of the Jews was that they looked for the

glory of the Messiah as something visible and in accordance
with their worldly conceptions. Even the disciples suffered
from this, and were all offended at their Lord. The glory of
the Spirit-life into which Christ has now entered and in
which He now works is a hidden mystery, the mystery of
godliness, working not in that which is outward or tangible,
but in the unseen, the inner life. When we read of Christ
manifesting himself, of His dwelling in the heart, we almost
always form some conception of joy and triumph, as at the
entrance of a king into his capital. And Jesus said that the
kingdom of heaven is as a seed. A seed is something that
contains life hidden in the most dead, unlikely looking form
possible. Who, not having ever heard of a seed growing,
could imagine the oak or the pine contained in its seed? And
this seed, with its hidden life, must itself again be hidden
under the earth. The kingdom of heaven comes to us in the
seed of the Word, so small and dead-looking that no one expects such mighty power from it. And it must be hidden, not
in the thoughts or feelings that we can recognize and watch
over, but deeper down, in the mysterious depths of the spirit. There Christ, who is in the unseen Spirit-life of the
Father, finds the unseen depths of our spirit-life and enters
there. He is himself the living word, the living seed; the
Spirit is the life of the seed.

False views of what glory is have been the great stum-
bling-block of the Jews and disciples of the Church and
individual believers. God's glory is His holiness revealed in
His good and perfect will. Christ's glory is, that having glorified God by entering into, doing, and suffering that will, He
was taken up into the fellowship of the Father's glory, of
that life of holiness and power in which God dwells. Christ is
glorified in us as we enter into His will by obeying and doing
it, and have His presence revealed within us in divine
power. That which in Christ was weak and despised, the
very opposite of human glory, the lowliness and suffering of
the cross, was the hidden seed of His divine glory. In lowliness and obedience, in poverty of spirit and the absence of

---

1. Compare Rom. 8:17, 18; 2 Cor. 4:16, 17; Heb. 2:9, 10; 1 Pet.
4:13-16.

what can be seen or felt, in the death of the flesh and the patient waiting on God, is the seed of Christ glorified within us by the Spirit.

NOTE 9

The Presence of the Spirit in the Church
(Chapter 14)

"The present enjoyment of the Spirit is but an earnest, a gift beforehand, a pledge of the coming fullness. St. Paul speaks (Rom. 8:23) of those 'which have the first-fruits of the Spirit,' and in his other epistles he uses equivalent expressions (Eph. 1:13, 4:30; 2 Cor. 1:22, 5:5). What can be meant by such words but that the spiritual life is a continual process, receiving with its widening capacities, richer gifts of the wisdom and holiness of God? The Church is in its infancy as to evaluation of spiritual blessing. It is also so much engaged in controversy that it can hardly be preparing itself for the completion of the holy promise. By mistaking the part for the whole, it is in danger of settling itself into premature satisfaction, as if it had exhausted the possibilities of prayer! Would it be uncharitable to suggest that the Church is too much engaged in that worst and most cankering of all worldliness—the elevation of one sect above another—and the jealous defense of forms, which are but transient conveniences? What is delaying the outpouring of the fullness of the Spirit? There is indeed a still sterner inquiry, which cannot be put without emotion, yet it may not be honestly suppressed. Is not the presence of the Holy Ghost in the Church less distinct today than in the apostolic age? Certainly there is not much appearance of Pentecostal inspiration in contemporary Christianity. Why has not a Church eighteen hundred years old a fuller realization of the witness of the Holy Ghost than had the Church of the first century? Has the Church accomplished all the purpose of

God, and passed for ever the zenith of her light and
beauty?"—*The Paraclete*

NOTE 10

The Outpouring of the Spirit (Chapter 15)

I will give another note from Professor Beck, on the Spirit and the work He does in the believers and the Church, as
well as in the world, in virtue of His being poured out on all
flesh (*Chr. Ethik*). Anything that helps us to meditate on
what was needed to prepare for the outpouring of the Holy
Spirit—what its object was, and how He comes now to do
that work—will help to free us from those very limited ideas
we have of who the Holy Spirit is and what is the blessed
work He has come to do in us.

"As concerns the relation of the Spirit to Christ, He is
the witness who takes of what Christ contains and possesses
and brings it to us, thereby revealing and glorifying Christ
(John 15:26; 16:7, 14). The witness of the Spirit has this peculiarity, that He acts as the power from on high, and that
where His witness enters, life comes in divine power. The
Spirit is the dynamic principle, in whom are concentrated
all the life powers that flow from Christ, and from whom
they are divided as the powers peculiar to each, as gifts and
graces. He is thus the formative power, which out of the substantial reality of what there is in Christ begets and develops the individual life. His witnessing mediates the begetting; as the dynamic principle He is also the generative principle. Through Him the Christ is born in us; becomes with
His life of grace our inner personal life, so that we are
clothed upon with the power from on high, with a supernatural life-power. We have the grace of Christ, not only as
an object without us, but within us as the power of God. In
the Spirit there dwells within us that power of divine grace,
in which all the powers of the new life concentrate. Spirit,
life and power are therefore in Scripture correlated ideas,
just as on the other side, flesh, weakness and death are one.
The eternal life system, which from its divine head is again

to bring the earth—the world of flesh—into organic union with the spiritual world can alone be built up on heavenly dynamics, on the action of the Spirit as the power of the heavenly life.

"This action of the Spirit is, however, only mediated for the world by the reconciliation which Jesus Christ has effected, and by His being glorified. Previous to this reconciliation, the divine Spirit worked on earth either as the Spirit in nature, as the power of the earthly life, or as the Spirit of the theocracy, with special temporary manifestations for special functions, as in the case of the prophets. It did not work yet in such a way that eternal life, as it belongs to the divine nature, and dwells in the Father and the Son, could become the personal life of man, the property of his inmost nature. In this special aspect the Spirit in the Old Testament was only a promise to be realized in Christ, and therefore bears the name of the Spirit of promise. In the New Testament Spirit the promise becomes fulfillment, actual bestowment, and possession. However, before this could take place with any human individual, the Spirit had to first form and secure for himself in human nature a center from which He might communicate himself. In this central nature the Spirit had to be brought into a free organic union with man's psychical and physical nature as existing in the flesh, and that nature likewise had to be formed into the organ of the Spirit. In one word, a man, anointed and permeated with the Holy Spirit, the anointed, had to be formed. Then, in this spiritually perfected central personality of Jesus Christ, the flesh had, by a voluntary sacrificial death, to be transformed into the true spiritual existence of the divine being, or glorified and lifted up into God, so that the reconciliation of the world with God was accomplished. Only in this way could this visible life-system, the organism of the actual soul-life, become judicially and ethically accessible to the operation and participation of the divine Spirit, out of the reconciler and through Him. In this way alone could the Spirit, in His new character, be set free out of the nature of Christ to be poured out as the power of the heavenly life, the power of eternal life, upon all flesh.

"The question now comes, 'How are we to identify with, or interpret this outpouring of the Holy Spirit?'

"The outpouring of the Spirit is not identical with the individual indwelling of the Spirit, but is the universal presupposition of the latter, for it is spoken of (see Acts 2:16, compare 33) as an outpouring down upon all flesh ($\xi\tau\mu$ indicates the direction), of which the being filled with the Spirit individually is only the consequence; the individual entering in of the Spirit is mediated by the universal outpouring. The relation is the same as that between the universal reconciliation, and the personal reconciliation. The personal is mediated by the universal. Each of these, the reconciliation of the world and the outpouring of the Spirit, stands as an all-embracing fact, accomplished once for all. They are each an objective universality, while in subjective realization only a few are partakers of either. The outpouring on all flesh is then, neither the inpouring in all flesh, nor a mere rhetorical expression for the inpouring in a few individual men, but indicates its direction and destiny for all men. But again, it is not presented as a mere ideal destiny, as it was in the Old Testament; in the New it is a fact that has taken place (Acts 2:33). Having received the promise of the Father, He has shed this forth. Corresponding to this destination for all flesh, there is also a world-embracing operation of the Spirit on the whole. Our Lord himself, speaking of the coming or outpouring of the Spirit (John 16:8), attributed to Him a work in the unbelieving world, even when they do not individually receive Him. It is thus a work independent of His reception—a judicial one.

"We are thus led to regard the matter in this light: that the Spirit, as sent down or poured out, has now, by His descendence out of His previous transcendence, become a power covering and influencing the world, a new universal power proceeding from Christ, on the ground of the accomplished reconciliation of the world in Christ, even while the Spirit—as an individual gift, a subjective possession—has become personally immanent in only a few. As the outpoured Spirit He is, and works in the world, independent of His indwelling in special individuals, even as the exalted Christ also exists and works as the Lord who fills heaven and earth, as a universal power. With the outpouring of the Spirit on all flesh, a new life-power has been set free from above, which now as Spirit, thus invisible, pervades the world system according to its own laws. It is the reaction of the holy universal power of the Spirit against the universal power of the spirit of falsehood and destruction which had until then ruled the world. This latter does not only exist as a spirit immanent in individual men, but as an independent power, the prince of this world. The operation of the new, holy, and spiritual world-power thus acts partly in a general sense, as it works in the world and partly in a special and individual sense, as it works in the church of Christ. With regard to His general work in the world, we have the world-judging work of the Spirit. The Spirit works as the fire cast upon earth from above, in its separating and judging power embracing not only the moral, but even the physical world (Luke 12:49, 51; 3:16; the baptism and burning up with fire, Rev. 4:5).

"This is the foundation and preparation for the more special operation, in which the Spirit, as the new life-stream from above, flows into the individual souls that are united with the Lord, and fills them (John 3:5; 7:38; 4:10, 14). Here, in His quickening power, the Spirit is in union with water, just as in His judging power, with fire. Compare Gen. 1:2 (water, spirit, light); Matt. 3:11 (spirit, fire, water); Rev. 4:5; 15:2; 22:1.

"Where the Spirit is thus represented as fire and water, it appears as a power in nature—but it is a power of nature divine and spiritual, making itself felt within the physical world as a universal power—not for daily tasks in connection with the world, but at special times for tasks in connection with the kingdom of God. As such a universal power, the outpoured Spirit forms the connecting link between the redeemer of the world—and the redemption and transformation of the world of flesh out of its natural state, into an actual spiritual body. The outpouring of the Spirit is thus, just as the reconciliation—of which it is the immediate result—a real, perfected plan in this earthly world of the holy Spirit-influence, through which, in opposition to the unholy spirit-influence, the operation and entrance of a substantial heavenly Spirit-life in humanity (Eph. 1:3; Heb. 6:4), and at last in all nature (Rom. 8:19), is mediated, and so the full destruction of satanic power obtained (1 John 3:8; 12:31; 16:8, 11)."

NOTE 11

The Spirit of Missions (Chapter 16)

The great International Missionary Conference has just been held, followed by what has been called a Missionary Crusade in Scotland. I have joined with many in the prayer to our Lord for His presence in the meeting, in thanking Him for success vouchsafed, in praising Him for the results. And yet I feel as if there is one remark I cannot withhold. I noticed with great interest a paper, issued before the meeting, in *The Christian*, by Dr. A. Pierson, pointing out what might be hoped for from such a gathering, and concluding with the remark that unless it issued in a great baptism of prayer it might still be a comparative failure.[1]. What I have felt in regard to some other large gatherings of God's servants in the holy ministry impressed me here also, that there was too little time given to the united confession of our need of, our expectation of, and our faith in, the power of the Holy Ghost. We all admit that what the steam is to the engine that draws the train, what the fire is to the cannon with its powder and ball, the Holy Spirit is to the work of the Church and of missions. Why shouldn't we, at such gatherings for eight or ten days, set apart the better part of the days for persevering, united supplication for the mighty indwelling and working of the Holy Spirit in God's servants, present or represented, for His mighty power in the assembly, and for the deepening conviction throughout the Church that the one thing needful is Christ's indwelling presence revealed by the Holy Spirit? Instead of the meetings for prayer being the smallest, they should be the largest and most important! It was ten days of continuing with one accord in prayer and supplication at the footstool of the exalted Lord that prepared that frail company of disciples for the struggle in which they defied the power of Jerusalem and Rome, and conquered. We need, above everything, to help each other to continue in prayer that we may be greatly strengthened by God's Spirit.

I feel confident that, if at such gatherings we would make waiting upon God our first priority, there would not only be the blessing at the time for those who meet, but it would also be a living testimony of unspeakable value to the blessed truth that it is by the Holy Ghost filling each individual believer that our blessed Lord is waiting to bless the world.

In reading the stirring reports of the Missionary Crusade in Scotland the same thought presented itself in a different form. When one or more men, full of a holy enthusiasm for missions, address large audiences, they may succeed in imparting somewhat of their fire to their hearers. The Spirit in them touches deeply those who come under their influence. And yet the permanent result is often very small, and the process has to be continually repeated.[2] What the Church needs, what our Lord asks and longs to give, is something more. It is not enough that Christians, living a weak, sickly Christian life, should from time to time be stirred. If the interest of the individual believer in missions is to be well-pleasing to the Master, and a real spiritual force in the world, it must come, not from continual appeals from without, but as the spontaneous outflow of a heart in which the Spirit of Jesus is dwelling. Every branch of the vine must bear its fruit from the direct inflow of the life-giving sap—the Holy Spirit. If the confessions that have been made in these past years of terrible shortcomings and unfaithfulness—while we have only been playing at missions—are to mean anything, we must all labor for the restoration of the half-forgotten truth that *every believer* is expected to be full of the Holy Ghost. All the Church's appeals for support and prayer must be accompanied by the teaching, in the power of the Spirit, that where the Holy Spirit dwells and rules, sacrifice for Christ and entire personal devotion to His interests is nothing but the natural outcome of a healthy Christian life. Christ did not call His Church to be His witness to the whole earth without first promising the power of the Spirit coming on her.

I must ask my readers to forgive me if I appear to repeat too frequently this one thought. I feel like one who has a message to bring, but is conscious that he stammers, and fears that his message will not be rightly understood. We are all so sure that we believe in the Holy Ghost, and that we understand how indispensable His operation is, that we don't look carefully at the deep spiritual truth that our almighty Lord Jesus is waiting, by His Holy Spirit, to work in every believer. It is through His Church that He works the greater works He promised, the exceeding abundantly above what we ask or think, according to the power that is working in us. The beginning of the change must come through the ordinary ministry of the Word. Every individual believer must be educated in the full consciousness that to be filled with the Holy Ghost is an absolute necessity for a life truly fruitful and well-pleasing to God. May every appeal for missions, every effort, in the light of the hundreds of millions whom we have been leaving to perish, bring the Church to a sense of her guilt, and a surrender to her glorious calling. May all speaking and writing and praying, may all our conferences and Church councils, lead to the deepening of the conviction—the Holy Spirit is the Church's power for all her work and missions, and that power will only act accordingly as the number increases of individual believers who give themselves to be possessed, to be led, to be used of the Spirit of Christ.

---

1. "There is one outcome for which we look with greater confidence and hope than for all other results combined. What the Church needs above all else is a baptism of prayer. . . . If that conference in London does not result in a new baptism of prayer, the highest result will not be attained. Let the whole Christian Church unite in one mighty and moving plea that in these latter days it may come to pass that God shall pour out His Spirit upon all flesh, and Joel's prophecy shall at last receive its complete fulfilment."

2. Dr. Pierson says in the same paper, "Dependence is frequently placed upon men's organization. A transient enthusiasm that is awakened is like the morning cloud or early dew, and passes as quickly away."

NOTE 12

Conscience (Chapter 21)

If man is the antitype of the temple, and his spirit the most holy place where God dwells, it is not difficult to identify the place and the meaning of that part of its furniture which typifies conscience. This is none other than the ark of the covenant. There are three marks of identification. The law of God was contained and carried in the ark. Conscience is the power which has God's law written in it. To the degree that the law is present, whether written in the heart of the heathen or transcribed in the heart of the believer by the Spirit, to the same degree conscience is able to do its work. Conscience is the receptacle or holder of the law as the ark. It was also on the ark that the mercy-seat rested, that the sprinkling of blood was effected, and the throne of grace set up for God to be worshipped. Likewise, it is to the conscience in particular that the blood is applied within us, and that the Spirit witnesses of our being well-pleasing to God.

The ark was called the ark of the testimony, containing God's law or His testimony to Israel. Likewise the Holy Spirit, writing the living law in the heart, is God's testimony to His redeemed people, the witness both of His will and of His favor. Conscience, sprinkled with the blood, and keeping watchful guard over the childlike life of obedience, is the spiritual organ within our spirit, to which, and through which, the Holy Spirit gives His witness: "My conscience bearing me witness in the Holy Spirit."

With what care was the ark treasured in Israel! With what confidence followed by the hosts when passing through Jordan to conquer Canaan and its hosts! With what quiet expectancy borne around Jericho! With what joy a place was prepared for it, and God's presence with it claimed! (Ps. 132). Christian, treasure above everything the ark of the testimony within you. The law of the Spirit is within it, the blood is upon it. It is the place where your God dwells and rests and communes with you. It is the meeting-place, the point of contact, between God and the soul—the seat of faith and the seat of God. Above everything, bow in fear and reverence before the holy presence which rests above the ark. Keep a conscious void of offence.

NOTE 13

The Light of the Spirit (Chapter 22)
(From *Christ Crucified*, by Dr. A. Saphir)

But it may be asked: God revealed himself and His purpose in Christ. Why is another light, another teacher, needed? The necessity is obvious from history. The heathen world by wisdom knew not God, and when Christ came He was rejected; they who received Him confessed it was owing to a supernatural illumination, to the Spirit of God. Israel taught by holy men inspired of God, in possession of the Scriptures, the perfect portrait of Him that was to come; Israel, thus highly favored and fully instructed, was not able to discern the divine features of that countenance, of which Moses and the prophets, of which all their institutions, testified. He came to His own, but His own received Him not. They crucified Him. What greater proof can we have that *Christ himself remains unseen light, unless the Spirit reveals Him?*

But look at the very disciples of our Lord. They were drawn to Jesus by the Father. Their knowledge that Jesus was the Messiah, the Son of God, came not by nature, by flesh and blood, but it was from above. They loved Jesus with all their hearts, cleaving unto Him with compassionate affection. And yet, while He was here, they did not fully understand the Scriptures. Even the instructions of the blessed Master, received with intense admiration and affection, were not sufficient. They stood at the threshold of truth: *the Holy Ghost alone can lead us into the truth.* God is in Christ; but the Holy Ghost alone reveals Him as God manifest.

But let us go higher than the proof of actual history and experience. God in His love reveals himself. It is His gracious will that I should know Him. In Christ Jesus He reveals himself perfectly. Jesus is light, full of brightness and sweet tenderness. *And yet I require another light to see the true light.* Why is this?

Simply because there is no other God but the Triune—Father, Son and Holy Ghost. God knows himself in His Spirit. It is in the Spirit of God that God is light in himself, and therefore by the Spirit He sends forth light into the world and into the hearts of His children.

God reveals himself. But who is God revealed? Who else but the Son? *And by whom does the Father know and love the Son? By that very Spirit by whom He reveals himself to man.* Scripture is of the Father; its substance is Christ, and it is revealed by the Holy Ghost. A revealing God, a revealed God, is the true God—Father, Son and Holy Ghost.

So it is in redemption. We do not exalt the Lord Jesus Christ, or approach Him more closely, when we forget the Father and the Spirit. It is the glory of Christ that He reveals the Father, and baptizes with the Holy Ghost. Father, Son, and Holy Ghost are one in majesty and glory; one in love and grace.

Remember, there is no bridge from this world into the land of glory; there is no ladder from this earth into heaven, unless from that shore and that height, the Triune God himself comes down and brings us salvation. *Amor descendit* was a saying of the ancients. Love descends from heaven. What God in His infinite love, wisdom, and power has treasured up in Christ Jesus, He *himself must give us by the power of the Holy Ghost.* By this we know and confidently believe that nothing shall separate us from the love of God, which is in Christ Jesus. Christ is ours, not by our own reason, not by our own energy, not by our own faithfulness, but by the Holy Ghost himself, who is very God and eternal God, who links us to the Lord Jesus, to be His for evermore.

The Holy Ghost, who is in essential and perfect communion with the Father and the Son, reveals unto us eternal realities. He alone knows the infinite love of God with which He has loved us, for He alone can fathom the depth out of which this love proceeds. Thus, what the Holy Ghost reveals and imparts is the knowledge of realities which are eternal in God.

He brings a *living* knowledge; His light is the light of life. It is not information, an insight into the connection of truths, or an appreciation of their beauty and grandeur. Men may have such vast and deep knowledge, and yet be destitute of the grace of God and be uninhabited by the divine Spirit. To know God and Jesus Christ whom He has sent is life eternal. This knowledge of God, beholding Him and Christ, is the spiritual, never-ending life which the Spirit creates within us. Dead knowledge is not the work of the Holy Spirit—knowledge which remains quiescent, silent, and lonely; for the knowledge which the Spirit gives is *communion*. We see the Father and the Son *as seeing us.* When we behold them by the revelation of the Spirit, it is as beholding us with infinite love, and bestowing upon us the blessings of grace. We know because we are known. "Thou Father, Thou Son, seest me," is the immediate consciousness of the soul, when there is a spiritual perception of God. In other words, adoration, love, petition, listening to God's voice, receiving the love and peace of Christ, and *communion*, are all invoked in this knowledge.

This knowledge is therefore also an *experience* of God; when we know, we possess and receive God and His gifts. We know the Father, and He *is* our Father; we know Christ, we see His mediation; we have come to the blood of the new covenant, and we *possess* Christ, and experience the power and efficacy of His death and resurrection. We know the spiritual blessings in heavenly places, and knowing them we possess them. We have not merely the picture or image, but the substance of divine realities.

It is the Spirit himself who teaches and enlightens. *The truth itself*, the preaching of the Gospel, the reading of the Scriptures, *has no inherent power to bring knowledge into the soul.* These are only the instruments, the Spirit is the agent; they are only the sword, the Spirit is the energy, the hand that wields it. They shall be taught of God. God causes the light of the Gospel to shine into our hearts. How little we realize this truth, so comforting and full of encouragement! *How apt are we to forget the living Spirit* in the gifts and channels which He uses! How fond we are of placing ourselves in God's place; if not in the Father's, in Christ; if not in Christ's, in that of the Spirit!

NOTE 14

The Spirit Guiding the Church (Chapter 23)

The whole teaching of the apostle to the Corinthians, in regard to the need of the Spirit's revelation—if the truth is to maintain its divine power and freshness, and if we are to be led farther and deeper into it, suggests to us the danger of creeds as the human expression of the truths of Scripture. While they have their very high value as temporary and secondary embodiments of the faith of the Church, they may so easily in practice usurp the place which theoretically we accord to the Word of God alone. They may become particularly harmful when they are regarded as a sufficiently perfect and final formula of what the Word has to teach us. We may unconsciously close the heart against the expectation of any further teaching of the Spirit for the clearer and fuller unfolding of what is revealed in the Word. The Holy Spirit has been given to the whole Church to guide her into all truth. We should trace the way in which, during the first five centuries, amid human controversy and weakness, some of the great outstanding truths of revelation were mastered and formulated. We thank God for the restoration at the time of the Reformation, of truths that had been lost sight of and displaced by error. But is there the danger that many consider the leading of the Spirit to have become less needful after our Reformation creeds had been settled? Many can hardly bear to think that the Holy Spirit may have more to teach His Church, or that a clearer and fuller setting forth of divine truth than is to be found in our standards may be expected. This attitude towards the Holy Spirit and His teaching is one of great danger. It closes the heart against that teachable and expectant spirit to which alone the divine Spirit can reveal the truth of God in power. It fosters that spirit of self-contentment with the correctness of our orthodoxy which unconsciously robs Holy Scripture of its authority, while at the same time we are insisting on our allegiance to it! It tends toward the position of the Jews in the time of Christ, in which, while they fondly imagined that God's Word was everything to them, it was their human exposition of it, their human image of God's truth, for which they were so zealous. We must learn to trust the Holy Spirit more in our theology. He has still much to teach us. As the life and work of the ministry comes more under the power of the Spirit, and the leading of the Spirit in every believer is acknowledged as a necessity and a privilege, we shall become accustomed to the fact of His leading the Church into the truth, and look in confidence to Him to do His work in ways we cannot beforehand perceive.

What makes many so unwilling to accept this truth is the apparent danger connected with it. They see a great number engaged in the task of reconciling the truth of revelation to the instincts of the human mind, to the spirit of the age, to the requirements of science. All these seek emancipation from the creeds, not in order to restore a more purely scriptural theology, but to be freed from all the restraints of a system of religion that will satisfy the religious consciousness of human reason. It is not difficult to see how far removed from each other these two parties stand, though both plead for liberty in regard to the creeds. The one pleads for liberty of judgment—to be free to follow the dictates of reason as spoken by our wisest men; the other for the liberty of the spirit—to be free to receive and to follow the teachings of the Holy Spirit, as revealed to the Church under His rule, waiting for His revelation of what Scripture contains. It is well, in the interest of the Church, to have these two parties carefully distinguished. The Church and the faith have no truer friends than those who, while acknowledging that in the Reformation a noble foundation of truth was laid, yet believe that in raising the superstructure there is still much that the Holy Spirit needs to do, and is willing to do, in revealing the full proportion of Scripture truth—if He finds the Church ready to listen and obey His leading.

The following remarks, from one whose attachment to the form of sound doctrine and deep insight into Scripture are above all question, are worthy of careful consideration. In his *Christ and the Scriptures*, Dr. Saphir says:

"There is among us an uneasy feeling, a secret consciousness that something is wrong. The development of doctrine, which is clearly opposed to that gospel which has proved the power of God to the heart and experience of man is one cause of alarm; and a return to the bulwark of the Reformation creed and theology is the natural recourse. But against this, two considerations are urged. In the first place, Israel ought never to look and turn back. The Lord himself (and not an image of Him) is a wall of fire round us. Life alone can combat the errors of death. But, in the second place, if the *creeds* could not even retain and preserve life (as history proves they were not able to do), how much less will they be able to rekindle a dying flame or to bring the dead to life. It is out of these very creeds that the present state of things has come, either as a development or as opposition, and our aim ought to be to find out whether, in these creeds, the absence of some scriptural element, or the false representation and emphasis of some scriptural element, be not the root of the disease which is manifesting itself.

"Here it is evident that two parties meet which may be essentially and radically different: those for whom the creeds contain too much of the scriptural element, and those for whom they contain too little of that element, or do not contain it in sufficient purity. The objectors to the creeds may be such because the creeds are too Shemitic, or because they are not Shemitic enough."

Let us still listen to the words of another. When John Robinson, pastor of a congregation of refugee Puritans at Leyden, was bidding farewell to the party of exiles who were leaving on the *Mayflower* for New England, and were to become celebrated under the name of "the Pilgrim Fathers," he spoke these memorable parting words: "I charge you, that you follow me no farther than you have seen me follow the Lord Jesus Christ. The Lord has more truth to break forth out of His holy Word. I cannot sufficiently mourn the condition of the Reformed Churches, which are come to a period in religion, and will go, at present, no farther than the instruments of their reformation. Luther and Calvin were great and shining lights in their times. Yet they did not penetrate into the whole counsel of God. The Lutherans cannot be drawn to go beyond what Luther saw; and the Calvinists remain where they were left by that great man of God. I plead with you to remember that it is an article of your church covenant—that you be ready to receive whatever truth is made known to you from God's Word."

The whole subject is one of deep importance and not without difficulty. The only safety for the Church is in renewed faith and the unceasing expectation of the Holy Spirit's working in the life of her believing members. Out of this will grow that intense surrender to Him which will quicken her capacity for taking in the whole truth of Holy Scripture, and reproducing it in life and testimony in words which the Holy Spirit teaches.

NOTE 15

Trusting the Spirit (Chapter 27)

In a little book entitled *Reminiscences of the Keswick Convention*, 1879, with addresses by Pastor Stockmaier, I find some most helpful thoughts with regard to the work of the Holy Spirit, as He enables us to die to self and to take Christ as our life. For the sake of preserving these, and introducing them to readers who may otherwise not have access to them, I give somewhat lengthy extracts here. The only way that the blessing of revival can become permanent is that each believer know that what he has received in the fellowship of the saints can be secured and increased to him personally, through the blessed ministry of that Holy Spirit dwelling in Him, of whom he knows so little.

"Phil. 2:12, 13, 'Work out your own salvation with fear and trembling, for it is God that worketh in you both to will and to do of his good pleasure.' We will fear to disobey, because we are not dealing with human work or persons, but with the Holy Ghost; it is not we ourselves who are working it out, but the Holy Ghost.

"When Moses came before the burning bush, the Lord said to him, 'Put off thy shoes from off thy feet, for the place whereon thou standest is holy ground.' This is holy ground, for it is God the Holy Ghost who works the willing and the doing. In all questions of sanctification or service we are in the presence of our God: on holy ground. It is God that works in us to will and to do; work out your own salvation with fear and trembling. What is it to work out our own sal-vation? The Apostle tells us in the same verse, 'Wherefore, my beloved, as ye have always obeyed.' I think that word 'wherefore' brings us back to verse 8, to Christ's work. Christ had *become obedient unto death.* In verses 5-11 we have the work of Christ—abasement; and then, because He was abased, He was exalted high; therefore you also obey.

"In verses 12, 13 we have the work of the Holy Spirit, working on the work of Jesus. Jesus has been obedient unto death; death is contrary to our nature. We do all we can to keep our own life; but as Christ, through the eternal Spirit, offered himself without spot to God, and by His death brought an end to His work of immolation, so does the work of the Holy Ghost bring us into fellowship with a dying Christ. He makes us willing to die by the power of Christ; He makes us take the position in which the death of Christ has placed us. He died 'that they which live should not henceforth live unto themselves, but unto him that died for them and rose again.' Such a position given to us by Christ, no man is willing to enter into; it is the Holy Ghost who takes us by the hand and makes us willing to enjoy and to seek the fellowship of the dying and of the risen Christ. 'Now also in my absence,' go on yielding to the Holy Ghost, who will teach you to follow the Lamb, making you willing to die with Christ that you may serve, and love, and walk in new-ness of life; and all this in fear and trembling, because it is God who works. The only fear we want is to follow the Holy Ghost in all His operations, renouncing self and yielding to Him, that He may be able to work for God's glory; to leave all the matter in His hands. As soon as our fears are concen-trated on that point—to grieve not the Saviour—we have nothing more to fear; we can then seek first the kingdom of God and His righteousness, and all other things shall be added unto us. As heaven surrounds the earth on all sides, so the work of the Holy Ghost leaves nothing out of His reach within our being, bringing all under His control and transforming power.

"We must come back to the holy ground we left. God ought to have what is His. We came from Him and were made for Him; we must learn to honor the Holy Ghost and to consider His working the most precious thing we have, fearing to lose even one of His promptings, because all that He works involves infinite labor. It is a matter of experience, that in the measure that we know more of the love of God, we know also more of the fear of God; one involves the other and regulates the other; there is no contradiction.

"In James 4:1 we read of 'lusts which war in your members,' but in the same passage (v. 5) we read of the lust of the Spirit, so you cannot put quite the same significance on the word which we generally put on it. The word here does not mean sinful lust. The Spirit of God cannot have sinful lust. We see here two tendencies, two powers, two worlds that have nothing in common, separated as completely as heaven from earth—the flesh and the Spirit. We are responsible moral beings. We must choose as to which of these two adversaries we will give sway in our interior and exterior life.

"I know a position in which no uprising from impure feeling takes place in the heart, or takes form as a flash in a second of time. Such a Christian has learned to allow himself be kept by Christ from such uprisings; they no more appear; and yet these same Christians have a consciousness of the tendency of the flesh to rise up.

"There are infinite degrees of purity; and only after we have been fully delivered from such impure uprisings can the Holy Ghost go deeper and deeper in His purifying work. This cannot be expressed, it must be realized; and we are not easily conscious of how much our experience and the experience of others, or the level of Christian life in the Church, influence our explanations of Scripture. Have you ever attended such meetings as those of Keswick and Oxford without experiencing that in the same measure that God the Holy Ghost draws nearer and nearer, your interior atmosphere is modified, and there comes a moment in which you breathe the mountain air? And in the same measure as we come under the shadow of the Holy Ghost, the power of the Holy Ghost in our lives is different than the ordinary. When we return to the experience of the first days of the Church at Jerusalem, we will know the power of the Holy Ghost to keep us sheltered against the tendencies of our flesh. But we are a family, and we cannot experience individually the fullness of Jesus Christ our head, without wanting the rest to follow us; we want the lives of all the members to realize the life of the Holy Ghost. It is difficult to abide under the shadow of the Almighty when you are surrounded by sick Christians, slumbering Christians, Christians who do not fully trust their Saviour. Our daily life, our conversation, our very countenance, must testify that we have found the abundant life in our good Shepherd. Oh, dear Christians, cease from saving your own life, defending your own life; the Holy Ghost works to cause to die every portion of your old life. Oh, beloved brethren, we are so *worldly*; our worldly life is the great hindrance to conversions, the great reason why the Gospel has so little success. Yet remember, every Christian at one time has given up all to his Lord; then you were happy, and the very reason for your unhappiness now is that you have not yielded your whole life. In daily life and conversation, in daily choices, sometimes you hesitate between your will and God's will. Oh, my brethren, I do not want to open my heart to mere human wishes or human desires, because it may hinder my seeing the countenance of my God; never would I take into my own hands, an afternoon, or even an hour, because I know it would be an unhappy day, an unhappy hour. I am too happy now not to put every day, every hour, in the hands of my heavenly Father; too happy to ever again take into my hands the threads of my life.

"John 16:7-11. Then in Acts 2:36 and following verses, we have the fulfillment of the promise. Now, dear brethren, there are in the text from the gospel of John, two distinct offices of the Holy Ghost, put forth by our divine master. His name for the disciples is Comforter, and He has also the office of convincing the world. But before He may convince the world through the disciples, more disciples must be filled with the Holy Ghost. At Pentecost that promise was fulfilled; the disciples were filled with the Holy Ghost, and having the Comforter dwelling in them, they were the instruments in God's hands of convincing the world of the sin of unbelief. How few disciples there are who know the Holy Ghost in His office of Comforter! And what is His comfort? The Holy Ghost will bring into our hearts, above all, the consciousness that we are pleasing the Father by the power of the Son; that we are reconciled children, pleasing our Father. Oh, how long will Christians introvert the offices of the Holy Ghost, and oblige Him to be in their daily walk more convincing than comforting? For I have a deep feeling in these days, and I must speak it out in the presence of our God, that the Holy Ghost has to do among us, generally speaking, more the work of convincing than of comforting—convincing of sin. What sin? The sin of unbelief. It is the fruit of unbelief that so many Christians, looking back a day, or a week, or a year, do not have the testimony in their souls that they have lived the life which pleased their God. Again and again the Holy Ghost is obliged to take up His office of convincing of sin, and as a result the children of God lose the very capacity to believe that they may come to a life which pleases their Father in heaven. The meetings at Keswick, nor any other meetings, cannot have the approval of God unless they have this fruit—that a week later, a month later, a year after the meeting, there will be at least some Christians who have learned by faith to please their God. We must not come back a year later, telling of the power of Jesus, and yet, when asked if we have proved the power of Christ in our lives, we must confess we have not habitually pleased God; we have not habitually the presence of the Holy Ghost as the Comforter.

"Remember, we are on holy ground, and we have no right to speak of the power of our God if we are not experiencing it. I would not go forward one step if I for one moment did not know that I experience all the things that I believe.

"And now, one passage more in I Peter 2:5-9. Beloved friends, may you fulfill that glorious mission which our God has given us! Only after having been convinced of the sin of unbelief, and having *left forever* the sin of unbelief, can we know the Holy Ghost acting in our souls as the Comforter. Those three thousand men on the day of Pentecost—how they saw their sins! 'What shall we do?' 'Repent'; that is to say, leave your sin—the sin of unbelief with regard to Jesus Christ. They did so; and in that very moment they received the Jesus they had crucified as Lord and Christ. So I would plead with you, leave that frightful sin of unbelief that you may know Jesus as the anointed Lord, who is waiting for children of God whom He may anoint as priests. Let us begin by believing that He is able to keep us trusting through our daily life, to keep us in faith, and in a walk that pleases our God. Can we go on any longer living a life that does not please our Father?

"Phil. 2:12, 13. I think that if there is not a more practical realization of the glorious truth brought before us, it is because the children of God have a definite trust in the work of Jesus, but they have not the same trust in the Holy Ghost who is working continually in the soul of every believer to will and to do all that concerns our salvation. This moment I know that I have air to breathe, and that my God will continue to give it to me every minute; even so, the Holy Ghost will not interrupt His work in the inmost parts of my soul. I am His temple, and He is working in me, for it is God the Holy Ghost 'who worketh in you, both to will and to do of his good pleasure.'

"Now, you are asking how to trust. How can I be sure that I am now trusting Jesus to keep me from sin; that this afternoon and this evening I shall be kept in communion with my God; that I shall abide in Jesus, that I shall go on trusting? Dear brother, the moment you present such a question, you are disbelieving the Holy Ghost. So long as you ask it, you will never continue in communion with God, because you are seeking to find in yourself the secret of trusting, and it is the *Holy Ghost* who 'worketh in you both to will and to do.'

"The reason so few Christians realize these things is that they do not have the same definite trust in the work of the Holy Ghost as they have in the work of Christ. We must be *Trinity believers*, realizing all that Christ has provided for us by His work; but we are in the economy of the Holy Ghost, and so long as we do not honor the Holy Ghost we cannot be practical Christians.

"Let us come to the Holy Ghost with all the details of our daily life. The Father, the Son, and the Holy Ghost are all working together; the Father is working hand in hand with the Holy Ghost. The Holy Ghost has His appointed work in my soul, and He can work freely in my soul only as long as I am looking to Jesus. The moment I begin to look at the work of the Holy Ghost, I interrupt it; the beginning and the end of the work of the Holy Ghost is to make me look to Jesus. When I am looking to Jesus, I am at the place where the Holy Ghost can work in me. The Father is working with the Holy Ghost from morning to evening; if He did not work, there would be temptation beyond my endurance. I could not remain under the state described in I Cor. 10:13. There can be no temptation beyond what we are able to bear, because the Father is preparing every evening the details of the following day for His child, and I know He will never permit a storm from without or from within beyond the spiritual strength I have by looking to Jesus. There are no hairs falling from your head without the permission of your heavenly Father. The work of the Holy Ghost can go on in our souls freely, fully, gradually, through the watchful power of the Father, who so arranges all details of the exterior life that it may work together hand in hand with the work of the Holy Ghost.

"You may ask, For sanctification, does the believer receive the Holy Ghost as spoken of in John 7:37-39 and 14:16, 17, or is the Holy Ghost a distinct gift from sanctification?

"Beloved friends, What is sanctification? In one word, I would say, by justification you are brought by the Holy Ghost into Jesus Christ. God takes away the burden of your sins and places you in a new world in Jesus Christ; sanctification to me, is nothing else than to *dwell* in Jesus Christ, to remain in the place where the Holy Ghost has put me. From the moment we first receive the Holy Ghost, we have nothing else to do but respect the Holy Ghost within us. 'Work out your own salvation with fear and trembling, for it is God which worketh in you both to will and to do of his good pleasure.' Many children of God are not truly full of living waters, and if the living waters are not flowing out from them, the reason is that they have not practically honored the Holy Ghost in all things. *'Work out'*—because we must obey the Holy Ghost *working within*—'with fear and trembling,' fearing to disobey the Holy Ghost in anything, and then we shall begin to become as living waters to others. God will subdue our nature, and will act in us as the sap acts in the branches—from the moment we give up our being to the Holy Ghost to work in us in all things.

"And again, how will this life of faith in Christ help us in common daily temptations, such as the difficulty of getting up in the morning so as to have time for reading and prayer before breakfast?

"The secret of realizing in daily experience what we teach here is to learn to yield in all things to the gentle leadings of the Holy Ghost. The Holy Ghost is not working in us as a master with his slave; He will make us become the bride of Christ. The true relation of husband and wife is that in which the wife is the equal of the husband; and in our relations with the Holy Ghost we must learn to yield to the slightest suggestions, to the 'still small voice.' That is a precious lesson to learn during all our life, to have our ears more and more open to that still small voice of our God. At first, for those Christians who are not accustomed to the still, small voice, there is trouble, because the voice of bad example, of teaching that is not according to the Holy Spirit, and other voices, are filling the understanding and the soul. They must learn to be deaf to all other voices, and to listen only to that still small voice. It is a holy thing to learn to distinguish that voice; and you will distinguish it as your soul, your imagination, your wishes, are on the side of God. Trusting in the goodness, kindness, tenderness, and delicacy of our Good Shepherd, we shall learn to listen. Listening to other voices, we are sure to go wrong. In Rom. 8:11, and I Thess. 5:23, we see the end of the ways of God—the work ends by being manifested in our *bodies*. You may read in the faces of Christians, by the look of their eyes, that they are not *young* Christians, but that they have lived long with God. In proportion as you learn to listen to the still small voice, 'the Spirit of him that raised up Jesus from the dead' will also begin to act in your mortal bodies and quicken them. Sometimes we are striving and struggling to rise early, to overcome our bodies and cannot; but in the same measure that we learn to yield to the Holy Ghost, the quickening power of the Spirit of God will manifest itself also in our bodies, and they will regain their vitality for all that is best in God's service. We shall learn to know from the voice of God what He would have us to do. The Spirit of God will never quicken our bodies for what our natural energies can perform; but I know and realize daily, hour after hour, that my God quickens this mortal body for every service He gives me. My English may be very poor, but I could not speak five minutes if the Spirit of God did not give it to me; and so for early rising, or anything else, the Holy Spirit will give us every moment just the strength that is needed and no more. The man who is living in full dependence upon God is not concerned whether he is tired or strong, whether he feels healthy or sick; he has learned to receive from his God promptings for service. If he feels he must rise early, for him that is the will of God, necessary in order that he may go safely through the day. He, childlike, goes to his Father, saying, 'Give me from the moment I rise my daily bread,' and that includes the Spirit of God working in the mortal body, so that body, soul, and spirit become, moment by moment, what the Lord wants them to be for His service.

"In Phil. 2:8 you read that Jesus Christ 'became obedient unto death'; and in some verses farther down you find the apostle saying, 'As ye have obeyed, not as in my presence only, but now much more in my absence, work out your own salvation with fear and trembling. For it is God which worketh in you both to will and to do.' To will what, and to do what? To become likeminded with Jesus, who was obedient unto death. The Holy Ghost makes us willing to die, and to be in every respect, from morning to evening, a living sacrifice on the altar of our holy God, to go freely in the glorious law of the New Covenant. We can only have His life in the same measure as we forsake our own life.

"Oh, what a glorious life Christ has brought us, and what a glorious life the Holy Ghost works out in us, if we believe that Jesus Christ's life is infinitely more precious than our own life.

"Why are so many Christians so often exhausted in their work for Christ? Because they are seeking their own life in their work. Our work can only be fruitful when we are not seeking our own life or our own pleasure in our work, but seeking the glory and the interest of Christ. We have resurrection life as long as we remain buried with Christ and live only in His life.

"In John 5:29 you read, 'Search the scriptures.' Jesus showed the disciples of Emmaus that all Scripture was filled with the name of Jesus. Why so few fully trust Jesus is because so few know the real Jesus, as we find Him in the Bible. We must come out from a Christ of imagination, a Christ of feeling, and come back to the Christ given us in the Scriptures—a true, living Saviour, dying for our sins, and living that we may live His own life of righteousness.

"Oh, search the Scriptures, and let the Holy Ghost lift up before your eyes the person of Jesus—living, dying, risen;

and in the measure that the Holy Ghost, answering your prayer, brings new light on the person of Jesus, you will no more ask how to trust Him. Become better acquainted with this friend, and you will no more ask, How shall I trust Him? You cannot do otherwise. Only remember this one thing: it comes through faith. Jesus does not reveal with the first step all of His loveliness. He asks us to trust Him. 'Can you believe that *my* life is more precious than your life? Then give me your life, and I will give you another life.' Jesus is waiting; the Holy Ghost is casting light on the person of Jesus; you are wrong to look back on yourself when the Holy Ghost has put Jesus before you. Oh, beloved, this is life abundant! To whom? To those who let the living Saviour guide them to the understanding of His work on Calvary—that is, His work of breaking the chains and the links by which we were entangled in our own life. We cannot die; we retreat from the thought of going with our divine Shepherd, not only in the green pastures, but through the valley of the shadow of death. In the Gospels, Jesus Christ says of Mary, 'This also that this woman hath done shall be told for a memorial of her. She hath done it for my burial.' Mary accepted the dying Christ (woman is the receptive one). She received what Simon Peter could not accept, that Christ should go to the cross. She poured forth her best to anoint Christ for His burial. Let us too fully accept a dying Christ, no longer claiming to live ourselves. Jesus Christ died and came to resurrection through death. Stay under the shadow of the life of Christ. You want rest and peace, so don't seek it only in green pastures and by still waters; the deepest comfort is in the valley of the shadow of death. 'I will fear no evil'— where! In the 'valley of the shadow of death.' I preach life through death, life in death. I know no other life than that. If Jesus is *all*, my life must yield to His life. His life must have preeminence over my life.

"Go deeper in searching the Scriptures, follow Christ in all His steps, and remember, by death He has taken away the power and the fear of death, that we might no longer be in bondage. Now the dying to self is no longer dreadful; it is life—it is the only life that will satisfy all my being; to be nothing, and to have Christ. Trust Jesus to bring you into full fellowship with His dying! Trust Him. Don't look to your nature, to your feelings. Behind the valley of death there is abundance of life, and the moment you give up all things, letting yourself go in the arms of Jesus, death will lose its terror. I have had the experience, and everyone who fully yields himself to Jesus has the experience—in Him is the only true life. If you want unity in your daily life, don't seek life; you will never find life if you are seeking it alone. We will always find power in Christ to die to ourselves, if that is the thing we are seeking; and unless we have died we cannot bring forth fruit. Do you want me to tell you what I have seen and felt to be the result of this entire trust? It is this: I allowed my Saviour, knowing Him better than before, to take me through every experience that He would. He brought me through deep waters; there is no servant of God who will not be purified by fire. The Lord brought the sons of Levi through fire, and there He purified them for service, because our Lord uses only pure vessels for fruitful service. God will not use habitually unclean vessels. I have also experienced that, in the deep valley of the shadow of death, I knew my Saviour, and He comforted me as never before. I assure you, I would never go to still waters or green pastures when my divine Shepherd chooses to lead me through deep waters and dark valleys. There are green valleys on one side, and dark valleys on the other, and He is just leading each of His sheep according to his special needs. Learn to look to Jesus, and in doing that, you will find that Jesus, by His look, is leading you under the direction of the Holy Ghost; and soon it will become the natural attitude of your soul to trust, and you could do anything more easily than distrust Jesus.

"Some may ask, Is a life of practical holiness compatible with an earnest, active business life, a life in which the mind is occupied with commercial affairs six days of the week, from nine in the morning until seven in the evening; and say nine out of every ten transactions are made with unconverted men?

"Let me introduce you to a businessman: In the first verses of Daniel 6, you read that there were in the kingdom of Darius a hundred and twenty princes and three presidents, and there was one man, Daniel, who was preferred above all the princes. Now this man went, risking his life, three times a day into his bedroom, and opened his window towards heaven, to 'breathe heavenly air.' The more business we have, the more we need to pray. Take a man in whom is incorporated the spirit of greed, or the spirit of covetousness; this man in every part of his daily life will never lose sight of the great goal of his life—to get money.

"Now a man in whom is incorporated the Spirit of God will never lose sight of the great purpose of his daily life—to glorify his God; but he must be dead to self in order to live such a life. The Christian businessman and father does not work for his children, but for his God, and God gives him bread for his children. Believe me, our Father in heaven understands business, and He will never let one of His children go through a day without the needed supply; but the child of God must be ready to stop and listen as soon as his Father suggests it: 'Child, come to me, I have something to say to you; there is some cloud overhanging you; come aside with me, that I may prepare you to meet it.'

" 'Go in peace'; you can go in rest, leaning on the arm of your divine Shepherd. Don't ask how you may keep resting. Remember, it is the Holy Ghost who will keep you trusting, every day and every hour, on the one condition: that you seek to trust, not in the strength of your own heart, but in the Holy Ghost. Then, guided by the mind and mighty hand of your Father, standing on the holy ground of the work of the Trinity—'Go in peace.' Amen.

"In the joy of work and service, let us apply the great lesson of heavenly life—the lesson of *love*. Let us learn to rejoice in the work of others, and not in our own work. Let us learn to 'rejoice with them that do rejoice, and weep with them that weep;' not weep our own tears of sorrow, nor rejoice only with our own personal joy. Let us come under the hand of our Lord, with only one purpose—to serve others in love. *There* is the secret of life. The Holy Ghost never looked for His own glory, never spoke of His own: His only purpose is to glorify Christ. 'In this my joy is fulfilled,' that was heavenly joy. 'He must increase, but I must decrease.' I *must*—it was not obligation, but the yearning of the heart."

NOTE 16

The Spirit of Christ and His Love
(Chapter 29)

"Know then that I am love incarnate; I have clothed my-self with flesh that I might reign in your hearts. Love one another as I have loved you, and you will no longer lack my presence. All my life and sufferings were to this end—that divine love should dwell permanently among men. I have been manifest in the flesh, I must be manifest in the Church. Love one another as I have loved you that the world, alarmed to see me ascending on high, may turn to you, and behold with glad relief, Christ in you. Love is about to have the highest revelation it has ever had; but when you gaze upon the cross, especially when the Holy Spirit enables you to look with an intelligent eye upon it, understand that the love there revealed is your example. He who dies upon the cross is to live in you. 'By this shall *all men* know': this is that evidence that none shall be able to resist—the mark of love among God's children.

"Having been introduced, in the person of Jesus, into our common humanity, love refuses to disengage itself, and makes provision for its own perpetuation. Whatever discoveries the disciples were yet to make of the love of Christ, from His death on the cross, and by the outpouring of the Holy Spirit, were discoveries of the love they were required to show for one another. They were each commissioned to carry on the loving life of Jesus.

"But how can this thing be? It is by virtue of the union of the believer to Christ that the heart of the former becomes the storehouse of the Saviour's own love for His people. The vocation of every believer is this: to be a communicator of the love of Christ.

" 'If ye abide in me, and my words abide in you, ye shall ask what ye will, and it shall be done unto you.' Is it difficult to see why the prayers of Christ's people are not more promptly fulfilled? They do not allow His word to abide in them; they do not practically recognize their obligation to love one another as He has loved them. Who knows how many priceless expressions of the Father's love toward us are effectually repressed by the fact that we are inattentive to the sweet mandate of Jesus, to give each other His love? We profess to desire earnestly the outpouring of the Holy Spirit, but we shall do well to note that one of the first things which the Holy Spirit will aim to produce in us will be this Christlike love to the brethren.

"My Christian brethren do not see the Saviour with their bodily eye, but I have been commissioned by the Saviour to provide for them, in some sense, a compensation for this deficiency. I am commanded to let the love which was manifested in His mortal person, now be manifested in my life—a command which would be utterly idle and futile, were it not that He, the ever-loving one, is willing to put His own love within me. The command is really no more than to be a branch of the true vine. I am to cease from my own living and loving, and yield myself to be the expression of Christ's love."—George Bowen: *Love Revealed*

NOTE 17

The Spirit's Coming (Chapter 5)

"The teaching of Jesus Christ with respect to the ministry of the Holy Ghost is so remarkable, as to raise the inquiry: Where was the Holy Ghost during the earthly ministry of the Son of Man? Where was the Spirit that had moved on the face of the waters, that had been poured out upon Israel? Was His ministry suspended? It may be suggested that the *fullness* had not been realized in the ancient Church, which is undoubtedly true; yet, though true, it is insufficient to account for the treatment of His descent as a new visitation and benediction of God. The answer would seem rather to be that the Holy Ghost as *in Jesus Christ himself*, and could not be given to the Church as a distinctively *Christian* gift, until the first period of the incarnation had been consummated in the ascension of the Son of Man. In

Him dwelt all the fullness of the Godhead bodily; when the influence of that Godhead was poured out upon the Church, it came from the very heart of Christ, and was impregnated with all the elements which made up the mystery and beneficence of the incarnation."—*The Paraclete*

OTHER BOOKS BY ANDREW MURRAY